FCE
Practice
Tests ▶ Plus 2

with key

Diana L. Fried-Booth

Longman

Exam Overview

The **First Certificate in English** is an intermediate level examination which is held three times a year in March, June and December. There are five papers in the exam and each paper receives an equal weighting of 20 per cent of the marks. Papers are:

Paper 1	Reading	1 hour 15 minutes
Paper 2	Writing	1 hour 30 minutes
Paper 3	Use of English	1 hour 15 minutes
Paper 4	Listening	40 minutes (approximately)
Paper 5	Speaking	14 minutes (for each pair of students)

- The examination questions are task-based and simulate real-life tasks.

- Questions in Papers 1–3 are text-based. This means that there is always something to read when doing the tasks.

- Rubrics are important and should be read carefully. They set the context and give important information about the tasks.

- For Papers 1, 3 and 4 you have to write your answers on a separate answer sheet.

Paper	Formats	Task focus
Reading four texts, 35 reading comprehension questions	**Part 1:** matching headings or summary sentences to the paragraphs in a text. **Part 2:** answering multiple-choice questions. **Part 3:** choosing which sentence or paragraph fits into gaps in a text. **Part 4:** deciding which of 4–6 short texts contains given information or ideas.	**Part 1:** reading for the main ideas in a text. **Part 2:** reading for detailed understanding of the text. **Part 3:** reading to understand text structure. **Part 4:** reading for specific information.
Writing **Part 1:** one compulsory task **Part 2:** one task from a choice of four	**Part 1:** using given information to write a letter of 120–180 words. **Part 2:** producing one piece of writing of 120–180 words, from a choice of five. Either an informal letter, a story, a report, an article or a composition.	**Part 1 :** selecting from and comparing given information to produce a transactional letter. **Part 2:** writing for a specific reader, using appropriate layout and register.
Use of English four texts, 65 questions	**Part 1:** multiple-choice cloze. Choosing which word from a choice of four fits in each of 15 gaps in the text. **Part 2:** open cloze. Writing the missing word in each of 15 gaps in a text. **Part 3:** key-word transformations. Using the key word to complete a new sentence which means the same as the one given. **Part 4:** proof-reading. Finding the extra words that do not belong in a text. **Part 5:** wordbuilding cloze. Changing the form of the word given so that it fits into the gaps in a text.	**Part 1:** vocabulary. **Part 2:** grammar and vocabulary. **Part 3:** grammatical accuracy and vocabulary. **Part 4:** grammatical accuracy. **Part 5:** vocabulary.
Listening four parts, 30 questions	**Part 1:** eight short texts each with one multiple-choice question. **Part 2:** long text with ten gap-fill questions. **Part 3:** five short texts to match to one of six prompts. **Part 4:** long text with seven questions. Either multiple-choice, true/false or three-way matching.	**Part 1:** understanding gist meaning. **Part 2:** understanding specific information. **Part 3:** understanding gist meaning. **Part 4:** understanding attitude and opinion as well as both specific information and gist meaning.
Speaking four parts	**Part 1:** the examiner asks each student questions. **Part 2:** comparing and contrasting two pictures. Each student has to speak for 1 minute. **Part 3:** interactive task. Students discuss something together using a visual prompt. **Part 4:** discussion. The examiner asks questions related to the theme of Part 3.	**Part 1:** giving personal information. **Part 2:** giving information and expressing opinions. **Part 3:** exchanging ideas and opinions and reacting to them. **Part 4:** expressing and justifying opinions and ideas.

Contents

PAPER 1

PART 1

Reading (1 hour 15 minutes)

You are going to read an article about surfing. Choose the most suitable heading from the list **A–I** for each part (**1–7**) of the article. There is one extra heading which you do not need to use. There is an example at the beginning (**0**).

Mark your answers **on the separate answer sheet.**

A	Warnings ignored
B	Future challenge
C	Scientists' involvement
D	Wetsuits on a mountain
E	Ideal surfing conditions
F	One man's influence
G	Origins of surfing
H	Scientific breakthrough
I	Dangers of surfing

Tip Strip

- Read the text quickly for general understanding.
- Don't worry if there are some words which you don't understand; focus on understanding the main point of each paragraph.
- Then look at the paragraph headings; don't expect the words from the text to match.
- Re-read each paragraph and find the heading which best summarises the main idea in the paragraph.
- Check your answers carefully.

Heading A: What does 'ignored' mean?

Heading D: 'Mountain' is not mentioned in the text but there is a reference to something that takes place on a mountain. Don't be deceived by Mount Everest!

Heading H: What is a 'breakthrough'?

The history of surfing

0   **G**

It is generally believed that the ancient Polynesians were the first to surf and to introduce surfing to the Hawaiian islands in the central Pacific Ocean. In fact, early records show that surfing was at its height in the late eighteenth century. During the next century the sport declined, but by the beginning of the twentieth century its popularity had increased again and it gradually became an established water sport.

1

Hawaii has the best surf in the world but the beaches are among the most dangerous, partly because they are overcrowded. During October each year there are huge swells in which the waves can be almost twenty metres high. These waves then move to the southern hemisphere in April.

2

If a surfer gets sucked into the centre of one of these waves and then flung onto the shore as the wave breaks, the force can be life-threatening. And if the weight of the water does not make them unconscious, then the wave can drag them under water long enough for them to drown.

3

To most people, a twenty-metre high wave is Nature's way of saying: stay away. It's the oceanic equivalent of a lion's roar: get closer and you will be killed. But there are some surfers who actually find these dangers one of the most attractive features of the sport.

4

In the second half of the twentieth century one man in particular was responsible for fresh enthusiasm in the sport. He was a Californian surfer called Jack O'Neill who was determined to create a suit that would keep people warm in the waters of northern California, and at the same time would allow complete freedom of movement.

5

He experimented with various materials without much success until, during a plane journey in 1952, he came across a substance called neoprene. Using this material he created a wetsuit made of rubber which kept surfers warm and made surfing a year-round activity in climates which would otherwise be too cold for part of the year.

6

Over the years wetsuits have been used for everything from deep-sea diving to board sports which take place on land, like skateboarding. In 1988 O'Neill's original wetsuits were used for the first ever snowboarding world cup event, reflecting O'Neill's belief that snow is only frozen water and snowboarding takes place over frozen waves.

7

One surfer who recently rode a giant wave off the Pacific island of Tahiti astonished onlookers by walking away without a scratch. This same man now wants to surf a wave called Jaws, which crashes onto the shore of Maui, one of the Hawaiian islands, for only a few days each year. Jaws can reach a height of over twenty-five metres and is known to the surfing world as the Mount Everest of surfing.

PART 2

You are going to read an article about a woman who runs a company called Peanuts. For Questions **8–15**, choose the correct answer **A, B, C** or **D.**

Mark your answers **on the separate answer sheet.**

Hungry pop stars

Valerie Jones runs a company called Peanuts whose job it is to look after pop stars and pop groups when they go on tour. She is the person who feeds the stars and she's been doing it for the past ten years.

When the stars are playing at a festival Valerie may have to cook for up to a thousand people which includes all the crew and the people who work backstage. She erects a marquee – a huge tent – and the food is served buffet style from a central serving area. She has to cater for different tastes, so there are normally four or more choices of menu. She also has to look after people who may be on a special diet or some singers who don't eat dairy food before a concert.

She drives an enormous truck full of kitchen equipment and hires at least three walk-in refrigerators, a dishwashing unit and portable cabins which act as storerooms and office.

All the bands have to queue up to be served and everyone has to have a meal ticket. The stars are usually more relaxed when they are eating as no one is bothering them for autographs, although Valerie says that sometimes the security men and the stars' managers are more trouble than the stars themselves.

There are certain things which she always has to keep in stock like herbal teas and her own particular mixture of honey, lemon and ginger which singers like to keep in flasks on stage with them when they're singing. Years ago bands used to drink quite a lot of alcohol, but these days they're much healthier. Most bands drink fresh fruit juice and prefer to eat salads.

A lot of people in the bands are quite young and they're not used to very expensive food, so Valerie prepares plain food unless a band sends her a 'rider'. This is a list of special requirements. When people are tired, unwell or homesick they like to have familiar 'comfort' food so she keeps a stock of people's requirements just in case. As a result of all this, Valerie says she has become an expert shopper and in less than an hour in a supermarket she can spend £1000.

A lot of bands won't eat before a concert because they're too nervous, so Valerie and her staff can end up working very long hours as they have to be around to provide what people want at two or three in the morning. One thing Valerie has noticed is that the more mad a band is on stage, the more normal they are when they are off it. She says she is amazed at the change in behaviour. A really wild singer can turn out to be really quiet and polite off stage.

Tip Strip

- Read the text carefully. You do not necessarily need to understand every word. The questions follow the order of the text.

- Underline the key words in the question, e.g. Valerie has to provide a range of food. Then try to find the part of the text which contains the answer and underline the key words there, e.g. She has to cater for different tastes ...

- Look at the options and decide which option best matches the key information in the text. Option C 'there is such a wide variety of preferences' is the only option to contain the idea of providing a range of different food for people's likes and dislikes.

Question 9: 'less nervous' is another way of saying 'more relaxed'

Question 11: Which word in the text describes food that is 'simple'?

Question 12: Do you need to refer to something earlier or later in the text?

Question 15: What amazes Valerie about the bands?

8 Valerie has to provide a range of food because

   A people are very fussy about what they eat.
   B people are used to eating in restaurants.
   C there is such a wide variety of preferences.
   D there is such a demand for special menus.

9 The singers are less nervous when they are eating because

   A their security men are with them.
   B there are no fans hanging around.
   C their managers fuss over them.
   D the bands enjoy eating together.

10 Why does Valerie have to keep a supply of certain drinks?

   A The bands rely on a special recipe.
   B The bands prefer herbal tea to coffee.
   C The bands take fruit juice on stage.
   D The bands like to drink alcohol.

11 What do most bands like best to eat?

   A rich food
   B cheap food
   C junk food
   D simple food

12 What does 'just in case' in line 43 refer to?

   A Valerie's supply of more expensive food
   B Valerie's list of 'riders' from the different bands
   C Valerie's supply of special food for various people
   D Valerie's understanding of people feeling sick

13 Why do you think Valerie has become an 'expert shopper'?

   A She has a lot of money to spend each week.
   B She has learnt to find what individuals want.
   C She has to buy as much as possible for £1000.
   D She has to shop very quickly in a supermarket.

14 Why is a band likely to be hungry after playing?

   A They feel more relaxed after a concert.
   B They work long hours with little food.
   C They only have a snack before a concert.
   D They like to wait until they eat together.

15 What does Valerie think about the singers?

   A They are completely crazy on and off stage.
   B They behave differently on and off stage.
   C They are less rude when they are off stage.
   D They are normally more noisy on stage.

You are going to read a newspaper article about teenagers learning the art of discussion and argument. Seven sentences have been removed from the article. Choose from the sentences **A–H** the one which fits each gap (**16–21**). There is one extra sentence which you do not need to use. There is an example at the beginning (**0**).

Mark your answers **on the separate answer sheet.**

WHY THE UNITED NATIONS WENT TO SCHOOL

Teenagers can talk for hours on the phone to their friends, but if you try to get them to talk about politics or the latest developments in agriculture, for example, they are likely to fall silent. | **0** | **D** | It is more to do with lack of confidence or experience in putting forward clear arguments in front of strangers.

In order to demonstrate the value of good communication skills, a boarding school in Bath, in the west of England, decided to organise an interesting and exciting way of teaching teenagers how to argue and debate in public. | **16** | The Model United Nations programme, which is a role-play exercise, was first developed in the US where it forms part of the curriculum in hundreds of schools.

As many as 600 student representatives, ranging in age from 13 to 18, attend from schools all over England and Northern Ireland. | **17** |

The important roles within the UN, like the president of the general assembly, and the topics, are chosen by the teachers, and they decide which subjects students will discuss. | **18** |

MUN starts on a Friday evening and lasts until Sunday evening. Before arriving all the students are given a country to represent and are expected to prepare for the discussion in advance. | **19** |

It is then up to the students to discuss their views with the other members of their committee to win support for their argument, before they reach a decision by voting on a particular topic. | **20** |

For some of the students it will be the first time they have spoken in front of an audience and it can be very nerve-wracking. | **21** | At the same time students become more aware of political affairs and as well as gaining in self-confidence they learn about international issues.

A The other roles are taken by the students who pretend to be diplomats and try to represent the views and opinions of different member states.

B However, it gives them an opportunity to develop their skills at persuading other people and interacting with other students.

C Who is then chosen to speak in the full assembly is up to the student who is the chairperson of that committee.

D This is not so much to do with lack of knowledge or opinions about these matters.

E They tried to destroy the other representative's argument.

F Once they are all together they are divided into five committees.

G They hold an annual Model United Nations (called MUN for short by teachers and students) based on the real United Nations General Assembly.

H In some years a few students from other countries such as Italy and Poland will also attend.

Tip Strip

- Read through the text carefully so that you have a general understanding.
- Look very carefully at what comes before and after each gap.
- Read through the sentence options and find one that fits in terms of topic and language links.
- Re-read the paragraph again to check that it makes sense.

Question 16: This is the first reference to the Model United Nations, its abbreviation MUN and the explanation of what it does. Without this explanation the last part of the paragraph would not make sense.

Question 17: Find other countries that link with 'England and Northern Ireland'.

Question 18: The paragraph begins with a reference to 'roles' so look for a sentence which continues this topic.

Question 21: Despite the fact that students may be nervous, the experience is obviously worthwhile. Look for a word that connects these contrasting ideas.

You are going to read a magazine article in which four actors talk about their profession. For Questions **22–35** choose from the actors **A–D**. The people may be chosen more than once. There is an example at the beginning (**0**).

Mark your answers **on the separate answer sheet**.

Tip Strip

• You do not need to read through the whole text first.

• Read each question and underline the key words.

• Scan the text by reading through it quickly to find the information. Ignore parts of the text which are not relevant to the point you are looking for.

• When you find the relevant part of the text, read it carefully.

• The questions and the text will not contain the same words. You need to look for and match meaning. e.g. Question 22 'has become successful at a young age' = 'just 21 and already a box office name'.

Question 29: 'out of work' is a similar way of saying 'unemployed'.

Question 30: Find another way of saying 'not interested'.

Question 32: Find another way of saying 'refuses'.

Which of the actors

had intended to do something else?	**0**	D
has become successful at a young age?	**22**	
was strongly influenced by their upbringing?	**23**	
had little warning before going on stage?	**24**	
comments on different acting techniques?	**25**	
accepted work without hesitation?	**26**	
was picked without having spoken?	**27**	
has not been professionally trained?	**28**	
used to worry about being unemployed?	**29**	
is not interested in reading scripts?	**30**	
had a difficult time before becoming famous?	**31**	
refuses quite a lot of work?	**32**	
tried to change their appearance?	**33**	
had to fight for parental support?	**34**	
thinks the acting process is quite charming and attractive?	**35**	

AN ACTOR'S WORLD

A Jake Armstrong

'I have a terrible problem reading through scripts,' admits Jake Armstrong. 'I find most of them very boring, although once in a while a script will really appeal to me and I am immediately attracted to the character the director has asked me to consider.'
Jake Armstrong was always going to end up doing something dramatic. His father and mother are both actors, and although neither of them pushed him into the profession, he feels his career path was inevitable as he saw so much theatre when he was a child. 'I would wait backstage until it was time to go home at the end of an evening performance. I met the most fantastic people. As a child you don't appreciate fame and I thought all these extraordinary people were really normal. But there was something fascinating about the whole business, why people dress up as different people and pretend to be other personalities. Unlike my parents, however, I am more interested in film work. The thing about filming is that you hang around for hours chatting away to people, then suddenly you've got to turn it on. I had to learn very quickly how to tone down for the camera, not to overact, whereas on stage in the theatre it's the exact opposite.'

B Laura Dyson

'I think I'm very lucky to have been noticed so early in my career. When I was at drama school I used to feel quite desperate meeting up with friends who had already graduated and who were out of work. I would listen to them talking about the temporary jobs they had, working in restaurants, supermarkets – whatever they could find, and going to one audition after the other. And they were only auditioning for really small parts in theatre or film and getting absolutely nowhere.'

Laura Dyson is just 21 and already a box office name. She was spotted whilst on stage in London and offered a film role by one of Hollywood's leading directors. 'It was unbelievable. I'd had hardly any experience and the play I was in was a walk-on role only. I didn't have to say a single word! Apparently the director was looking for someone who could play a 16-year-old schoolgirl, so I suppose I'm fortunate in that I don't look my age. The irony is that I used to spend hours making up my face so that I'd look older. I used to get so fed up with people refusing me entry to adult films because nobody believed me when I said I was over 18.'

C Emmy Mason

'My parents have always been interested in the arts and I remember being taken to the cinema and the theatre at a very early age. When I said I wanted to go to drama school they were horrified. In fact, my father refused to agree but he eventually gave in because I threatened to go off around the world on my own at 17 doing any old job just to pay my way.'

Emmy Mason was determined to succeed and although it has not been an easy ride to stardom she has finally achieved the kind of recognition that most actors can only dream about. 'My big break came quite by accident. I was an understudy at the National Theatre for months on end. It was such hard work, learning the lines and yet knowing that you were unlikely ever to say them in front of an audience. Don't get me wrong, though. I was glad to be earning some money and at least I got to see the famous names each night. Anyway, one day the leading lady went down with flu and in the afternoon I was told I would be on stage that evening. There wasn't time to be frightened. I had sat through all the rehearsals so I knew the moves by heart. And that was it. The critics loved my performance and I've never been out of work since.'

D Luke Demain

'I guess I ended up acting by accident. I wanted to go to university but couldn't decide what to study. So I thought I'd take a year out, do different things and give myself a breathing space before applying. But during that year I got involved with a local theatre group and suddenly realised I was happier than I'd ever been.'

Luke Demain has never looked back. Unusual in this day and age, he didn't go to drama school and has had no formal training. Instead he found himself an agent who was willing to put him forward for auditions. 'To begin with I was mostly doing advertisements for TV and film, which was fine but not serious acting. Then one day my agent got a call from a film studio and the next day I was on the film set. There hadn't even been time to send me the script. Looking back I don't think I even asked what the film was about, it didn't matter. But I'm quite choosy now and turn down more scripts than I accept!'

PART 1

You **must** answer this question.

1 You want to do an activity course abroad during your summer holiday. You have seen the advertisement below in a magazine and made some notes about things you want to know. Read the notes you have made. Then, write to the company covering all the points in your notes and adding any relevant questions of your own.

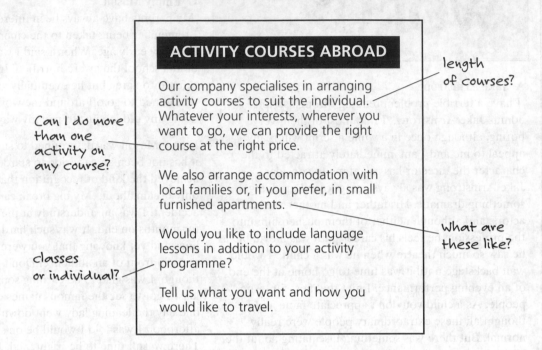

ACTIVITY COURSES ABROAD

Our company specialises in arranging activity courses to suit the individual. Whatever your interests, wherever you want to go, we can provide the right course at the right price.

length of courses?

Can I do more than one activity on any course?

We also arrange accommodation with local families or, if you prefer, in small furnished apartments.

What are these like?

Would you like to include language lessons in addition to your activity programme?

classes or individual?

Tell us what you want and how you would like to travel.

Write a **letter** of between **120** and **180** words in an appropriate style. Do not write any addresses.

Tip Strip

- You don't have to use your imagination. Read the instructions carefully and underline key words and phrases: e.g. <u>covering all the points in your notes</u> and <u>adding any relevant questions of your own.</u>
- Read the input material. What information does the advertisement ask for?
- Base your answer on the input material, but try to use your own words as far as possible.
- Think about who you are writing to. Which style is best: more formal or less formal? Should you end the letter with *Yours sincerely, Yours faithfully* or *Best wishes*?
- Plan your answer. Paragraph 1: express your interest in the activity course and give information about your own requirements. Paragraph 2: request the extra information (based on your handwritten notes). Paragraph 3: add a question of your own relevant to the input material.
- When you have finished, read the input information again. Have you included everything?
- Check the word limit, but don't waste time counting every word.
- Check your grammar and spelling.

Write an answer to **one** of the Questions 2–5 in this part. Write your answer in **120–180** words in an appropriate style.

---

2 You have been studying the environment in your English lessons and your teacher has asked you to write on the following topic for homework:

Taking care of our planet: the things we can all do to help.

Write your **composition**.

3 Some English friends are coming to stay with you for a week. They want to know about some of the special tourist attractions in your area, and have asked for some suggestions for things you think their children would especially enjoy.

Write your **letter**. Do not write any addresses.

4 An international magazine is publishing articles from readers about a person who has had an important influence on their life.

Write your **article**.

5 Answer **one** of the following two questions based on your reading of **one** of the set books.

Either (a) Write a **composition** describing one of the events in the book which you have read, saying why you have chosen it and what you find memorable about it.

Or (b) Your teacher has asked you to write a report for your class on whether you think the book which you have read would be suitable for a radio or television play. Write a **report** giving the reasons for your choice.

Tip Strip

Part 2

- Read the questions carefully. Choose a question you have ideas and vocabulary for.
- Underline the key points in the question and include them in your answer.
- Before you start writing, think of the main point you will include in each paragraph.
- Make a few rough notes if it will help you to organise your ideas clearly.
- Make sure you always write in paragraphs.
- Leave yourself enough time to read through what you have written in order to check your spelling and grammar.

Question 2:

- Make sure you have two or three concrete suggestions that you can make specific reference to.
- Use a formal or neutral style.

Question 3:

- Start and end the letter appropriately and deal with both tourist attractions and suggestions for things children can do.

Question 4:

- Use a neutral style; you do not know the reader.
- Introduce the person in your first paragraph.
- Explain why they are influential in your life and give some examples to support what you say.

Question 5(a):

- Choose one event which you know well, so that you can refer to the plot and the characters etc. Explain why you have chosen it.
- Use a formal or neutral style.

Question 5(b):

- Decide on radio or television.
- Organise your ideas. You can use subheadings if you wish for a report.
- Choose two or three examples of scenes/events etc. from the book and explain how these would make good radio or television.

PAPER 3   Use of English (1 hour 15 minutes)

For Questions **1–15**, read the text below and decide which answer **A, B, C** or **D** best fits each space. There is an example at the beginning (**0**).

Mark your answers **on the separate answer sheet.**

Tip Strip

- Read the text for general understanding.
- A, B, C and D are all plausible at first sight, but only one fits the gap.
- The word must fit in the context of the text as a whole.
- Check the words before and after the gap. Some words can only be used with certain prepositions, some words will be part of fixed expressions.
- Read through the text and check that your answers make sense.

Question 1: Which word can only apply to the length of something like a bridge?

Question 8: Which phrasal verb means 'to become'?

Question 12: Which word can stand alone without another phrase to complete the sense?

Example:

0   **A**   watch   **B**   find   **C**   see   **D**   look

0	A	B	C	D

ØRESUND BRIDGE

Imagine driving along a bridge that is so long that you can't even (**0**) ..... the other end. The Øresund Bridge, one of the (**1**) ..... bridges in the world, (**2**) ..... so far ahead into the (**3**)..... that you can't even tell where the blue of the water (**4**) ..... the blue of the sky.

The Øresund Bridge is an amazing example of modern engineering design that (**5**) ..... the Scandinavian countries of Denmark and Sweden. It is 8 kilometres long and was (**6**) ..... in July 2000. It crosses the Flinte Channel, the chilly waterway (**7**) ..... the two countries.

At one stage the bridge turns (**8**) ..... a tunnel under the sea. This tunnel is also a (**9**) ..... breaker in its own right as it is the longest road and rail tunnel in the world. The engineers built an artificial island near the Danish coast that (**10**) ..... to support part of the bridge (**11**) ....., as well as being the point at which the road disappears (**12**) ....., before coming out in Copenhagen, the capital of Denmark.

The bridge, which was built (**13**) ..... by the two countries, is expected to bring huge advantages. It will (**14**) ..... time compared to traditional ferry connections, as well as being of (**15**) ..... to the economy of both countries.

1	**A** longest	**B** furthest	**C** deepest	**D** hardest
2	**A** travels	**B** leans	**C** stretches	**D** pulls
3	**A** space	**B** distance	**C** horizon	**D** range
4	**A** comes	**B** meets	**C** lines	**D** starts
5	**A** links	**B** contacts	**C** holds	**D** relates
6	**A** done	**B** ended	**C** brought	**D** completed
7	**A** splitting	**B** cutting	**C** breaking	**D** separating
8	**A** down	**B** into	**C** out	**D** back
9	**A** performance	**B** world	**C** record	**D** account
10	**A** helps	**B** aids	**C** attempts	**D** tries
11	**A** scheme	**B** plan	**C** structure	**D** form
12	**A** down	**B** underground	**C** below	**D** underneath
13	**A** commonly	**B** doubly	**C** similarly	**D** jointly
14	**A** save	**B** spare	**C** spend	**D** spread
15	**A** good	**B** benefit	**C** quality	**D** comfort

For Questions **16–30,** read the text below and think of the word which best fits each space. Use only **one** word in each space. There is an example at the beginning (**0**).

Write your answers **on the separate answer sheet.**

Example:

0	an

ARTIST DEVELOPMENT MANAGER

Patti Wilkins is (**0**) ....an......... Artist Development Manager. She specialises in pop music and is (**16**) .... for managing the production (**17**) .... a pop singer's new single or album and (**18**) .... that it involves.

She is the person who selects the songs for the album, the photographs for publicity purposes, who shoots the video and chooses the clothes the singer (**19**) .... for that video. In (**20**) .... typical day she will meet the people designing the artwork for the album, the singer's manager, journalists and marketing managers.

(**21**) .... the week she will have to listen to the hundreds of tapes that are (**22**) .... to the record company by singers and bands hoping to (**23**) .... famous one day. She needs to understand (**24**) .... makes a good pop band and at the same time has to be (**25**) .... to spot star potential. In (**26**) .... of working long hours she feels it is (**27**) .... it when a song finally gets into the pop charts.

She learnt about the pop industry by (**28**) .... work experience and editing pop magazines (**29**) .... well as taking a business course. In that way she (**30**) .... out how to go about marketing and selling in the highly competitive music industry.

Tip Strip

- Read the text for general understanding.
- The word must make sense in the text as a whole.
- Decide which word each gap needs, e.g. preposition, relative pronoun, conjunction, verb, adjective, etc.
- Look out for fixed expressions, dependent prepositions after certain verbs and linking words and phrases.
- Read through the text and check it makes sense.

Question 20: What type of word goes here? Which two words are possible in the context? Which one makes more sense if we are talking generally?

Question 24: What type of word goes here? What other word can replace a noun?

Question 30: Look at the preposition after the gap. What verb can you put with this preposition to mean 'discovered'?

PART 3

Tip Strip

• Look at the **key word**. What type of word is it? What usually follows it, e.g. an infinitive, a gerund, a pronoun?

• Write your answer **on the question paper** and read **both** sentences again.

• Make sure you haven't added any extra information **or** missed out any of the original information.

• Write only the missing words on the answer sheet.

• Check your spelling.

• Contracted words count as two words, e.g. don't = do not.

Question 35: Which preposition follows 'prevented'?

Question 38: What auxiliary verb do you have to have in order to make a question here?

Question 40: Active to passive: make sure you keep to the same verb tense.

For Questions **31–40,** complete the second sentence so that it has a similar meaning to the first sentence, using the word given. **Do not change the word given.** You must use between two and five words, including the word given. Here is an example (**0**).

Example: 0   The bag is not big enough for all my luggage.

small

The bag .... for all my luggage.

The gap can be filled by the words 'is too small' so you write:

0	is too small

Write **only the missing words** on the separate answer sheet.

---

31 I had no idea about Rona's engagement.

unaware

I .... engagement.

32 I haven't seen a good film for months.

since

It's .... a good film.

33 Mark did as I suggested and bought a new computer.

advice

Mark .... and bought a new computer.

34 No teacher will tolerate bad behaviour in class.

put

No teacher will .... bad behaviour in class.

35 The heavy snow meant that no trains were running.

prevented

The trains .... the heavy snow.

36 Can I borrow your camera for my holiday, please?

lend

Can .... your camera for my holiday, please?

37 Jim was horrified to find his new car had been stolen.

horror

To .... his new car had been stolen.

38 When are you hoping to go to university?

want

When .... to go to university?

39 If only I spoke Russian.

could

I .... Russian.

40 Brazilian farmers grow much of the world's coffee.

is

Much of the world's coffee .... farmers in Brazil.

PART 4

For Questions **41–55**, read the text below and look carefully at each line. Some of the lines are correct, and some have a word which should not be there.

If a line is correct, put a tick (✔) by the number **on the separate answer sheet**. If a line has a word which should not be there, write the word **on the separate answer sheet**. There are examples at the beginning (**0** and **00**).

Example:

0	✔
00	up

Tip Strip

- Read the text for general understanding.
- Expect between four and six lines to be correct.
- Look at the whole sentence, not just at the numbered lines.
- Underline the words you think are wrong and read the sentence (not the line) without it. Does it sound right?
- Incorrect words can only occur **once** in a line.

Line 48: Is it a preposition or a participle which isn't needed here?

Line 50: Where do the 'famous personalities' appear?

Line 55: Look at the tense used throughout this fairly long sentence. Where is the mistake?

Red Nose Day

0 .... Every March in Britain there is a special day called Red Nose

00 .... Day during which the charity, Comic Relief, expects to raise up

41 .... millions of pounds. One third of all money collected together

42 .... goes to UK projects to help disadvantaged groups of people

43 .... such as like the disabled or refugees. The rest of the money

44 .... goes to Africa, where because twenty of the world's poorest

45 .... countries are situated. In these countries the money is used

46 .... to provide clean drinking water, health care for, education and

47 .... safe housing. So how are the British public persuaded to give

48 .... money to Comic Relief? The BBC plays a large part by being

49 .... broadcasting on hours and hours of programmes. Many famous

50 .... personalities appear here on the various programmes and ask

51 .... people to give over some money. Hundreds of schools are also

52 .... involved and students and teachers pay to dress up for the day.

53 .... Supermarkets, shops and garages sell red plastic noses and

54 .... millions of people wear these about for fun; some people even

55 .... buy extra large noses which they had fix to the front of their cars.

PART 5

For Questions **56–65**, read the text below. Use the word given in capitals at the end of each line to form a word that fits the space in the same line. There is an example at the beginning (**0**).

Example:	**0**	*exciting*

Write your answers **on the separate answer sheet.**

ABORIGINAL STORIES

Australian Aborigines are famous for their (**0**) ......*exciting*.... stories,   **EXCITE**

which are read not from a text but from their (**56**) .... These   **SURROUND**

(**57**) .... stories form the body of Aboriginal culture and   **TRADITION**

(**58**) .... , which make up their unique world view.   **KNOW**

The stories, which are often very (**59**) ...., are told by pointing   **THEATRE**

out and walking along large tracks of land; it can be said, therefore, that

the (**60**) .... of Aborigines are lived out as if in a giant natural   **LIFE**

storybook. It is also (**61**) .... that Aboriginal land has a strange   **BELIEF**

way of creating its own (**62**) ....   **PERSONAL**

When they talk about a place of (**63**) .... Aborigines say that   **IMPORTANT**

the land has a *gi* that either likes you or makes you feel disturbed and

(**64**) .... In fact, if you sit under a tree there is a   **COMFORT**

(**65**) .... that it is watching you, listening to you and that it   **POSSIBLE**

may even talk to you.

Tip Strip

- Read the text for general understanding.
- Decide what type of word you need for each gap (e.g. noun, adjective etc.).
- Look at the whole sentence, not just at the line containing the gap.
- You should make no more than two changes to the word.
- You may need to add a prefix or suffix to some words.
- Some words may be positive or negative. Check the meaning of the text.
- Read through the text and check that your words make sense.
- Check your spelling very carefully.

Question 58: Is a noun, a verb or an adjective needed here?

Question 64: Read this sentence very carefully. Is this word going to express a positive or negative idea?

Question 65: Is this word going to be singular or plural?

PAPER 4   Listening (approximately 40 minutes)

PART 1

You'll hear people talking in eight different situations. For Questions **1–8**, choose the best answer, **A, B** or **C**.

Tip Strip

- Read the **question** before the options and underline the key words.
- Each question is based on a different listening text and carries a separate mark.
- Focus on each new text as you hear it; don't look back at the one you have just done or look ahead to what comes next.
- Decide on one of the options after the first listening.
- Use the second listening to check that you are correct.
- If you are not sure, make a sensible guess.
- Do not listen for single words, but for the general meaning.
- Don't worry about words that you don't know.
- Be prepared for short dialogues as well as monologues.

Question 2: You'll hear the speaker mention plants, flowers and butterflies, as well as 'all kinds of tiny creatures crawling around'.

Question 3: What was the secretary's message?

Question 5: What can't the man find?

1 You hear a radio announcement about a transport problem.
What is the problem to do with?
- **A** the railways
- **B** the roads
- **C** the airports

1

2 You hear a man being interviewed on the radio.
What is the topic of his new book?
- **A** insects
- **B** flowers
- **C** butterflies

2

3 You hear a woman talking to her friend on the phone.
What has happened?
- **A** Her meeting was cancelled.
- **B** Her meeting was boring.
- **C** Her meeting was difficult.

3

4 You hear an advertisement for a concert.
What is being offered?
- **A** two tickets for the price of one
- **B** a ticket which includes supper
- **C** a special ticket for a family

4

5 You hear a man talking to a hotel manager.
What is he asking for?
- **A** a new suitcase
- **B** a small lock
- **C** a spare key

5

6 You hear an artist talking about a trip to an exhibition.
What is she looking forward to?
- **A** seeing her work on display
- **B** meeting some new artists
- **C** buying an oil painting

6

7 You hear a business woman talking to her assistant over the phone.
What is the reason for her call?
- **A** She's left her laptop on her desk.
- **B** She's left her diary behind.
- **C** She's left her passport in a drawer.

7

8 You hear a man phoning through an order for a takeaway meal.
Where does he want it delivered?
- **A** to his car
- **B** to his office
- **C** to his studio

8

You will hear part of a radio interview with a man who is the director of an Environmental Centre. For Questions **9–18,** complete the sentences.

Tip Strip

- The questions follow the order of the text.
- Before you listen, read the questions. Think about the kind of information which is missing.
- The words you need to write are on the tape, but not in the same order as the question sentences. It is not a dictation.
- Write 1–3 words in each space. If the answer is a number, you can write it in figures or words.
- Don't repeat the words and ideas which are already in the question sentence.
- Check that your word or phrase is grammatically correct and makes sense.
- Check your spelling.

Question 9: What kind of information would you expect to complete this sentence?

Question 10: Are you listening for a verb or a noun for this gap?

Question 14: What kind of things would the Centre not want people to do inside?

The Environmental Centre has been open for [**9**]

The Centre has working displays of sun and wind [**10**]

School children visit the Centre to carry out a [**11**] on the environment.

The majority of courses take [**12**] , apart from ones in the summer.

Accommodation is provided in basic [**13**] made of wood.

The Centre does not allow anyone [**14**] inside.

The course on garden wildlife and different plants is called [**15**] gardening.

The most popular course shows people how to save [**16**]

The cost of a course depends on whether people have a [**17**] or not.

The Centre has a [**18**] to make sure nobody is refused a place on a course.

You will hear five different people talking about the importance of modern inventions. For Questions **19–23**, choose from the list **A–F** the reason each speaker gives for the importance of the invention to them personally. Use the letters only once. There is one extra letter which you do not need to use.

A It entertains me.

B It guarantees contact.

C It helps my memory.

D It provides an escape.

E It's removed a pressure.

F It's always with me.

Speaker 1 ☐ **19**

Speaker 2 ☐ **20**

Speaker 3 ☐ **21**

Speaker 4 ☐ **22**

Speaker 5 ☐ **23**

Tip Strip

- There are five different speakers talking on a similar topic. You hear all five once, then all five are repeated.
- Read the instructions carefully. What will the people be talking about?
- Before you listen, read the options A to F.
- During the first listening, note down each speaker's main idea. Mark the option closest to this idea.
- During the second listening, check your answers. You may need to change some of them.

B: Listen out for the speaker who talks about the ways of guaranteeing contact with other people.

E: Two people mention relaxing, but only one of them speaks about it in the context of the invention which is most important for them personally.

F: What is another way of saying that something is always with you?

PART 4

You will hear a radio interview with a research scientist. For each of the Questions **24–30**, decide which of the statements are True and which are False. Write **T** for **True** or **F** for **False** in the boxes provided.

24 The 'smart pill' is a new drug. `24`

25 It's easy for some people to take the wrong medicine. `25`

26 People don't mind about making mistakes. `26`

27 Most people are impressed with the new system for reading labels. `27`

28 People can hear personal information with the new system. `28`

29 The labels are designed to speak aloud. `29`

30 Most people are afraid of the new technology. `30`

Tip Strip

- The questions follow the order of the text.
- Before you listen, underline the key words in the statements. Verbs and adjectives are often important.
- The ideas in the statements will be mentioned on tape; listen carefully to check that the statement reflects what is said.

Question 24: Does Andrew say that the smart pill is a new drug or is it something else?

Question 26: Andrew says that people 'worry about getting things wrong'. How is this comment reflected in the statement?

Question 30: Andrew says that people 'become confident'. Does this mean they are afraid of something?

PAPER 5

Speaking (14 minutes)

PART 1 (3 minutes)

The examiner (interlocutor) will ask each of you to speak briefly in turn and to give personal information about yourselves. You can expect a variety of questions, such as:

Where do you come from?
Have you always lived there/here?
Can you tell us what it's like? Would you like to live anywhere else?

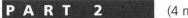

PART 2 (4 minutes)

You will each be asked to talk for a minute without interruption. You will each be given two different photographs in turn to talk about. After your partner has finished speaking you will be asked a brief question connected with your partner's photographs.

Eating out (compare, contrast and speculate)

Turn to pictures 1 and 2 on page 151 which show people eating out in different places.

Candidate A, compare and contrast these photographs and say why you think the people have chosen to eat in these particular places. You have a minute to do this.

Candidate B, which of these would you like to eat in?

Television (compare, contrast and speculate)

Turn to pictures 1 and 2 on page 152 which show people making a television programme.

Candidate B, compare and contrast these photographs and say how you think the people are feeling in these photographs. You have a minute to do this.

Candidate A, do you enjoy watching television?

PART 3 (3 minutes)

You will be asked to discuss something together without interruption by the examiner. You will have a page of pictures to help you.

People and travel (discuss and evaluate)

Turn to the pictures on page 153 which show different forms of transport. How popular do you think these different forms of transport are with different people?

PART 4 (4 minutes)

The examiner will encourage you to develop the topic of your discussion in Part 3 by asking questions such as:

Is it important to have a cheap public transport system? Why (not)?
Do you think people should pay more to use their own cars? Why (not)?
What do you think is the safest form of transport? Why?
If you go on a long journey, what form of transport do you choose? Why?

Tip Strip

Part 1
- The examiner (interlocutor) will ask you questions in turn. Don't prepare a little speech about yourself. Listen carefully to the examiner's questions which will be about you, your family, your interests and other things to do with the life you lead. Answer the questions as fully and as naturally as you can.

Part 2
- A minute is quite a long time to talk. If you do not clearly understand what you have been asked to do, ask the examiner to repeat the task for you. (within reason you won't lose any marks for doing this).Don't speak too fast.
- If you don't know a word in one of the photographs, try to describe it using other words to explain what you mean.
- Don't give separate descriptions of each picture. Compare and contrast them from the very beginning.
- Don't interrupt your partner's turn. Listen carefully and then respond briefly to the question which the examiner will put to you at the end of your partner's turn.

Part 3
- Ask your partner for his/her opinions, don't just say what you think.
- You have to talk for 3 min, so don't decide or agree too soon – talk about all the pictures first.
- You don't have to agree with your partner.

Part 4
The examiner may ask you questions in turn, or may ask general questions for you both to answer. For example, the examiner may say 'And what about you? What do you think? Do you agree?'
You don't have to agree with your partner, but try not to interrupt; let your partner finish, then say what you think.
Try to give reasons for your opinions and make your answers as full as possible.

TEST 2

Reading (1 hour 15 minutes)

You are going to read a newspaper article about living and working in Antarctica. Choose the most suitable heading from the list **A–I** for each part **1–7** of the article. There is one extra heading which you do not need to use. There is an example at the beginning (**0**).

Mark your answers **on the separate answer sheet.**

A	Avoiding human contact
B	Forced to remain
C	The most lonely place on earth
D	A choice of routine
E	Freezing temperatures
F	Alternative routes
G	Looking ahead
H	A varied community
I	The need for human contact

Tip Strip

- Part 1 asks you to match summary sentences or headings to parts of an article.
- Read the text for general understanding and don't worry if there are some words which you don't recognise; focus on understanding the **main point** of each paragraph.
- Then look at the paragraph headings; don't expect the words from the text to match.
- Check your answers carefully.

Heading A: Why might people at Davis Station want to avoid others occasionally?

Heading B: This talks about being 'forced to remain'. Which paragraph talks about people having no choice but to stay where they are?

Heading E: Could this heading be redundant as the whole article is about living in freezing conditions?

Heading H: This mentions 'a varied community'. Which paragraph illustrates the variety of people?

Dark days

0   C

The last ship of the season has left; the next will not be here until December. There will be eight months of isolation, cut off from the rest of the world on the edge of the world's coldest, remotest continent: Antarctica.

1

The people who spend the winter at Davis Station in Antarctica regard the departure of the last ship not with fear but with something like a feeling of relief. Gone are the busy days of summer, the helicopters, the crowd of people. Now life starts again.

2

There are more than 40 research projects being carried out in Antarctica but many of the scientists have left by the time winter arrives. The station is home to physicists, biologists, weather observers, mechanics, communications technicians, electricians, carpenters, plumbers, a doctor and a chef. There is also a station leader whose job it is to keep everyone happy and productive and to look after all the paperwork. When most of the team arrive each year in December, the sun never sets. By the beginning of the following June it will never rise, so people have to get used to many dark days.

3

It doesn't matter what hours people choose to work so long as the work gets done, so they can start and finish work at whatever times suit them. The first real meal of the day, a hot breakfast, is served at 10am. There is a hot lunch and a hot supper but putting on weight is a potential problem for many people. The doctor is there to advise on diet and exercise and a gym is available to help people keep fit.

4

Inevitably, small social groups develop within this isolated community. There is usually a group of smokers, a group of video watchers, a group of people who sit and chat. As people try to maintain contact with home so the cost of phone bills increases, but in any case there is nothing else to spend money on.

5

It is quite common for the sea to freeze during April and instead of waves lapping the beach, thick plates of ice lift and move with the tide. Once the sea ice has been checked to see if it is strong enough to walk on, one can ski over and fish through the holes. Eventually it becomes strong enough for vehicles to drive on it and the researchers can open up a new road system to enable them to drive around the coast in minutes, to huts which could only be reached after hours of walking in summer.

6

Trips to the huts are the only means of physically escaping from life on the station. Some trips are for science, others for recreation and a way of having some personal and private space. Some trips can be made on foot or skis, but in winter they are usually in vehicles.

7

There are no animals as they all leave for the winter, but in spring seals and seabirds and penguins arrive. Only humans stay in Antarctica for the full year, and although their lives are comfortable they are still isolated and imprisoned. They have good food, comfortable buildings, telephones, entertainment, the internet, but for many months at a time no chance of leaving.

You are going to read an article about one young English person's experience of a 'gap year', a year spent overseas, in China, between leaving school and going to university. For questions **8–14**, choose the correct answer **A**, **B**, **C** or **D**.

Mark your answers **on the separate answer sheet**.

INTO THE GAP

2 I am led into a large, whitewashed room to face a jury of 99. They are arranged in rows, and we look at each other through a cloud of yellow chalk dust. They have never met a foreigner before and eye me nervously as I step forward. I am in China for a year to work with 20-year-old students learning English. It felt odd being younger than my students, but I never felt too inexperienced to cope.

It had not been an easy choice to take the opportunity of doing a gap year. I was afraid of not being able to settle down to a life of studying when I returned and of losing touch with my friends. But once 16 the decision was made, I looked for somewhere challenging to live and work, with the possibility of travelling around the country at the end of my work placement.

I worked at a huge, concrete institute in a city with a million inhabitants and I grew to love it. The size of the class which could sometimes include up to 99 students, of very mixed ability and enthusiasm, left me feeling exhausted, but rewarded.

One of the best things about the work 29 was that I met hundreds of people, and felt appreciated and welcomed by them – people who had had practically no contact with the West. In China,

everyone wants to be your friend. My best Chinese mate was Mr Chow, a 35-year-old electronics teacher with a son, wife, and a cheerful face like a full moon. I helped him with his English and he coached me at table tennis, and taught me how to ride a motorbike. Best of all, he was a great storyteller, and some of my best nights were spent eating with him and his family. In China I learnt that fun takes on different forms. 43

In the more remote areas of China where life and landscape have changed little in hundreds of years, you can really feel like a cross between a celebrity and a creature from outer space. I've been on train journeys when kids have asked me to sign their clothes, been on television a few times – and just what do you say when Chinese men are stroking your legs, amazed by the fact that they are so hairy?

So, what have I come away with? I had no choice but to adapt, budget, bargain and become more independent. There's no faster way to grow up than having to stand in front of those 99 students, all older than yourself and tell someone off for turning up late again to a lesson.

Most of all I loved the experience of living in a different country and the challenge of trying to understand it.

Tip Strip

Question 9: Always read what has come before as well as what comes after with this kind of question.

Question 10: Don't be mislead by word-spotting; at the beginning of the text the writer mentions the fact that the students eyed him 'nervously'.

8 What does the use of the word 'jury' suggest about the writer's feelings in line 2?

A He thinks he has committed a crime.
B The students already find him boring.
C He cannot understand their behaviour.
D He knows they want to see what he is like.

9 What does the word 'decision' in line 16 refer to?

A going to university
B returning home
C going abroad
D contacting friends

10 Which phrase best sums up the writer's feelings about his job?

A concerned and nervous
B tired but fulfilled
C enthusiastic but worried
D successful and excited

11 How do the 'hundreds of people' react to the writer? (line 29)

A They were suspicious of him.
B They were amused by him.
C They were sociable to him.
D They were puzzled by him.

12 What does the writer suggest by saying 'fun takes on different forms' in line 43?

A He was surprised at his enjoyment of simple things.
B He got more fun from learning than teaching.
C He missed Western forms of entertainment.
D He enjoyed meeting his students outside lessons.

13 The children wanted the writer to sign their clothes because he was

A famous.
B unusual.
C popular.
D funny.

14 What does the writer conclude about his gap year?

A It enabled him to learn Chinese.
B He learnt how to control a class.
C He learnt to cope with foreigners.
D It helped him become more mature.

You are going to read a magazine article about a man who used to work at London Zoo. Eight paragraphs have been removed from the article. Choose from the paragraphs **A–I** the one which fits each gap **15–21**. There is one extra paragraph which you do not need to use. There is an example at the beginning (**0**).

Mark your answers **on the separate answer sheet.**

RATTLING THE CAGE

When Oliver Graham-Jones first arrived at London Zoo in 1951, he came across a number of difficulties. The zoo had changed little since it was built in 1823 and the keepers who looked after the animals were used to organising things their own way.

0	G

However, a new law changed all that in 1948 and only qualified vets were allowed to treat animals. The keepers, used to being in charge, disliked having a clever young boss with new ideas.

15	

He made such a fuss in the first year that many of the keepers refused to speak to him. He quarrelled with almost everybody and after a year the zoo management decided that his job would remain on a temporary contract.

16	

On one occasion when Mr Graham-Jones ordered that the heating in the animal houses should be switched off, the keepers went on strike.

17	

Despite all the arguing, the young vet was responsible for some major new improvements and most importantly for setting up the zoo's animal hospital.

18	

Today Mr Graham-Jones, now in his eighties, is against animals being in cages. 'In an ideal world, there wouldn't be places like London Zoo. We would have only safari parks as these are the best places to keep animals.'

19	

'However, to be fair to London Zoo, the management has done the best possible and opened up the animals areas as much as they can. But people nowadays have cars.' The situation is clearly different from 1948.

20	

Things have certainly changed. When Mr Graham-Jones first joined the zoo he actually lived in the zoo grounds.

21	

Later on he moved to live off site and eventually in 1966 he left the zoo altogether and became a college lecturer.

Another task in Part 3 asks you to replace paragraphs into an article.

• Read through the text carefully so that you have a general understanding.

• Look very carefully at the whole paragraph, before and after each gap.

• Read through the paragraph options and find one that fits in terms of topic and language links.

• Re-read the text and the paragraphs again to check that they make sense.

Paragraph C: Look at the tone of this paragraph as another clue for fitting it into the text.

Paragraph D: Another clue: look the way in which OGJ's words echo what has just been mentioned in the previous paragraph.

Paragraph E: The phrase 'at last' summarises the end of OGJ's battle to get things changed.

A 'The lion and monkey houses were shut up at 4pm when the keepers went home, leaving all the heating turned on. This resulted in the overnight temperatures being too high and, not surprisingly, a number of animals became ill.'

B According to Mr Jones, the moment you start to put cages around animals you've got a man-made artificial environment which doesn't suit animals.

C 'Nobody really wanted me,' said Mr Graham-Jones. 'The zoo keepers had their own ideas about nutrition, about what the animals should eat and these ideas had been handed down over the years from keeper to keeper. It took two years for me to settle in.'

D 'I didn't care if the job was temporary for 10 years; the zoo needed me and I was determined to improve the conditions for the animals.'

E He felt that he was at last in charge of a proper clinic where he could give the animals the quality of care he felt they deserved. The facilities included a fully equipped operating theatre in a clean and healthy environment.

F 'They don't need London Zoo – they can go to the country and visit safari parks, which are much better for animals. I'm not anti-zoo, all I'm saying is that places like this have served their purpose. Modern zoo keeping is rather different.'

G They only ever called in a vet – someone who specialised in treating sick animals – when it was absolutely necessary.

H The plan was a disaster. He ran out of money, decided that he didn't want to continue working as a vet and that he would re-train as a doctor.

I To enable him to look after the zoo's 800 animals he had a flat situated between the seals and the hippos! Although very convenient, the flat was decidedly noisy, especially in the early morning.

You are going to read a magazine article in which four different women talk about the importance of their own personal space. For questions **22–35,** choose from the people **A–D**. The people may be chosen more than once. When more than one answer is required, these may be given in any order. There is an example at the beginning (**0**).

Mark your answers **on the separate answer sheet.**

Which of the women

spends her day in conversation with others?	**0**	D
would like to take exercise during the day?	**22**	
worries she might upset other people?	**23**	
builds in a special time to be alone at home?	**24**	**25**
escapes outside to find peace and quiet?	**26**	
likes to prepare mentally for what is to come?	**27**	
gets annoyed if she has no time to herself?	**28**	**29**
thinks other people may feel equally stressed?	**30**	
relies entirely on her home environment for space?	**31**	
feels pressurised by too many demands at work?	**32**	
relies on personal space early in the day?	**33**	
creates space for herself even if she is not at home?	**34**	
has no time to relax during her working day?	**35**	

Tip Strip

Question 22: Look for someone expressing a wish.
Question 26: What word expresses the same idea as 'peace and quiet'?
Question 32: Look for how a list of things conveys how the person feels.

MY OWN PERSONAL SPACE

A Katrin

I always need to get away from other people at some point during the day. It's not that I don't get on with others, I've loads of friends. But I work in a really busy office in the centre of town and from the moment I leave home each morning it's non-stop. Crowds on the buses, busy streets, office bustle, phones, e-mail, do this, do that ... By the time the end of the day comes, I'm desperate for some peace and quiet. Even if I'm going out later in the evening, I always make sure I have at least an hour to myself without anyone being able to disturb me. I arrive home, make myself a drink and lie on the sofa. I close my eyes and relax by concentrating on each part of my body in turn, beginning with my neck. Even if I'm away from home, I try to find the time just to be alone in order to unwind and recharge my batteries. If I don't make this space for myself, I feel really tense and irritable.

B Lia

I share a student flat with three others, so there's never a quiet moment. When I come back from college in the evenings it's quite likely that there'll be other people there as well and we'll all have supper together. It's great fun but towards the end of the evening I feel really tired and so I like to disappear by myself for a while. It's hopeless to try and find any privacy in the flat, so I go out for a walk. Whatever the weather, I walk through the park which is quite close. Late at night it's usually empty. There are just shadows and the rustle of animals and birds. It's very peaceful and it gives me the opportunity to reflect on the day and to think about what I have to do the next day. When I get back to the flat I like to go straight to bed. Usually I fall asleep pretty quickly even if the others are still up and chatting or listening to music. If I don't get this time to myself, I'll be like a bear with a sore head the next morning and not nice to know!

C Beatriz

I'm a night owl and I absolutely hate getting up in the mornings. If people try and talk to me before midday, I really snap at them. Being an actress means that I work late so it's important that I create space for myself at the beginning of each day. And because I use my voice so much, in fact totally depend on it, I like to rest my voice and just listen to music when I wake up. I don't even want to hear other people's voices. Some people find this very hard to understand and get quite cross when I tell them not to contact me before noon. I tell them it's nothing personal but they still sound offended. I'm sure it must be the same for singers and, who knows, maybe teachers and lecturers get fed up with hearing the sound of their own voice and simply long to be by themselves somewhere, in complete silence.

D Natalie

I work in a call centre, which means I'm constantly on the phone. Apart from lunch and two short breaks during the day I'm speaking to people all day long. And of course you never get to see who you're speaking to! By the end of my shift I'm exhausted, not because I'm rushing around or I'm on my feet all day but simply because I've spent the day talking and listening. The breaks are so short that there's no time to do anything other than get a drink and something to eat. I'd love to be able to go for a walk but there's nowhere to escape to within easy walking distance. The building where I work is in the middle of an industrial estate, you can't even see a single tree. So my flat is full of house plants and when I get home it's wonderful to be able to relax, surrounded by all the greenery. I lie on the floor, stretch out, look up at the plants and try to imagine I'm in a tropical rainforest miles away!

Writing (1 hour 30 minutes)

You **must** answer this question.

1 You and your friends are organising a class trip. You have seen the advertisement below, but you need more information. Using the notes you have made, write to *Out of Class*, giving necessary details and asking for further information.

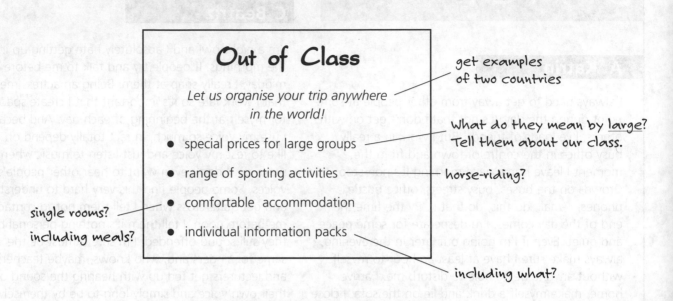

Out of Class

Let us organise your trip anywhere in the world!

- special prices for large groups
- range of sporting activities
- comfortable accommodation
- individual information packs

get examples of two countries

What do they mean by <u>large</u>? Tell them about our class.

horse-riding?

single rooms?
including meals?

including what?

Write a **letter** of between **120** and **180** words in an appropriate style. Do not write any addresses.

Write an answer to **one** of the questions **2–5** in this part. Write your answer in **120–180** words in an appropriate style.

2 An international magazine is asking young people to send in articles which will be published in a special edition. The title of the article is:

The person in the world I would most like to meet and why.

Write your **article**.

3 You have decided to enter a short story competition. The rules of the competition are that your story must **begin** with the following words:
Joni closed the door very quietly and waited.

Write your **story**.

4 This is part of a letter you receive from an English-speaking pen friend.

> I didn't know you were going camping with your friends. What was it like? Do tell me all about it when you next write.

Write your **letter** telling your pen friend about your camping experience. Do not write any addresses.

5 Answer **one** of the following two questions based on your reading of **one** of the set books.

Either (a) Which of the characters in the book is your favourite?
With reference to the book you have read, write a **composition** explaining why you especially like this character.

Or (b) 'This book is a really good read.' Write a **composition** saying whether you agree or disagree with this statement and giving your reasons why.

Tip Strip

Question 2:
• Remember you are writing for young people. Pick somebody you know something about (pop star? actor?) so you can say why you would so much like to meet him/her.

Question 3:
• Plan your story **before** you start writing. Has it got a beginning, a middle and an end?
• Think about verb sequences, e.g. Past simple /Past perfect.
• Try to make your story as interesting as possible.
• Remember that stories don't have greetings or headings.

Question 4:
• Explain to your friend why you hadn't mentioned you were going camping.

• Tell him/her who you went camping with; mention a few things that happened whilst you were camping and whether or not you enjoyed yourself.
• Use an informal style, but start and end the letter in an appropriate letter format.

Question 5(a):
• Choose a character whom you feel you know well from the story so that you can include plenty of reasons as to why he/she is your favourite.
• Use a neutral to formal style.

Question 5(b):
• Say whether you agree or disagree with the statement.
• Include examples from the book to justify your opinion, and to make it clear why you enjoyed/didn't enjoy reading it.
• Use a neutral to formal style.

PAPER 3

PART 1

For Questions **1–15**, read the text below and decide which answer **A, B, C** or **D** best fits each space. There is an example at the beginning (**0**).

Mark your answers **on the separate answer sheet**.

Tip Strip

Question 4: The writer does not believe people go for the coffee.

Question 7: Which word can be used without needing an object?

Question 11: Which verb is invariably used with 'business'?

Example:

| 0 | **A** hopped | **B** looked | **C** jumped | **D** popped |

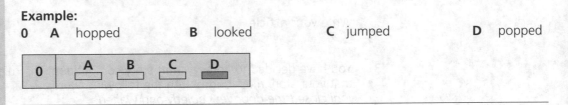

COFFEE CULTURE

The other day I wanted a cup of coffee, so I (**0**) ..... into the bank. I sat in a soft armchair and watched the world (**1**) ..... , which, in this case, was the (**2**) ..... for the services of the bank clerks. I'm joking, of course, but this could soon be common in banks in big cities.

The (**3**) ..... for 'real coffee' in Britain, like that for mobile phones, seems never-ending. However, the (**4**) ..... is that the attraction for many British people (**5**) ..... not so much in the coffee as in the 'coffee culture' that surrounds it. This is to do with big, soft sofas and the idea that if you sit on one, you too can (**6**) ..... the actors in the American TV comedy *Friends*.

In London, the first café opened in 1652. Men would (**7**) ..... there, often at (**8**) ..... times during the day, to (**9**) ..... news and gossip, discuss (**10**) ..... of the day and (**11**) ..... business. The cafés acted as offices and shops in which merchants and agents, clerks and bankers could carry out their (**12**) ....

In London today it is (**13**) ..... that there are more than 2000 cafés and the number is (**14**) ..... . It won't be long before coffee is sold everywhere. You can already buy it in hospitals, motorway service stations, supermarkets and at tourist (**15**) ..... throughout the country.

1	**A** fly past	**B** go by	**C** pass on	**D** walk along
2	**A** queue	**B** line	**C** wait	**D** search
3	**A** demand	**B** development	**C** claim	**D** supply
4	**A** sense	**B** suspect	**C** suspicion	**D** style
5	**A** leans	**B** lies	**C** occupies	**D** rests
6	**A** be	**B** feel	**C** join	**D** contact
7	**A** bring	**B** fetch	**C** take	**D** gather
8	**A** regular	**B** right	**C** correct	**D** perfect
9	**A** give	**B** exchange	**C** offer	**D** establish
10	**A** thoughts	**B** issues	**C** feelings	**D** circumstances
11	**A** make	**B** perform	**C** do	**D** form
12	**A** trading	**B** transactions	**C** information	**D** works
13	**A** estimated	**B** guessed	**C** taken	**D** told
14	**A** raising	**B** growing	**C** succeeding	**D** remaining
15	**A** scenes	**B** points	**C** attractions	**D** matters

For Questions **16–30,** read the text below and think of the word which best fits each space. Use only **one** word in each space. There is an example at the beginning (**0**).

Write your answers **on the separate answer sheet.**

Example:

0	their

SPORTS TOURISM

Hundreds of thousands of fans travel worldwide to watch (**0**) ......*their*........ favourite sport – an international match, a tennis championship, a Formula One Grand Prix.

In recent years (**16**) .... has been a huge increase in sports tourism. (**17**) .... longer are people content to (**18**) .... in an armchair to watch their teams or sporting stars on television. They want to be (**19**) .... the action is, (**20**) .... they pack their bags and head straight for the airport.

In (**21**) .... to the usual sporting events, the Olympic Games are held (**22**) .... four years. The Olympics may only last a couple of weeks, but (**23**) .... affect the host city for several years before. New facilities (**24**) .... to be built, not just for the Games themselves (**25**) .... also for the thousands of international visitors (**26**) .... come to stay. The effects are also felt outside the host city (**27**) .... many visitors choose to explore the surrounding region, and this (**28**) .... a lasting effect on tourism in the country. For example, (**29**) .... the 1992 Olympic Games were held in Barcelona, in Spain, the city has (**30**) .... an extremely popular tourist destination.

Tip Strip

Question 21: The word both before and after the gap and the second part of the sentence should help you decide what kind of word is missing.

Question 26: What type of word goes here? What word can stand in for a noun?

Question 29: What kind of word are you likely to need when referring to a date in the past?

For Questions **31–40,** complete the second sentence so that it has a similar meaning to the first sentence, using the word given. **Do not change the word given.** You must use between two and five words, including the word given. Here is an example (**0**).

Example: **0** The bag is not big enough for all my luggage.

small

The bag .... for all my luggage.

The gap can be filled by the words 'is too small' so you write:

0	is too small

Write **only the missing words** on the separate answer sheet.

Tip Strip

Question 32: What kind of word do you need to put after 'wish'?

Question 35: What preposition do you need to make this word into a phrasal verb meaning 'scold'?

Question 40: Careful – you will need to replace 'expensive' with another word.

31 'Don't speak so loudly, John,' said Petra.

asked

Petra .... so loudly.

32 I'm sorry I can't meet you this evening.

wish

I .... this evening.

33 It may rain later so take an umbrella.

case

Take an umbrella .... later.

34 David carried on working despite feeling very sleepy.

even

David carried on working .... very sleepy.

35 Marie scolded her son for breaking the vase.

told

Marie .... for breaking the vase.

36 I am not interested in computers.

interest

Computers .... me.

37 We were all surprised to see Kitty at the party.

surprise

To .... to the party.

38 The Beatles are thought by many people to be among the world's best pop groups.

that

Many people .... the world's best pop groups were The Beatles.

39 Is it all right for me to borrow your car?

if

Do .... your car?

40 The rent for this flat is more expensive than I had expected.

as

The rent for this flat is .... I had expected.

For Questions **41–55**, read the text below and look carefully at each line. Some of the lines are correct, and some have a word which should not be there.

Tip Strip

Line 46: Which conjunction isn't needed here?

Line 49: Which word could be used in this sentence but is in the wrong position here?

If a line is correct, put a tick (✔) by the number **on the separate answer sheet**. If a line has a word which should not be there, write the word **on the separate answer sheet**. There are examples at the beginning (**0** and **00**).

Example:	0	✔
	00	into

TIME TRAVEL

0	....	Have you ever wished you could travel back into the past
00	....	to change into some moment in your life? Have you ever
41	....	wanted to visit some important event in the history? Time
42	....	travel is a wonderful idea but it is full of difficulties. One
43	....	famous scientist, is Stephen Hawking, has said that if time
44	....	travel was possible we would be visited by time tourists. But
45	....	as we are since obviously not visited by such people, then time
46	....	travel is impossible. Other scientists, and however, disagree
47	....	with him and argue that our planet, Earth, is so far tiny a part
48	....	of the universe that time travellers have not yet visited this time
49	....	and place. Would it be possible so to travel into the future?
50	....	Scientists say that there this is almost certainly impossible,
51	....	although there is a faint ray of hope. It is believed that in the
52	....	future the universe will stop or expanding and start to grow smaller.
53	....	This may allow travel into the future although there is one major
54	....	problem: it will take on another few billion years before the
55	....	universe reaches to this stage.

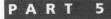

PART 5

For questions **56–65,** read the text below. Use the word given in capitals at the end of each line to form a word that fits the space in the same line. There is an example at the beginning (**0**).

Example:

0	organisation

Write your answers **on the separate answer sheet.**

VOICES FOUNDATION

Voices Foundation is a music education (**0**) <u>organisation</u>. Its founder,   **ORGANISE**

Susan Digby, believes (**56**) .... that learning to sing is the   **PASSION**

best way to introduce children to music. 'Playing a (**57**) ....   **MUSIC**

instrument is difficult, and the (**58**) .... of children who begin   **MAJOR**

usually give up, but everyone has a voice,' she says.

Digby's (**59**) .... for the Foundation came when she was   **INSPIRE**

travelling in Hungary. 'People there believe that a child's

(**60**) .... benefits from music education, and it has   **DEVELOP**

a (**61**) .... effect on other skills, like   **SIGNIFY**

(**62**) .... and linguistic skills. Music education provides a   **MATHEMATICS**

training which extends children's (**63**) .... and listening   **COMMUNICATE**

powers.' Digby believes that if children get (**64**) .... from   **ENJOY**

singing, they are more likely to learn an instrument (**65**) ....   **WILL**

when they are older.

Tip Strip

Question 56: Is an adverb, a verb or an adjective needed here?

Question 58: Is the word required more frequently used in its singular or plural form?

Question 63: Take care with the spelling of this word.

PAPER 4

Listening (approximately 40 minutes)

PART 1

You'll hear people talking in eight different situations. For Questions **1–8**, choose the best answer, **A, B** or **C**.

Tip Strip

Question 2: What do you learn when the woman says 'I'd make it and take it with us when we're out walking'?

Question 6: Where did these early plays take place?

Question 8: Listen out for when the woman says 'what's really attractive'; this will help you focus on the answer.

1   You hear part of a radio programme about a sports personality.
    What has he recently achieved?
    A   a new sporting record
    B   another gold medal
    C   a financial reward

1

2   You hear a woman asking for a recipe.
    What does she want to make?
    A   something for supper
    B   something for a party
    C   something for a picnic

2

3   You hear man talking about animals.
    What is he recommending?
    A   feeding a pet a balanced diet
    B   giving a pet plenty of exercise
    C   making sure a pet is looked after

3

4   You hear part of a radio programme about travelling abroad.
    Who is speaking?
    A   a journalist
    B   a tour guide
    C   a travel agent

4

5   You overhear a student talking about one of her classes.
    What has she done?
    A   missed attending a class
    B   withdrawn from a class
    C   complained about a class

5

6   You hear a woman talking about a new book on the theatre.
    What is the best title for the book?
    A   Popular Street Theatre
    B   Travelling Theatre Players
    C   Open-air Plays and Players

6

7   You overhear two people discussing a museum they have recently visited.
    What kind of museum was it?
    A   a costume museum
    B   a natural history museum
    C   a transport museum

7

8   You hear a woman discussing a new fashion.
    What does she like about it?
    A   the colours
    B   the designs
    C   the materials

8

You will hear part of a radio programme in which a man talks about his childhood in Australia. For Questions **9–18,** complete the sentences.

Tip Strip

Question 10: Are you likely to need a noun or a verb to complete this sentence?

Question 13: Can you predict what kind of word might fill this gap?

Question 14: William mentions that 'winter nights were very cold'. What might people leave on overnight?

William could hear rain falling on the [**9**] of his house.

People used [**10**] to stop their windows breaking.

William's parents had [**11**] and torches when the electricity failed.

In the wet season the [**12**] were unusable because they flooded.

People relied on using a [**13**] to receive whatever they wanted.

William enjoyed cycling through fields where [**14**] was grown.

Bandicoots are more commonly known as [**15**]

In Alice Springs the [**16**] are left on overnight.

Boarding school in Australia may be [**17**] from where you live.

People stay [**18**] during the hottest part of the day.

You will hear five different people talking about what they like about their favourite restaurant. For Questions **19–23,** choose from the list **A–F** what each speaker says. Use the letters only once. There is one extra letter which you do not need to use.

Tip Strip

Speakers 2, 3, 4 and 5 mention food, but none of them talks about a varied menu. 'Blue potatoes', however, are mentioned as being original. Which option contains this idea?

A: What other words do we use when we want to talk about 'scenery'?

D: Listen for someone who mentions their need to be away from the rest of the world.

A I love the scenery.

B I enjoy the varied menu.

C I like the fact that it's so ordinary.

D I like being cut off from reality.

E I enjoy observing everyone.

F I like it because it's different.

Speaker 1 [**19**]

Speaker 2 [**20**]

Speaker 3 [**21**]

Speaker 4 [**22**]

Speaker 5 [**23**]

PART 4

You will hear an interview with a woman who has left her own country to live abroad. For Questions **24–30**, choose the best answer **A, B** or **C.**

Tip Strip

Another task in Part 4 asks you to choose the best answer in multiple choice questions.
• Before you listen, read through the questions and underline key words.
• Listen to find the answer to a question, then choose the option (A, B or C) which is the closest.
Most questions will be about people's feelings, ideas, attitudes and opinions.

Question 24: Karin says that 'there was no reason why I shouldn't stay'. Which option reflects this feeling?

Question 26: Think about other words or expressions for these adjectives; you will not hear the identical words in the options.

Question 28: Once again, think of other similar words that Karin might use to express her feelings.

24 What made Karin decide to move to Italy?
A There was nothing to stop her.
B Her friends were already there.
C She wanted to learn Italian.

25 Why did Karin return to the UK for two weeks?
A to collect her furniture
B to buy a new car
C to sort out her affairs

26 How did Karin feel after a few weeks in Italy?
A worried
B lonely
C unhappy

27 How did Karin find a job?
A She asked her landlord's wife.
B Her landlord offered her some work.
C She wrote to a language school.

28 How did she feel about her job?
A very afraid
B quite helpless
C very impatient

29 When Karin first took a customer's orders,
A she smiled and spoke very softly.
B she couldn't understand what the person said.
C she managed without any problems.

30 How does Karin feel about her experience?
A Things were quite easy.
B She was very fortunate.
C She took a very big risk.

PAPER 5   Speaking (14 minutes)

Tip Strip

Part 1

• Listen to the instructions. Make sure you do what is asked.

• Don't be afraid to ask your partner or the examiner to repeat something if you haven't understood.

• Listen to the questions the examiner asks your partner, and listen to what your partner says. The examiner may say 'And what about you?' or 'Do you agree?'

• Don't give short answers. Say what you think and why.

 **PART 1**   (3 minutes)

The examiner (interlocutor) will ask each of you to speak briefly in turn and to give personal information about yourselves. You can expect a variety of questions, such as:

What subjects are you studying? / What job do you do?
What are you hoping to do when you leave school/college?
What are your plans for the future?

PART 2   (4 minutes)

You will each be asked to talk for a minute without interruption. You will each be given two different photographs in turn to talk about. After your partner has finished speaking you will be asked a brief question connected with your partner's photographs.

Travelling (compare, contrast and speculate)

Turn to pictures 1 and 2 on page 154 which show people traveling.

Candidate B, compare and contrast these photographs and say what you think the people in the photograph are feeling about travelling. You have a minute to do this.

Candidate A, do you like travelling with or without a lot of luggage?

Playing a musical instrument (compare, contrast and speculate)

Turn to pictures 1 and 2 on page 155 which show people playing musical instruments.

Candidate A, compare and contrast these photographs and say what you think the people in the photographs are feeling. You have a minute to do this.

Candidate B, do you play a musical instrument?

 **PART 3**   (3 minutes)

Communications (discuss and evaluate)

Turn to the pictures on page 156 which show the different ways we can keep in touch with what is happening in the world. What are the best ways of finding out what is going on?

PART 4   (4 minutes)

The examiner will encourage you to develop the topic of your discussion in Part 3 by asking questions such as:

Is it important to know what is happening in the world? Why (not)?
Do you think computers will eventually replace books and newspapers?
How interested are you in keeping up with the news in your own country?
Do you think there is too much news on the radio and television? Why (not)?

TEST 3

PAPER 1   Reading (1 hour 15 minutes)

You are going to read an article about a photographer who specialises in taking photographs of birds called storks. Choose from the list **A–H** the heading which best summarises each part (**1–6**) of the article. There is one extra heading which you do not need to use. There is an example at the beginning (**0**).

Mark your answers **on the separate answer sheet**.

A Storks will nest anywhere	**D** An important factor affecting stork numbers	**G** The photographer's first task
B An impressive sight		**H** Storks able to guarantee their existence
C Storks unlikely to find new nesting areas	**E** The reason for the photographer's visit	
	F Storks don't mind where they feed	

White Storks

0   *E*

As I walked along the narrow streets of a small Spanish village, I felt excited at the prospect of being allowed up onto the roof of a beautiful church. My purpose in being there was to take photographs of the white storks which had been seen nesting in the bell tower high above the village streets. In fact, storks had been my ticket into many similar adventures over the years.

1

Storks are large, beautiful birds with long necks and taking pictures of them is not easy. In towns and villages storks build their nests, which are like platforms made out of twigs, high up on rooftops or treetops. So my initial job was to collect a huge key, let myself into the church, and climb up the bell tower so that I could at least see the white stork nest on the roof of the tower.

2

I eventually reached the top and lifted the door above my head. After the hot, dry streets below there was a wonderful cool breeze and staring at me from their nest about forty metres away were three half-grown storks. It was a marvellous scene, especially in view of the fact that towards the end of the twentieth century there was great concern about the future of the white stork.

3

The numbers of storks had been decreasing for various reasons. The major cause for this decrease was probably due to the lack of rain in West Africa. Storks traditionally escape the European winter and depend on insects and other animals for their food supply. The severe drought caused by hardly any rainfall for years in West Africa had reduced the storks' supply of food with disastrous consequences.

4

Human development has also affected the stork's ability to survive, but in this case the bird has proved to be very adaptable. In natural environments, the stork nests in trees and on rocks. However, as buildings began to spread onto the storks' natural nesting sites, the birds adjusted to this loss by carrying their twigs even higher. Radio towers, road signs, statues, monuments, chimneys and even pylons carrying electricity have become loaded with piles of twigs.

5

Another example of the stork's amazing ability to adjust to changes in the environment is its diet. If a stork can't find sufficient food in its natural habitat, then it seems it will quite happily feed off what it can find in rubbish tips. This reliable source of food is probably one of the reasons why a sizeable percentage of the stork populations in Spain no longer migrate by flying off to Africa for the winter.

6

However, there is a new threat to storks on the horizon. European Union rules and regulations may affect the source of food found on rubbish tips, as governments are now being asked to clean up rubbish tips by covering them over. This will obviously cut off a valuable food supply for the storks. Nevertheless, like any animal or bird which has so successfully adapted to human development, the stork will no doubt find a way to ensure it will survive long into the future.

You are going to read an extract from an article about an unusual form of storytelling. For Questions 7–14, choose the correct answer **A, B, C** or **D**.

Mark your answers **on the separate answer sheet**.

Unusual storytelling

'It's the seventh minute into a match and we're up against one of the top clubs in Britain. We're expected to lose. I get the ball and I'm running as fast as I can for the goal. The goalkeeper runs towards me. Do I try to get round him or shall I shoot?'

'Go round him,' calls out one voice. 'Shoot!' shout a few of the kids gathered on the floor.

'I decide to shoot and I can see the ball going wide. But then I look up and see my mum blowing hard on her whistle from the side of the pitch, and the ball swings to the right and falls inside the goal post. I've just scored and we're one-nil up against the favourites.'

It's gripping storytelling and not a single child has moved. It also happens that every word is true, with the exception of
21 the bit about his mum! The speaker is a former football player, Barry Morgan, who now works as a community relations officer in a large city in southern England.

Part of Barry's job involves visiting clubs, schools and libraries along with a professional storyteller, Rick Taylor, in order to try and reach the kids who mainly sit at the back of classrooms and don't want to take part in lessons. They want to both excite the children's imaginations and encourage them to read, and so far they are delighted with the success of the project.

The original idea for the project was Rick Taylor's. Over the years he had collected a huge number of folk tales and stories and had earned his living travelling around the world telling them. After a one-off event with Barry Morgan, which was a tremendous success, Taylor decided that they should try and do more. **44**

'It was particularly good for the kids to have strong male role models involved. Many boys grow up wanting to be professional footballers and they'll listen to what we have to say far more readily than they would listen to their teachers. It's not just the boys who get a lot out of it; even though a lot of the stories are football based, the girls never get bored,' says Taylor.

But there are other groups for whom the storytelling has been a learning process. On one occasion, for example, Barry Morgan took some young professional footballers with him to one of the storytelling sessions. The players explained to the kids how relaxing with a book before a big game could improve their performance. 'Footballers have a fairly short career,' says Morgan, 'and most of them move on to other jobs in the leisure industry, running a business or public speaking. For all these careers you need good communication skills and telling stories to a bunch of school kids is great practice for the future. When I first started playing football I had almost no self-confidence but nowadays I'm quite happy standing up in front of 500 children.'

Tip Strip

Question 7: Make sure you read far enough into the text before you answer this question!

Question 10: Remember that this kind of question may require you to read both backwards as well as forwards in the text.

Question 11: The key information is not explicitly stated. What can you tell from the boys' attitudes?

7 Where is the speaker at the beginning of the article?

   A running on a football pitch
   B playing football with some children
   C reliving an earlier football match
   D sitting in a football stadium

8 What does 'the bit about his mum' (line 21) add to what the speaker says?

   A It's intended to praise his mother.
   B It's intended to make his listeners laugh.
   C It's important to involve your mother.
   D It's unusual for a woman to referee a match.

9 What do we learn about the children involved in the storytelling project?

   A They love reading stories in the classroom.
   B They enjoy being part of a club.
   C They are not interested in being at school.
   D They dislike having to go to libraries.

10 What does Taylor mean by 'do more' (line 44)?

   A He wanted the opportunity to earn more money.
   B He needed more stories from other parts of the world.
   C He felt the stories they told could be more successful.
   D He thought they could organise much more storytelling.

11 What is the attraction of this form of storytelling for many boys?

   A They admire the people telling the stories.
   B They enjoy listening to some good teachers.
   C They hope to become storytellers themselves.
   D They like the fact that girls are not included.

12 What did the young footballers recommend about reading?

   A It can make you play better.
   B It helps you to feel relaxed.
   C It makes you more confident.
   D It makes you a better storyteller.

13 What does the writer suggest about footballers in general?

   A They are not particularly well educated.
   B They adapt well to other professions.
   C They have trouble communicating with people.
   D They have to be prepared to look for other jobs.

14 How has Morgan benefited from storytelling?

   A He could take up another career.
   B He has become more sure of himself.
   C He became a good businessman.
   D He enjoyed meeting new people.

You are going to read a newspaper article about a writer's experience of winter in Siberia. Eight sentences have been removed from the article. Choose from the sentences **A–I** the one that fits each gap (**15–21**). There is one extra sentence which you do not need to use. There is an example at the beginning (**0**).

Mark your answers **on the separate answer sheet**.

A few years ago I decided I needed some peace and quiet to write a book. On the grounds that nothing from the real world could possibly disturb me out there, I arranged to swap my London flat for a little town in the middle of Siberia. **0** **C** I had heard that it was cold enough to make your eyes water and freeze the teardrops on your face.

I wasn't going to Siberia to get a tan. But writing a book in a cosy flat when it was cold outside was one thing. **15** I had picked the town because it was so remote and it had the reputation of being one of the coldest places on Earth. **16**

Anyway, off I drove to find my apartment in a block which I knew would be warm and well-heated by a communal central heating system. I must confess that when I got there I was not prepared for the fact that I had to break the ice off the door before I could open it. **17** I discovered later that these radiators continued to push out heat for seven or eight months of the year.

18 Every passer-by wore a huge hat and went about covered in a personal cloud of steam. Enormous sheets of ice hung from the trees, walls and balconies and the pavements looked like marble, millions of years old.

Siberian children, I was pleased to see, got their kicks from sliding on ice and attacking each other with snowballs. **19**

A fortnight after my arrival, we were informed on the news that temperatures were going to drop even further. **20** 'Are you ready for it?' Now when I went to market I found women with their faces wrapped to the eyeballs, standing behind piles of fish, frozen solid. Ice cream was sold in unpackaged, naked lumps and for a few days we went around with hats and collars covered in frost.

In these bitterest days, heard no word in the tram stations or the bus stops, just the sound of crunching snow and silence. We all knew that there was no shortage of energy and if our flats were warm and we could make ourselves cups of tea there was nothing to worry about. **21** In the local theatre, I heard that a group of dancers had to practise their movements while wearing huge boots. Buses drove around in pairs in case one of them broke down, and schools had to close.

Walking home through the town centre one night with the temperature at -38°C, I came across people who had built fires from cardboard boxes, still trying to sell their goods and hoping people would stop to look at what was on sale. That same evening I wandered out to admire the glittering snow under brilliant stars.

I eventually finished my book as the temperatures reached zero, the pavement snow turned grey and another Siberian winter appeared to be almost over.

A Some people did worry, however.

B Out in the streets I found a certain pleasure in the extreme cold.

C In fact it was so far from anywhere else that most people didn't even know whether it counted as being in Europe or Asia.

D Moreover, on arriving and leaving the aeroplane, the immediate effect of the moisture freezing on my eyelashes was extremely unpleasant.

E The ice on my windows has finally melted.

F But once inside the flat I found there were radiators heating every room twenty-four hours a day.

G Writing a book when it was -45°C was quite another.

H In the centre of the town was an ice-chute and the children would spend long hours sliding down the chute with their feet in the air.

I 'Have you heard?' people kept asking me, in excitement.

Tip Strip

Sentence A: This suggests that it will contradict something which has just been stated in the text.
Sentence B: Could this sentence occur at the beginning of a paragraph?
Sentence G: There is a parallel structure in the text which is another kind of clue.

You are going to read a magazine article about five people who use computers. For Questions **22–35,** choose from the people **A–E**. The people may be chosen more than once. When more than one answer is required, these may be given in any order. There is an example at the beginning (**0**).

Mark your answers **on the separate answer sheet.**

Which of the people uses a computer

for entertainment?	**0**	*D*
to help keep appointments with colleagues?	**22**	
to find out about business competitors?	**23**	
for planning rough copies of their work?	**24**	
to create better pictures?	**25**	
while on a journey?	**26**	
to catch up on new things in their specialist areas?	**27**	**28**
because other people rely on you to have one?	**29**	
to reduce feelings of loneliness?	**30**	
even though it does not feel very individual?	**31**	
because it cuts down on costs?	**32**	
even though it is not the latest model?	**33**	
to advertise what they do?	**34**	
because they've depended on one for so long?	**35**	

Tip Strip

Question 25: Who might need to include pictures in what they do?

Question 29: Look for a similar way of saying that you can't work without a computer.

Question 32: What other expression do you know for 'cuts down on costs'?

I NEED MY COMPUTER

A Tara

I'm a poet and I spend a large part of my life travelling around the world. I have a laptop computer, which means I can work on trains and buses, wherever I happen to be. My poems always begin in a notebook (and I mean the paper variety) where they stay for a while, moving from notes I have made, sometimes just individual words and phrases, to more developed pieces. The only way I can keep in touch with my family and also stay in contact with other writers is by using e-mail. Actually, I also use e-mail for sending work – poems, articles, reviews – to magazines, publishers and newspapers. Through my PC I am in constant communication with writers all over the world and we're able to swap poems and ideas within seconds. It's brilliant.

B Maisse

I'm a surgeon and I work in a large teaching hospital. Although I have a PC at home, I also have a little pocket PC, a PDA – personal digital assistant. I carry my PDA around with me all day as it's small enough to fit into my coat pocket. I use it like a diary and it has an alarm which I can set to remind me about meetings with other doctors in the team. I wouldn't be nearly as organised without it; having all the necessary information in one place and not on scraps of paper is invaluable. There are lots of things available over the internet which are great for doctors. There's always a lot of reading to be done, and it's often cheaper to download journals online than buy the printed copy. It also use the internet to find out about the latest discoveries in drugs and developments in medical research.

C Konrad

I'm my own boss and I run my business from home. I bought a computer when I set up the company a couple of years ago, and I know that I couldn't operate without one. In any case everyone expects you to have a computer these days. The first thing I do in the morning is check my e-mail. I get about 40 e-mails a day; using e-mail is often much more convenient for communicating with my customers. It means you can choose when to reply, unlike the telephone, which interrupts whatever you happen to be doing when it rings. My computer helps me manage my time better, but it is not as personal as a phone call. I also use the internet for finding out what other companies like mine are offering. Once upon a time I would have asked for a company's brochure or information pack, but nowadays most companies advertise on their own websites.

D Suzy

I am 12 years old and in my first year at secondary school. My parents have recently bought a new computer, so they let me have their old one, which is still very good. It has made a big difference to the way I do things, particularly my school work. It is a quick and easy way to do my homework. Instead of having to draw pictures I can get them from the art work package on the computer and just add them to whatever it is I need to illustrate. It also saves mess – no rubbing out and no cutting things up. My computer also has an internet connection which gives me access to all sorts of information. I can also use the encyclopaedia and dictionary that are on the computer. Lastly, my computer has lots of games which I can play after I have done my homework.

E Fergus

I love computers. I owned one of the early laptops and today I have both a PC and a laptop. My life as a freelance musician would be a real struggle without my computers. I have to run myself like a small business, and I simply wouldn't be able to do that without a computer. You have to keep in touch with music agents, concert promoters and conductors, and there are lots of letters to write. I use my computer to send out information about myself each week by e-mail. I can even send a picture of myself that way too. It saves a lot of money on stationery, stamps and so on. I also keep all my accounts up-to-date on it and use the internet to research new music. The other thing I love about having a computer is that being a professional musician can be a solitary business, because you spend a lot of time on your own at home. My e-mail is like having a friend in the flat.

Writing (1 hour 30 minutes)

You **must** answer this question.

1   You and a friend would like to work for a year on a volunteer programme. Your friend has written to you and sent you the advertisement below. Read the letter and the advertisement, together with his/her notes. Write a letter to the World Support Programme asking for the information which your friend suggests and adding any relevant questions of your own.

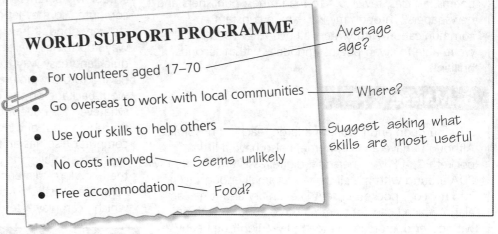

> This programme sounds just what we want. I've added some comments but I shall be away next week, so perhaps you could write for more information and ask about anything else you think we need to know'.

WORLD SUPPORT PROGRAMME — Average age?

- For volunteers aged 17–70
- Go overseas to work with local communities —— Where?
- Use your skills to help others —— Suggest asking what skills are most useful
- No costs involved —— Seems unlikely
- Free accommodation —— Food?

Write a **letter** of between **120** and **180** words in an appropriate style. Do not write any addresses.

Write an answer to **one** of the Questions **2–5** in this part. Write your answer in **120–180** words in an appropriate style.

Tip Strip

Question 2:
- You need to write clearly on two or three ways in which you spend your free time. Your writing should communicate a feeling of enthusiasm for what you do so that the reader is interested in what you say.

Question 3:
- Plan your story before you start writing. Has it got a beginning, a middle and an end?
- Think about verb sequences, e.g. Past simple/Past perfect.
- Try to make your story as interesting as possible.
- Remember that stories don't have greetings or headings.

Question 4:
- Organise your ideas into a clear report: either rely on paragraphing or use subheadings (or both).
- Briefly introduce the programme, include its title and say what it is about.
- Mention a few things about the programme that support your recommendation from the foreign learner's point of view.

Question 5(a):
- Say why you have enjoyed reading the book. What was especially enjoyable? The storyline, the characters, the language level, the fact that you could identify with the theme etc?
- Use an informal style.

Question 5(b):
- Describe an event which you think will give a flavour of what the book is about without giving away the plot. Explain why what you have chosen is a suitable 'advertisement' for the book. Organise your writing into clear paragraphs.
- Use a formal style.

2 Your local newspaper is going to include a weekly article in English on 'The Best Ways to Spend Free Time'. You have been asked to write the first article on what you do in your free time.

Write your **article**.

3 You are going to enter a short story competition. The competition rules say that the story must **begin** with these words:

I promised to keep the secret, whatever happened.

Write your **story**.

4 Your teacher wants to recommend a television programme for students who are learning your language. Write a report on a television programme which you know well, saying why you think it would be helpful and interesting for foreign learners.

Write your **report**.

5 Answer **one** of the following two questions based on your reading of **one** of the set books.

Either (a) A friend has asked you to recommend a book in English which she would enjoy reading. Write to your friend recommending the book you have read, saying what you find especially enjoyable about it.

Write your **letter**. Do not include any addresses.

Or (b) You have been asked to choose an event from the book you have read in order to advertise the book in a class library exhibition. Write a **report** on which event you think would be the most suitable and why.

Use of English (1 hour 15 minutes)

For Questions **1–15**, read the text below and decide which answer **A, B, C** or **D** best fits each space. There is an example at the beginning (**0**).

Mark your answers **on the separate answer sheet.**

Tip Strip

Question 2: There may be many theories; which word is right in this gap?

Question 5: All these words can precede 'on' but only one makes sense in this sentence.

Question 9: Look at the word 'it' to help you decide on the correct answer.

Example:

0 **A** produced **B** written **C** considered **D** sung

MUSIC – A UNIVERSAL LANGUAGE

Music is universal – it is (**0**) ..... by all cultures. Some scientists believe that music came before speech and (**1**) ..... as a development of mating calls. In fact, there is (**2**) ..... theory that the (**3**) ..... languages were chanted or sung rather than spoken. Indeed, in some cultures, music is a form of (**4**) ..... history. The Aboriginal Australians, for example, use music as a means to (**5**) ..... on stories of the land and spirits to the next (**6**) ..... .

New evidence suggests that music does not just (**7**) ..... the feel-good factor but it is also good for the brain. A study of intellectually (**8**) ..... children showed that they could recall more (**9**) ..... after it was given to them in a song than after it was read to them as a story.

Researchers also report that people (**10**) ..... better on a standard intelligence (**11**) ..... after listening to Mozart. The so-called 'Mozart effect', has also been (**12**) ..... by findings that rats (**13**) ..... up on Mozart run faster through a complex network of paths or passages, (**14**) ..... as a maze. Overall, it seems that in most instances people who suffer from any form of mental (**15**) ..... benefit from listening to music.

1	**A** was	**B** swelled	**C** reacted	**D** arose
2	**A** one	**B** every	**C** such	**D** that
3	**A** earliest	**B** newest	**C** easiest	**D** simplest
4	**A** enjoying	**B** making	**C** recording	**D** stating
5	**A** move	**B** pass	**C** hand	**D** happen
6	**A** children	**B** people	**C** tribe	**D** generation
7	**A** convince	**B** satisfy	**C** please	**D** prefer
8	**A** disabled	**B** inactive	**C** incapable	**D** disordered
9	**A** facts	**B** knowledge	**C** memory	**D** information
10	**A** examine	**B** prepare	**C** score	**D** achieve
11	**A** form	**B** scheme	**C** demonstration	**D** test
12	**A** supported	**B** given	**C** marked	**D** remembered
13	**A** held	**B** brought	**C** stood	**D** set
14	**A** called	**B** heard	**C** regarded	**D** known
15	**A** badness	**B** hurt	**C** illness	**D** pain

For Questions **16–30**, read the text below and think of the word which best fits each space. Use only **one** word in each space. There is an example at the beginning (**0**).

Write your answers **on the separate answer sheet.**

Example:

0	one

FOLLOW YOUR NOSE

Of the five senses, smell is probably the (**0**) ......*one*...... that you value the least. Yet your sense of smell is the most direct link (**16**) .... the brain and the outside world. It (**17**) .... two seconds for a smell to (**18**) .... the nose and travel to the part of the brain (**19**) .... controls emotions and memories. Exactly (**20**) .... your sense of smell influences your emotions, however, is (**21**) .... fully understood.

Nevertheless, a sense of smell can even influence your relationships (**22**) .... other people. Apparently, you (**23**) .... in love through your nose, not your eyes or your ears. Moreover, people tend to smell of what they eat and (**24**) .... can also influence what people think of you.

In one famous study, 84 per cent of people taking (**25**) .... said they were more (**26**) .... to buy a particular brand of trainers, when they (**27**) .... placed in a room smelling of flowers. This kind of knowledge can be (**28**) .... to influence people's spending habits at a sub-conscious (**29**) ...., and could obviously be useful in (**30**) .... all sorts of things from clothing to cars.

Tip Strip

Question 32: What preposition follows 'apart'?

Question 34: What rule governs the use of 'it's worth ...'?

Question 39: 'ought' is a modal verb – can it be made into a past tense?

For Questions **31–40,** complete the second sentence so that it has a similar meaning to the first sentence, using the word given. **Do not change the word given.** You must use between two and five words, including the word given. Here is an example (**0**).

Example: 0   The bag is not big enough for all my luggage.

small

The bag .... for all my luggage.

The gap can be filled by the words 'is too small' so you write:

0	is too small

Write **only the missing words** on the separate answer sheet.

---

31   The company director was respected by all his employees.

up

All the employees .... the company director.

32   Judith was the only member of the family who had never married.

apart

All the members of the family .... got married.

33   Most people find Finnish is not an easy language to learn.

difficulty

Most people .... Finnish.

34   There is no point in asking Denise to the party as she's so busy.

worth

It .... Denise to the party as she's so busy.

35   As I had plenty of time before my flight, I was able to do some shopping.

not

If I had not had plenty of time before my flight, I ....
to do some shopping.

36   Taking photographs in the art gallery is forbidden.

allowed

You .... photographs in the art gallery.

37   My brother never listens to what I say.

takes

My brother .... what I say.

38   This milk is sour, so throw it away.

gone

This milk ...., so throw it away.

39   You were supposed to do your homework before today's lesson.

ought

You .... your homework before today's lesson.

40   A friend is decorating my bedroom next week.

am

I .... by a friend next week.

For Questions **41–55**, read the text below and look carefully at each line. Some of the lines are correct, and some have a word which should not be there.

Tip Strip

Line 44: How many examples are there?

Line 45: Read the whole text carefully; are the young people forced to visit the elderly?

Line 55: What fixed expression is used in this line?

If a line is correct, put a tick (✔) by the number **on the separate answer sheet.** If a line has a word which should not be there, write the word **on the separate answer sheet.** There are examples at the beginning (**0** and **00**).

Example:	0	✔
	00	*was*

0	....	I am writing in response to an article which you printed
00	....	in your magazine last week and which was criticised young
41	....	people like me. The article said that teenagers are rude and
42	....	noisy and not interested in other people. I think that comment
43	....	is very unfair and while then it may apply to some young people,
44	....	it is certainly not true of me and my friends. For one example,
45	....	every Saturday morning we must work in our local community
46	....	by visiting elderly people in their own homes. Sometimes do they
47	....	want help with their shopping, other times they ask to us
48	....	to do some work in their garden. We give up two to three hours
49	....	of our time and we don't get paid. I also know by other friends at
50	....	school who help out in the local hospital once a week simply at
51	....	talking to patients who may not have any visitors, and even generally
52	....	just making themselves like useful in all sorts of ways. If we are noisy
53	....	it's usually because we're enjoying ourselves, and if we ever appear
54	....	rude, I can assure you it's probably because we're having chatting
55	....	and laughing together, because you're only young that once!

PART 5

For Questions **56–65,** read the text below. Use the word given in capitals at the end of each line to form a word that fits the space in the same line. There is an example at the beginning (**0**).

Example:

0	*scientists*

Write your answers **on the separate answer sheet.**

RECOGNISING A LIAR

Recent research has led many (**0**) .....*scientists*..... to believe that the   **SCIENCE**

(**56**) .... to recognise whether or not someone is telling the   **ABLE**

(**57**) ...., or is about to break bad news has more to do with   **TRUE**

science than a magical (**58**) .... sense.   **SIX**

The human body and brain subconsciously pick up signals so small that

they would not (**59**) .... be noticed. If someone is telling lies,   **NORMAL**

for (**60**) ...., their body language is slightly   **INSTANT**

(**61**) .... The brain picks up on these changes, which   **DIFFER**

may include a bead of sweat or a slight (**62**) ..,.............. in tone   **ALTER**

of voice. Upon the (**63**) .... that the person has been lying,   **REALISE**

the brain has a 'told you so' sensation. Scientists argue that people

should trust their own (**64**) .... ; their instinctive reactions   **JUDGE**

will tell them if a person is (**65**) .... and not to be trusted.   **RELY**

Tip Strip

Question 58: You may recognise what is needed here if you know the fixed expression!

Question 59: Is a noun, a verb or an adverb needed here?

Question 65: Read this last sentence carefully; is the missing word going to be positive or negative in this context?

Listening (approximately 40 minutes)

You'll hear people talking in eight different situations. For Questions **1–8**, choose the best answer, **A, B** or **C.**

Tip Strip

Question 3: How will the company check the battery?

Question 5: This is an advice line; visitors cannot be forced to do things – listen for how advice is offered using the modal verb 'may'.

Question 7: What does the man say to describe his feelings as he sat through the lecture?

1 You overhear a man arranging an interview.
Who is he talking to?
A his boss
B a customer
C an agent

| | 1 |

2 You hear a girl talking about a sports injury.
How did she injure herself?
A She fell over.
B She hit a post.
C She hurt her arm.

| | 2 |

3 You hear a woman talking to a mobile phone company.
What is she told to do?
A take her phone back to the shop
B charge the battery for longer
C return her phone to the company

| | 3 |

4 You hear two people trying to arrange a meeting.
What do they decide to do?
A postpone their meeting
B meet at the weekend
C cancel their meeting

| | 4 |

5 You hear a recorded message about hospital visiting times.
What advice is being given?
A Visitors can get a meal if they want.
B Visitors should avoid coming by car.
C Visitors must register on arrival.

| | 5 |

6 You hear a woman talking about being a pianist.
What does she dislike most about her career?
A the loneliness
B the hours of practice
C the travelling

| | 6 |

7 You hear a man talking about a lecture he attended.
How did he feel during the lecture?
A bored
B cross
C confused

| | 7 |

8 You hear a woman talking about a relative.
Who is she complaining about?
A her mother
B her sister
C her daughter

| | 8 |

PART 2

Tip Strip

Question 9: Remember you can answer this question using a number or you can write the number in words.

Question 13: Are you listening for a noun or a verb to fill this gap? How do you know which one is right?

Question 17: Listen carefully for the word which is used to describe all kinds of things – don't be tempted to guess!

You will hear part of a radio programme in which a woman called Amelia Unwin talks about one of the most successful football clubs in the world. For Questions **9–18**, complete the sentences.

Manchester United paid [**9**] for one player.

The Club sells anything from shorts to a [**10**]

A Manchester United strip will cost you about [**11**] to buy.

The Club sells its goods throughout the [**12**] at official shops.

Any company can use the Club's facilities to hold a [**13**] for its employees.

Many supporters buy a [**14**] in advance.

The Club's matches are [**15**] to bring in more money.

The Club profits from being involved in [**16**] and championships throughout the year.

The players wear the names of various [**17**] on their shirts.

The players' [**18**] cost the Club an enormous amount of money.

You will hear five different people talking about what they enjoy about going on a cruise ship holiday. For Questions **19–23,** choose from the list **A–F** what each speaker says. Use the letters only once. There is one extra letter which you do not need to use.

A I love shopping in all the different places.

B It awakens my sense of history.

C I appreciate the varied scenery.

D It gives me the excuse not to do anything physical.

E I like the entertainment on board.

F It gives me a chance to explore.

Speaker 1	**19**
Speaker 2	**20**
Speaker 3	**21**
Speaker 4	**22**
Speaker 5	**23**

You will hear a radio talk given by a TV actress called Zoe Fisher. For each of the Questions **24–30,** decide which of the statements are True and which are False. Write **T** for **True** or **F** for **False** in the boxes provided.

24	Zoe did not expect to be a teacher after leaving school at sixteen.	**24**
25	Zoe did not continue her studies at college.	**25**
26	Zoe believes she is a born teacher.	**26**
27	Zoe misunderstood the taxi driver's remark.	**27**
28	Zoe settled down the moment she arrived in Britain.	**28**
29	Zoe wants her book to attract readers of different nationalities.	**29**
30	Zoe thinks life turns out as we intend it to.	**30**

Speaking (14 minutes)

PART 1 (3 minutes)

Answer these questions:

Can you tell me something about your family?
What's the most interesting thing you have ever done with your family?
Can you briefly describe your family to me?
Who are the most important people in your life after your family?

PART 2 (4 minutes)

Being alone (compare, contrast and speculate)

Turn to pictures 1 and 2 on page 157 which show people sitting by themselves.

Candidate A, compare and contrast these photographs and say why you think the people enjoy being alone. You have a minute to do this.

Candidate B, do you like doing things by yourself?

Being creative (compare, contrast and speculate)

Turn to pictures 1 and 2 on page 158 which show people doing things with their hands.

Candidate B, compare and contrast these photographs and say why you think people enjoy doing things like this. You have a minute to do this.

Candidate A, do you like making things or drawing?

PART 3 (3 minutes)

Belonging to a club (discuss and evaluate)

Turn to the pictures on page 159 which show different clubs. What do these different clubs offer, and which of these clubs would you be interested in joining and why?

PART 4 (4 minutes)

Answer these questions:

Why do some people dislike belonging to clubs or societies?
Do you or your friends belong to any clubs? Which ones? Why did you decide to join?
Are there any disadvantages in belonging to a club?
Do you think clubs are more useful when people get older?

PAPER 1   Reading (1 hour 15 minutes)

You are going to read a magazine article about a woman who works for the film industry. Choose the most suitable heading from the list **A–I** for each part **1–7** of the article. There is one extra heading which you do not need to use. There is an example at the beginning (**0**).

Mark your answers **on the separate answer sheet**.

A Initial career move	**D** Determination is essential	**G** Chance of stardom in future
B The purpose of an audition	**E** Looking good on the screen	**H** Turning down promising actors
C Huge effort to attend auditions	**F** Choosing an alternative career	**I** The pressures in holding auditions

My Kind of Life

*Fiona Bartlett is a talent scout for a film company.
It is her job to find the right faces for the right film.
She has spent the last month selecting the final cast
for a new soap opera for teenagers.*

0	**B**

I studied Theatre Arts at university and had intended to end up working as a stage manager in a theatre. However, during one summer holiday I did some voluntary work with a children's theatre group and I met a number of casting agents – people whose job it is to look for children to take part in any new production. They do this by holding auditions – which are rather like interviews – where they can assess a child's acting ability.

1	

It was fascinating sitting in on the auditions. Children whom I thought were brilliant, who could sing and dance and had such confidence were not always the ones who got the parts. The casting agents would explain that one of the things they were looking for was how photogenic the child would appear in front of the camera, so each audition is videoed and watched on a monitor at the same time as the child is performing live.

2	

Three people usually sat in on each audition and the director made the final decision. The schedule was always very tight and auditions were held in a different place each day for a period of up to two weeks at a time. So they were constantly on the move and might audition up to a hundred young hopefuls in one day. I spent two days accompanying children to these auditions, and it was that experience that attracted me to the profession.

3	

However, when I first left university I worked as a personal assistant to the Production Manager of a children's animation and cartoon company. It was my job to look after his diary, arrange meetings, book actors and musicians for recording sessions and so on and in that way I met hundreds of different people. Then one day I heard that a TV company was looking for a casting agent and I applied for and got the job.

4	

I was prepared for the hard work and the travel but one thing that I was completely unprepared for was the emotional strain of the job. You arrive at the hall where the auditions are being held to be greeted by hundreds of young people all desperate to be chosen. And sometimes, however good they are, they are simply not right for the part, so you end up disappointing the vast majority of these kids.

5	

Obviously they've all worked and rehearsed enormously hard to get as far as the first audition. Most of them are accompanied by their teachers or a parent, they may have travelled miles to reach the place on time and spent money on fares and new clothes and so on. And they've got probably no more than five minutes to show us what they can do. Some of them are so nervous they just freeze, others are over-confident and burst into tears when you have to tell them they are not what you're looking for.

6	

In an ideal world you'd like to be able to offer everyone a job. But it is a very competitive world and if you can't survive these knocks early on when you're still a teenager, the chances are you've picked the wrong profession. But if you believe in yourself and you can cope with these setbacks, it is worth auditioning over and over again. Sometimes people wait years before they get through an audition and there are no guarantees that you'll succeed in this business.

7	

But on the positive side there's enormous job satisfaction to be gained from choosing the right actors for a new production. I know that all the hours I've spent this last month will have been worth it when the first episode of this new soap is broadcast, and perhaps some of these new young faces will go on to become big names in the years ahead.

You are going to read a magazine article about a businessman. For Questions **8–14**, choose the correct answer **A, B, C** or **D**.

Mark your answers **on the separate answer sheet**.

ROAMERS

In 1989 a young, intrepid Australian was travelling around Europe and found himself at his British hotel after closing time – at 10 in the morning. Whilst most of us might take this as an opportunity to find a cosy bed and breakfast or at least a dry bench in a railway station, Matt Lassiter spotted a business opportunity. Knowing that he was not alone and that thousands of backpacking youngsters were wandering the world with heavy bags and fat wallets, Lassiter came up with a plan to start his own hostels that made young visitors feel at home whenever they arrived. 'I realised there was not so much a gap in the backpackers' market, but rather a canyon!'

A couple of years later, Lassiter formed his own company which he called Roamers. His intention was to focus on creating hostels which would provide accommodation for the dynamic youth tourism market. 'The average backpacker, around 18–21, is likely to be highly educated, often taking time off between school and university and usually has quite a lot of money to spend and these are the people Roamers sets out to attract,' says Lassiter.

Today, Roamers operates in more than 20 countries, has 70 hostels and provides 1.5 million bed nights each year. Lassiter says that each hostel is like a kindly aunt or uncle looking after young people. Backpackers like that and their parents like it even more, not because Roamers is a fun environment, but because Roamers offers a safe and secure form of accommodation.

A typical hostel has showers and toilets on each floor, a 'chill out' room with television, food, bar and drinks facilities, a laundry room and internet access with free e-mail usage. Lassiter was very aware that his young, bright customers would all be familiar with the internet and that it would play an important part in marketing his company.

Part of Lassiter's success is knowing that backpackers want to feel like explorers. 'We have to be very careful how we market our products – it must be their decision and not seen as a package holiday – we make them think they are independent.' The Roamers technique is to offer pre-booked two or four-day tours, a couple of nights recovering from jet-lag, a welcome pack, clean sheets – no sleeping bags – and a free call home. The formula is certainly working, which just goes to show that Lassiter's instincts are exactly right for this growing holiday market.

Tip Strip

Question 8: Look carefully at how the information, while not stated as such, is clearly implied.

Question 11: Look back to the previous sentence. Pay careful attention to the word 'like'.

Question 13: Look at the fourth paragraph of the text. What does 'Lassiter was very aware' suggest?

8 How did Matt Lassiter react to the British hostel closing in the morning?

   A He looked for alternative accommodation.
   B He decided to continue his journey.
   C It put him off travelling in Europe.
   D It gave him an idea for the future.

9 What did Lassiter think would help young travellers?

   A to be less spoilt financially by their parents
   B to be more aware of looking after their money
   C to accept that accommodation can vary
   D to find more welcoming accommodation

10 Roamers hostels are designed for young people who

   A are studying part-time.
   B have freedom and leisure.
   C are living on a small budget.
   D have an interest in marketing.

11 What does 'that' in line 35 refer to?

   A the hostels' caring attitudes
   B hostels run by relatives
   C the hostels' generous facilities
   D hostels available worldwide

12 Why are parents in favour of Roamers?

   A They can pay extra for secure arrangements.
   B They approve of the entertainment on offer.
   C They don't worry about their children's safety.
   D They like the fact that their children have fun.

13 Lassiter's use of the internet

   A saves him time and money.
   B shows good business sense.
   C attracts business partners.
   D helps him market computers.

14 Lassiter is successful because

   A he has researched his market.
   B he operates a very fair formula.
   C travellers can depend on his advice.
   D explorers benefit from his hostels.

You are going to read an article about a woman pilot. Eight sentences have been removed from the article. Choose from the sentences **A–I** the one which fits each gap (**15–21**). There is one extra sentence which you do not need to use. There is an example at the beginning (**0**).

Mark your answers **on the separate answer sheet.**

FLYING INTO THE RECORD BOOKS

Polly Vacher is no ordinary woman pilot. **0** __*I*__

15 _____ It ended only three days behind schedule when she landed her Piper Dakota at Birmingham in central England in May, five months later.

16 _____ This included storms and a cyclone in Fiji, a country in the South Pacific Ocean. Nor was the journey without incident for Polly, who only learned to fly at the age of forty-nine.

One of the trip's most frightening moments came, worryingly, on the same route where Amelia Earhart, the American pilot, went missing when she was attempting to fly around the world in 1937. **17** _____ In fact, she allowed herself to be photographed as she stood beside a Banyan tree, which Amelia Earhart had planted in 1935, before setting off for the 16-hour section of her flight from Hawaii to California.

According to Polly all went well for the first part of her journey. **18** _____ Then suddenly it started to get very bumpy. Checking the outside air temperature Polly discovered it was zero degrees. To her horror she found streams of ice-cold rain running back along the wings and starting to freeze. **19** _____

Though Polly immediately dropped her height to prevent the weight of ice pulling her plane into the ocean, there was more drama when the cabin suddenly went quiet. **20** _____ As a result the main tank had run dry an hour early, but fortunately the emergency tank went into action and she was able to land safely.

The lonely hours spent flying were a great contrast to the warm welcome she received wherever she landed. **21** _____ The publicity she attracted also raised money for a charity which provides flying scholarships for disabled people.

A Polly's 46,000km record-breaking journey began in January.

B This is the most dangerous kind of ice as it is difficult to see it forming.

C Polly, however, was determined not to let what had happened in the past cause her anxiety.

D Strong winds meant that she had used more fuel than expected.

E Up there in the sky you are completely free.

F The delay was the result of uncooperative weather.

G There was tremendous media interest and on one occasion she gave up to seven interviews in a single day.

H The moon and the stars appeared and she even had time to do some sewing.

I In 2001 she flew to the ends of the Earth and into the record books by becoming the first woman to fly the smallest aircraft around the world via Australia and the Pacific.

Tip Strip

Sentence B: 'This' is likely to refer to something just mentioned.
Sentence D: Where is fuel stored on a small plane?
Sentence F: What words in the text are linked to the idea of 'delay'?

Tip Strip

Question 24: Look for a similar way of expressing the idea of including people.

Question 28: Where might you expect to buy things other than in a shop?

Question 33: What is the word for someone who doesn't eat meat?

You are going to read about four countries that offer work experience opportunities for young people. For Questions **22–35,** choose from the countries (**A–D).** The countries may be chosen more than once. When more than one answer is required, these may be given in any order. There is an example at the beginning (**0**).

Mark your answers **on the separate answer sheet.**

Which of the countries

makes special mention of its city-based projects?	**0**	C
offers different types of schools?	**22**	
has a European feel to it?	**23**	
will accept you directly into the community?	**24**	
can rely on parental support for its education programme?	**25**	
would you choose if you want to work with pre-school-age children?	**26**	
offers a variety of sporting activities?	**27**	
is recommended for its shopping?	**28**	
is benefiting from its own people's experience abroad?	**29**	
might require you to learn a local language?	**30**	
gives you a choice of accommodation?	**31**	**32**
would appeal to someone who doesn't eat meat?	**33**	
suggests that it offers unique opportunities?	**34**	
offers a stimulating classroom atmosphere?	**35**	

PROJECTS ABROAD

A INDIA

Magical India is a land of many contrasts. It is impossible to generalise about this subcontinent and everyone has a different experience and different opinions. To live in India is to be part of a way of life totally unlike anything else.

People who volunteer to work in India spend up to six months at a time in the south of India. It's an area with a special feel to it – the villages and farms feed local people well, while the temples, sometimes built on great rocks overlooking the plain, satisfy people's spiritual needs.

South Indian community life is very close; if you work there you will be treated as an addition to any school or family that you join. The food is famous for its variety of spices, vegetables and fruit and many people are vegetarians.

You will find yourself helping with both primary and secondary schoolchildren. Some schools also have children as young as nursery age, and you may well have the chance to work with them as well.

Travelling in India offers great opportunities. The rainy seasons in June and July and October keep the climate cooler, and do not interfere with daily life.

B GHANA

Ghana is a colourful country of thick tropical forests, wild savannah or bush and great beaches. It is home to one of Africa's friendliest and most welcoming people. The Ashanti built their kingdom on Ghana's gold – their country used to be called the Gold Coast. Modern Ghanaian culture is open and varied.

In recent years Ghana has attracted new money, and many Ghanaians have returned home from working or studying abroad bringing new investments and ideas with them.

In Ghana people attach great importance to social and community events and many people are deeply religious. The official language is English but the main spoken languages are Ewe, Twi and Ga.

Children and their parents see education as a way to better jobs and good lives and children work hard at school. If you are working with young children in a primary school, you will find that teaching lively songs and rhymes is very popular.

Travelling around is cheap. Local minibuses, buses and trains operate throughout most of the country and wherever you go you will be given a warm welcome.

C NEPAL

If you choose to work in Nepal, you will find a well-established programme for volunteers, particularly in the capital Kathmandu.

You will be offered opportunities in schools both in and around the city, ranging from well-equipped independent and state schools to much smaller ones set up to help children who, without an education, would have no future.

Volunteers spend up to six months at a time working with children from the ages of five to seventeen. You have a choice of working in busy Kathmandu, one of the villages in Kathmandu Valley or in the peaceful town of Pokara at the base of the great Annapurna mountain range by the shores of the beautiful Phewa Lake. Accommodation is either with host families or local hostels.

The surrounding countryside is excellent for walking and climbing, boating on the lake, and white-water rafting in the mountain rivers.

D TOGO

Togo in West Africa is situated between Ghana and Benin. The capital city, Lome, is on the coast close to the Ghanaian border.

Togo's official language is French and although Togo has been independent since 1960 the French influence is still evident, from the architecture to the food.

Lome is said to have the best market in West Africa and the Togolese are warm and hospitable people. Accommodation is cheap; you can choose to stay with a host family or you may prefer to find your own room or apartment.

The south of the country is flat with lagoons along the length of the coast, but as you travel north the land becomes hilly and rich with coffee plantations.

We can offer you work opportunities in secondary schools where the classes range in age from 11–20.

PAPER 2   **Writing** (1 hour 30 minutes)

You **must** answer this question.

1   You are in charge of the arrangements for your friend's birthday party. Your friend has given you a list of requests to which you have added your own notes. Write a letter to the restaurant manager asking for information and giving relevant details.

Can you check on these things when you write, please? Thanks!

- any chance of a private room? ———— *expensive?*

- must have music - bring our own ———— *equipment?*

- maximum number of people —— *will depend on size of room*

- costs < *food* / *drink*

- special effects, e.g. lighting ———— *& decorations*

- times < *start* / *finish - what time does restaurant close?*

Write a **letter** of between **120** and **180** words in an appropriate style. Do not write any addresses.

Write an answer to **one** of the Questions **2–5** in this part. Write your answer in **120–180** words in an appropriate style.

Tip Strip

Question 2:
• Organise your information clearly. You want your letter to make a good impression on the person reading it.
• Remember to say something about the level of your spoken English.
• End your letter appropriately.

Question 3:
• Plan your article so that you write about your day in an organised way. Try to make your article as interesting as possible so that the reader has a clear idea of what a typical day in your life is like for a person in your country.

Question 4:
• Organise your ideas into a clear report: either rely on paragraphing or use subheadings (or both).
• Say where you took the visitors and what you showed them. Mention the visitors' reactions to some of the things they saw.

Question 5(a):
• Choose two characters who you know well.
• Say why you would want to meet both of them, but avoid repeating the same reasons for each character.
• Use a formal style.

Question 5(b):
• Briefly describe the book (e.g. plot, setting, characters etc.). Explain why you think it is worth reading (e.g. what did you find uninteresting / enjoyable / exciting / amusing about it?). Did you think it was well written?
• Use a formal style.

2   You are interested in applying for the holiday job described in the advertisement below.

> A large department store needs English-speaking assistants to work in the store during the summer. The store is very popular with tourists.
>
> You should have a good level of spoken English. If you are interested, please write explaining why you think you are a suitable person for the job.

Write your **letter** of application. Do not include any addresses.

3   An English-language magazine is publishing articles from young writers around the world. The title for each article is:

My Typical Kind of Day

You decide to send in an article based on the country where you live.

Write your **article**.

4   You recently spent a day showing foreign visitors around your town. Your teacher has asked you to write a report of the day for the *Learning English* page of your school newspaper.

Write your **report.**

5   Answer **one** of the following two questions based on your reading of **one** of the set books.

Either   (a)   If you could meet two of the characters from the book you have read, who would you choose, and why?

Write your **composition**.

Or   (b)   A magazine called *Bookworm* wants readers to send in articles on books in English which they think are worth reading. Write an **article** for the magazine saying why you think the book you have read is worth reading.

Use of English (1 hour 15 minutes)

For Questions **1–15**, read the text below and decide which answer **A, B, C** or **D** best fits each space. There is an example at the beginning (**0**).

Mark your answers **on the separate answer sheet**.

Tip Strip

Question 2: Which verb is usually used with 'association' when it is a new one?

Question 7: Which phrasal verb means 'established'?

Question 13: People stood on piles of earth until a more professional arrangement; which word has the best meaning?

Example:

| 0 | **A** years | **B** rule | **C** period | **D** reign |

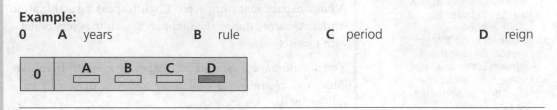

THE EARLY DAYS OF FOOTBALL

Football became the game we know today during the (**0**) ..... of Queen Victoria in the nineteenth century. So many different (**1**) ..... of the game were being played in Britain at that time, that in 1863 the Football Association was (**2**) ..... in order to draw up and agree the (**3**) ..... of the game.

Throughout the country new football (**4**) ..... were built and the development of the railways (**5**) ..... that football teams and their (**6**) ..... could travel to the matches. In 1888 the Football League was (**7**) ..... up with twelve clubs, and football became a national sport, (**8**) ..... to rugby by many people as the more popular game of the (**9**) ..... .

Sometimes people played the game in just a field. In one town, Burnley, in the north of England, the field had a river (**10**) ..... along the side of it in which players (**11**) ..... baths after matches. People stood on banks (**12**) ..... from earth and it was not until the early 1900s that (**13**) ..... stands were built. The players would have had two wooden (**14**) ..... for the goals with tapes across the top instead of a cross bar, and nets were not (**15**) ..... until 1891.

1	**A** methods	**B** conditions	**C** forms	**D** ways
2	**A** formed	**B** made	**C** joined	**D** offered
3	**A** techniques	**B** laws	**C** rules	**D** lines
4	**A** grounds	**B** places	**C** lands	**D** courses
5	**A** helped	**B** intended	**C** said	**D** meant
6	**A** organisers	**B** fans	**C** partners	**D** helpers
7	**A** put	**B** got	**C** set	**D** made
8	**A** wanted	**B** preferred	**C** liked	**D** favoured
9	**A** two	**B** both	**C** other	**D** one
10	**A** lying	**B** moving	**C** running	**D** causing
11	**A** got	**B** took	**C** ran	**D** picked
12	**A** produced	**B** made	**C** consisted	**D** worked
13	**A** accurate	**B** right	**C** proper	**D** correct
14	**A** pins	**B** nails	**C** points	**D** posts
15	**A** invented	**B** composed	**C** completed	**D** presented

For Questions **16–30,** read the text below and think of the word which best fits each space. Use only **one** word in each space. There is an example at the beginning (**0**).

Write your answers **on the separate answer sheet.**

Example:

0	with

FAST TRACK TO FLUENCY

A couple of generations ago, a bilingual child – in other words a child who spoke more than one language – was regarded (**0**) ....with...... suspicion. People thought that such (**16**) .... child would be slow (**17**) .... develop academically, would feel confused and even (**18**) .... up with a split personality.

Today, however, research shows the advantages of a bilingual upbringing, including an awareness (**19**) .... other cultures and an increased ability (**20**) .... language learning.

Tests (**21**) .... out in Canada presented small children with two apartment blocks made (**22**)................. of building bricks; the larger apartment contained fewer bricks. Children who (**23**) .... not bilingual said that the larger apartment had more bricks, (**24**) .... bilingual children correctly saw that the (**25**) .... one had more bricks. The bilingual children appeared to have the ability to ignore misleading information (**26**) .... dealing with problems, in much the (**27**) .... way as they 'edit out' one language when using the (**28**) ....

According to the research, as (**29**)................. as developing problem-solving skills earlier than those who only speak one language, bilingual children also understand written languages faster (**30**) .... learn to read more easily.

PART 3

Tip Strip

Question 32: What happens to the form of the verb after 'let'?

Question 36: What is the third conditional pattern?

Question 40: Which word is needed with 'rather' when expressing a preference for one thing over another?

For Questions **31–40,** complete the second sentence so that it has a similar meaning to the first sentence, using the word given. **Do not change the word given.** You must use between two and five words, including the word given. Here is an example (**0**).

Example: **0**   The bag is not big enough for all my luggage.

small

The bag .... for all my luggage.

The gap can be filled by the words 'is too small' so you write:

0	is too small

Write **only the missing words** on the separate answer sheet.

---

31 The shop assistant told me to keep my receipt for my new shoes.

hang

'You .... your receipt for your new shoes,' the shop assistant said.

32 Alex speaks fluent French although he has never been to France.

spite

Alex speaks fluent French .... been to France.

33 You do not need to reserve a seat on regional trains.

necessary

It .... to reserve a seat on regional trains.

34 'Shall we go to the café?' said Flora.

suggested

Flora .... to the café.

35 Richard's parents did not allow him to drive their car.

let

Richard's parents .... drive their car.

36 I didn't have Rob's phone number because I had lost my mobile.

had

If I .... , I would have had Rob's phone number.

37 Someone will meet you at the station.

be

You .... at the station.

38 Philip started to laugh when he heard the joke.

burst

Philip .... when he heard the joke.

39 Lucy doesn't like people to phone her late at night.

objects

Lucy .... her late at night.

40 I prefer staying in bed to getting up early at the weekend.

rather

I'd .... get up early at the weekend.

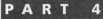

PART 4

For Questions **41–55**, read the text below and look carefully at each line. Some of the lines are correct, and some have a word which should not be there.

If a line is correct, put a tick (✔) by the number **on the separate answer sheet.** If a line has a word which should not be there, write the word **on the separate answer sheet.** There are two examples at the beginning (**0** and **00**).

Tip Strip

Line 44: How does the wrong word double the superlative?

Line 49: 'power' and 'strength' are abstract nouns; how does that help you decide which word is wrong?

Line 54: What fixed expression is used in this line?

| Example: | 0 | ✔ |
| | 00 | lot |

0 .... A tree is a symbol of man's connection to nature and reminds

00 .... people lot of the basic values that remain unchanged over the

41 .... centuries. In Estonia, in this northern Europe, people say that

42 .... if you have planted at least one tree during your life, your life

43 .... has not been for wasted. Trees have always played a very

44 .... important part in Estonian culture and the most oldest tree

45 .... in the country is an oak tree which is grown eight metres thick.

46 .... Many centuries ago, Estonians believed in that some trees were

47 .... holy and these trees were worshipped by people who sacrificed

48 .... their crops and cattle. In many other countries throughout the

49 .... world oak trees are symbols of power and the strength.

50 .... The wood is used much in the building and furniture industries

51 .... and even the fruit of the tree, the acorn, is well useful. Acorns

52 .... are fed to pigs and in the past when conditions were hard

53 .... some people turned dried acorns into kind flour to make bread.

54 .... In a fact, the story goes that the poorest people in one country

55 .... were saved from starvation and death by eating acorn bread.

PART 5

Tip Strip

Question 58: Will you need a singular or plural word here?

Question 61: This word needs a short suffix.

Question 63: Watch your spelling!

For Questions **56–65,** read the text below. Use the word given in capitals at the end of each line to form a word that fits the space in the same line. There is an example at the beginning (**0**).

Example:

0	furniture

Write your answers **on the separate answer sheet.**

THE MAN WHO FURNISHED THE WORLD

Ingvar Kamprad runs the most successful (**0**) ...furniture.. business in   **FURNISH**

the world. His (**56**) .... of paying extra for already expensive   **HATE**

goods in terms of (**57**) .... costs gave him the idea of   **DELIVER**

producing build-it-yourself items. (**58**) .... could see the   **SHOP**

items on display in self-service stores, pick up their (**59**) ....   **CHOOSE**

of goods and take them straight home. In (**60**) .... , he   **ADD**

offered car roof-racks, which made it even easier for people to take

their purchases with them.

There are now more than 150 stores (**61**) .... 30 countries.   **THROUGH**

Kamprad dislikes the (**62**) .... that his stores create the same   **ACCUSE**

kinds of homes all over the world. His (**63**) .... is that there   **ARGUE**

are millions of different ways that people can use his

(**64**) .... , and each nationality puts items together in   **PRODUCE**

different (**65**) .... to suit their own living styles.   **COMBINE**

PAPER 4 Listening (approximately 40 minutes)

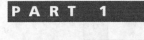

You'll hear people talking in eight different situations. For Questions **1–8**, choose the best answer, **A, B** or **C**.

Tip Strip

Question 1: If a person is 'after something' in this context, what does it mean? Look at the prompt question to help you.

Question 4: Look at the list of jobs. What kind of vocabulary do you associate with these jobs?

Question 7: How do we often express a desire for something we miss? You will hear the woman use this structure.

1 You overhear a woman talking in a library.
   What does she want?
   A a railway timetable
   B a book about trains
   C a video film on trains   **1**

2 You hear two people making arrangements for a party.
   What are they celebrating?
   A someone's birthday
   B a friend's wedding
   C passing a driving test   **2**

3 You hear a man talking about making an appointment to see his doctor.
   What was the problem?
   A The doctor couldn't see him for a week.
   B His usual doctor was away on holiday.
   C He was told to go to the local hospital.   **3**

4 You hear a part of a radio play in which a woman is describing her job.
   What does she do?
   A She's a writer.
   B She's a dancer.
   C She's a lawyer.   **4**

5 You hear a school tutor talking to a student about his report.
   What is her advice?
   A He should study medicine.
   B He should take a year off.
   C He should visit a university.   **5**

6 You hear a man talking about opening a new restaurant.
   What is he hoping will happen?
   A He will be able to expand later on.
   B He will find a new business partner.
   C He will attract customers from abroad.   **6**

7 You hear part of a radio programme in which an old woman is talking about her past life. What does she miss most?
   A her ability to travel
   B her large house
   C her sports car   **7**

8 You hear part of a weather forecast on the radio.
   What does the forecast warn about?
   A the danger of storms
   B low cloud and fog
   C the risk of floods   **8**

Listen carefully – this kind of answer is more difficult to predict, but think about the kind of word (e.g. verb or noun) that will fill the gap.

Question 14: Look at the word after the gap – that should help you predict what you're going to hear.

Question 18: Although this answer may be something you've never heard of, the words you need to complete the sentence are basic words. Just write down what you hear.

You will hear part of a radio programme which talks about modern music. For Questions **9–18,** complete the sentences.

The students' concert will take place in the next [ ] **9**

Lucy was amazed to see a large [ ] **10** made of iron as an orchestral instrument.

The name of Max Sinclair's piece is [ ] **11**

The piece takes [ ] **12** to play.

The concert will consist of [ ] **13** new pieces of music.

Another piece of music is arranged to look like a [ ] **14** pitch.

Max got his idea for his piece by hearing a [ ] **15** at work.

Tim Travis usually plays [ ] **16** in the orchestra.

Tim Travis uses a [ ] **17** which is quite heavy to play Max's piece.

Max Sinclair's music has been described as ' [ ] **18** modern'.

PART 3

Some of these speakers mention things that they did not like at school.

A: What would you expect to hear from someone who describes where their school is situated?

C: Speakers 1, 2, 4 and 5 all mention their teachers. Does anyone say that the teachers were excellent?

E: Think about what an 'exchange holiday' involves and this will help you focus on the right information.

You will hear five different people talking about what they enjoyed best about their schooldays. For Questions **19–23,** choose from the list **A–F** what each speaker says. Use the letters only once. There is one extra letter which you do not need to use.

A	I liked where the school was situated.
B	I enjoyed all the academic subjects.
C	I thought the teachers were excellent.
D	I made friends for life.
E	I liked the exchange holidays.
F	I loved the long breaks.

Speaker 1 [ ] **19**

Speaker 2 [ ] **20**

Speaker 3 [ ] **21**

Speaker 4 [ ] **22**

Speaker 5 [ ] **23**

You will hear part of a radio interview with a woman called Hayley Jones who spent a year in Antarctica. For Questions **24–30**, choose the best answer **A, B** or **C**.

Tip Strip

Question 25: How does Hayley refer to feeling depressed? She doesn't use the actual word.

Question 26: Don't be tempted to assume that what you hear e.g. 'I didn't feel nearly as tired' is the right answer because it is similar to one of the options!

Question 30: Listen for how Hayley expresses her feelings about her experience.

24 Why did Hayley go to Antarctica?
    A   to join the other scientists there
    B   to do research into waste material
    C   to study in the laboratory there

24

25 What did Hayley find depressing?
    A   not being able to listen to the radio
    B   the environment being one colour
    C   being without her family for so long

25

26 While in Antarctica, Hayley had not expected to
    A   feel so tired.
    B   work so hard.
    C   sleep so little.

26

27 What did Hayley find different about Rothera?
    A   She could go skiing at any time of day.
    B   She could walk alone without worrying.
    C   She could sit in on music rehearsals.

27

28 In order to keep warm, Hayley says she wore
    A   lots of thick clothes.
    B   her skiing clothes.
    C   lightweight clothes.

28

29 Hayley thinks that in the future Antarctica
    A   is unlikely to see many more tourists.
    B   may be less expensive for tourists.
    C   will become fashionable for tourists.

29

30 How does Hayley feel about her year in Antarctica?
    A   She found it a very worthwhile time.
    B   She thinks she learnt a great deal.
    C   She didn't like living so far away.

30

PAPER 5

Speaking (14 minutes)

PART 1 (3 minutes)

Answer these questions:

How do you usually spend your holidays?
Where did you go for your last holiday?
Where would you most like to go for your next holiday?
What do you think you gain from visiting other countries?

PART 2 (4 minutes)

Young children (compare, contrast and speculate)

Turn to pictures 1 and 2 on page 160 which show very young children.

Candidate A, compare and contrast these photographs and say how you think these young children might be feeling. You have a minute to do this.

Candidate B, do you remember when you were very young?

Seeking information (compare, contrast and speculate)

Turn to pictures 1 and 2 on page 161 which show people seeking information.

Candidate B, compare and contrast these photographs and say how difficult it is for people to find the information they need. You have a minute to do this.

Candidate A, do you find it easy or difficult to read maps?

PART 3 (3 minutes)

Raising money (discuss and evaluate)

Turn to the pictures on page 162 which show ideas for raising money. Your school or college wants to raise money to buy a minibus. What is the best way to do this? What kinds of problems might students come across trying to raise money?

PART 4 (4 minutes)

Answer these questions:

How easy or difficult is it to raise money?
Have you ever been involved in a project to raise money for something?
How would you set about raising money for something like a school minibus?
Do you like giving money to people who stand in the street with collecting tins? Why (not)?

TEST 5

PART 1

You are going to read a magazine article about *tweenagers*, a word used to describe an age group of children who are not yet teenagers. Choose the most suitable heading from the list **A–I** for each part (**1–7**) of the article. There is one extra heading which you do not need to use. There is an example at the beginning (**0**).

Mark your answers **on the separate answer sheet.**

A *Tweenagers* readily accept what they're told

B Factors affecting *tweenage* behaviour

C The young are getting older every day

D The commercial value of the *tweenage* market

E Basically a *tweenager* remains a child

F *Tweenagers* have real spending power

G *Tweenagers* are in control of what they do

H The end of childhood for *tweenagers*

I The need to belong is very strong

Tweenagers

0	C

Tweenagers. It's one of those labels that marketing and advertising people stick onto new consumer groups to persuade them to buy more of the products that are suitable for their life-stage and their life-style. In the case of *tweenagers*, it's the eight to twelve-year-olds who want to grow up as fast as they can, and who copy the fashions and behaviour of the teenagers they can't wait to become.

1	

In the UK there are about four million children in this age group and in the last ten years this group has become a clearly separate social and economic unit. The market for children's clothes, music, mobile phones and so on in this category is estimated to be worth about £30 billion.

2	

Most of these children have lived through a period of economic wealth and, according to recent research, pocket money has risen by 32% over six years. Consequently, *tweenagers* are a marketer's dream.

3	

From a psychologist's point of view, up until the age of eight, a child's family is his or her most important reference point and biggest influence. From eight onwards, other influences become important – particularly friends of the same age and sex, and role models from the world of entertainment and sport.

4	

Eight to twelve is a broad age range and includes various levels of maturity. There are still ten-year-olds who are secretly happier playing with dolls or toy cars than shopping for the latest fashion labels or watching soaps on television. But the pressure of friends means it's quite hard for them to follow their real interests as they want to fit in with their peer group.

5	

Before the age of eleven or twelve children have not developed the capacity for abstract thinking. This means that they receive information from the media but are not very likely to question what they see and hear. A teenager can watch something and ask questions like: 'Are they just trying to sell me something?' Teenagers rebel and protest but *tweenagers* take it all at face value, so are much more easily persuaded.

6	

Many teachers of this age group also comment on the fact that *tweenagers* are into pop culture and fashion from the age of eight onwards. Most children of today get a lot less physical freedom than previous generations, but a lot more freedom of choice. Many stay up late to watch what they like on television and make friends with who they like.

7	

One teacher who has taught this age range for a number of years said, 'I like *tweenagers*. By the time they are eight or nine most of them have developed a wicked sense of humour, and they can really make me laugh. Below that age they're still sweet, still want to please the teacher and do well. In spite of their fashionable life styles, however, they are still quite innocent. The important thing is that they may look like teenagers, speak like teenagers and want to be teenagers, but they are still just children.'

You are going to read an article about a UK journalist called Paul Howells who gives advice on how to design web pages for the internet. For Questions **8–15**, choose the correct answer **A**, **B**, **C** or **D**.

Mark your answers **on the separate answer sheet**.

Design your own website

What I love about my job is the variety. I get enquiries from people all over the world asking me how they should go about setting up their own website. I've been asked about so many subjects – anything from someone wanting to teach people how to throw boomerangs to another person selling paper flowers which they make at home in their spare time.

Obviously with all the thousands of websites available at the click of a button, you want to create an impression with your website so that it becomes a must-see destination. Not everyone is prepared, however, for the way in which a website can become so popular that it actually has to be closed down.

When people first set up their website they probably pay their web advertiser a monthly fee based on the number of hits or page impressions their site receives. If they can pay their monthly fee without it costing them too much, that is the best that most people hope for. One guy, Pete Bennett, whom I helped, wanted to set up a one-stop shop to provide decent images of the world's flags. He'd been fascinated by flags since his boyhood and had no idea that thousands of other people shared his passion. Anyway, in one month his web page had over 1.5 million hits. As a result his internet provider trebled the fee that he was being charged. He wasn't a rich person and he couldn't afford to spend that amount of money on a hobby without any benefit to himself, so he decided to carry advertising on his site. He found a company which specialises in smaller sites and adverts were added to the pages on his website. So, although he doesn't make a huge profit, at least his hobby provides him with a small income.

If you have specialist skills or expertise, it can pay you to sell the products that people want. I helped one woman design a page to advertise the fact that she tells fortunes, based on the information that her clients supply her with. If you want her to tell your fortune, you fill in a questionnaire online – your age, date of birth, hobbies, interests and so on and for a small fee she e-mails you back your fortune. You can print it out and it looks really good, decorated with moons and stars, your zodiac sign and your birthstone. I tried it myself and although I'm not sure I believe it, my future according to her is positive and exciting. I also found out that for someone born in August, like me, the birthstone is a peridot, a pale green stone which I'd never even heard of!

I also get a fair number of complaints from people e-mailing me to say that they can't access a website. When they click on the site a message appears on their screen saying 'An error has occurred in the script on this page'. This usually happens when someone has tried to achieve fancy effects on their website by using programming techniques based on a scripting language. This means that unless they really know what they are doing, whoever designed the site has probably made a mistake in their programming. This is where people like me come in. Most computer instruction guides make things appear quite straightforward, but unless you're very skilled, you're likely to run into problems. It's generally worth getting a professional to help you set up your site in the first place – otherwise people like me would be out of work. And let's face it, this is big business.

Tip Strip

Question 9: If you haven't come across the expression 'must-see' before, you should be able to guess what it means.

Question 11: What does 'a small income' allow you to do?

Question 12: The word 'clients' can be used in many different contexts; here it means 'customers'.

8 What does Paul Howells enjoy most about his job?

   A dealing with different people
   B his worldwide contacts
   C teaching design skills
   D the range of topics

9 What does Paul mean by 'a must-see destination' in lines 14/15?

   A a website that can no longer be seen
   B a website that everyone wants to visit
   C a website that does not make a charge
   D a website which has been well prepared

10 Why did Pete Bennett set up a website on flags?

   A He knew lots of people shared his interest.
   B He hoped to make a lot of money.
   C A web advertiser wanted to sell flags.
   D He'd been interested in flags for years.

11 Why did Pete Bennett accept advertising on his website?

   A to attract more hits
   B to repay the huge fee
   C to add more interest
   D to help him earn same money

12 Who are the 'clients' referred to in line 49?

   A interested people
   B web page designers
   C internet providers
   D product advertisers

13 Why do error messages sometimes appear?

   A People make a mistake in their e-mail address.
   B People try to put too much on the web page.
   C People have used a program incorrectly.
   D People have clicked on the wrong button.

14 What comment does Paul make about setting up a website?

   A It is usually fairly easy to do.
   B You must use a good instruction guide.
   C It can be quite complicated.
   D You should rely on your own skills.

15 What does Paul's final sentence suggest about his work?

   A There's a lot of money to be made in designing websites.
   B There are far too many websites on the internet.
   C There's a big chance of becoming unemployed.
   D There are more web page designers than necessary.

You are going to read an article about a university professor. Seven sentences have been removed from the article. Choose from the sentences **A–H** the one which fits each gap (**16–21**). There is one extra sentence which you do not need to use. There is an example at the beginning (**0**).

Mark your answers **on the separate answer sheet.**

SHE'S THE FIRST EVER PROFESSOR OF POP

Sheila Whiteley is Britain's first Professor of Popular Music at the Open University. **0** **A** Although she is now in her sixties, Professor Whiteley, like many women of her generation, had a short career before getting married and having children. **16**

She completed a degree as well as qualifying as a teacher. At that time, at the beginning of the eighties, a number of university lecturers were developing the academic study of popular culture, including film, TV, radio and music.

17 The course combined art, music and politics and Sheila Whiteley became a tutor on the OU course.

Today, Sheila Whiteley says that popular music is sexist. 'In the music industry, the number of women holding top positions is few. **18** The same is true of the lead guitar players in most pop and rock groups. In a recent list of the 100 best guitarists of all time published by a music magazine, only three were women. Boys get together and learn how to play at around 12 or 13. **19** While boys grow up wanting to be famous footballers or rock stars, girls want to marry footballers and rock stars.'

20 Now, however, when she listens to the latest bands she discusses hip-hop, rap, techno, ragga and reggae with young would-be rock musicians who are studying on the Popular Music course. **21** 'Because the study of popular music is so new there is a freedom which other academic subjects don't have,' she says.

Topics under research in her department include the politics of certain kinds of music, and the influence of Norwegian folk music on Norwegian jazz.

A Popular music is such a new area for serious academic study that it has very few professors in the world, let alone Britain.

B And some recent research suggests that things are not likely to change in the near future.

C Her publications include three successful books and numerous articles.

D The Open University led the way in developing a course which laid the foundations for the study of popular culture in universities.

E Professor Whiteley remains as enthusiastic about modern music as she was in her youth when the Beatles were around.

F If you go into a recording studio, it is a strongly male environment.

G This course is a mixture of theory and practical musicianship.

H Once her children had grown up, however, she turned to studying.

Tip Strip

Sentence D: What does 'led the way' mean? At the head of something or following behind?

Sentence E: What examples of modern music can you find in the article?

Sentence H: What does the word 'however' contribute to the meaning of this sentence?

You are going to read a magazine article in which three writers describe the best places to visit if you want to see the biggest cats on Earth. For Questions **22–35,** choose from the people **A–C**. The people may be chosen more than once. When more than one answer is required, these may be given in any order. There is an example at the beginning (**0**).

Mark your answers **on the separate answer sheet.**

Who

finds lions most interesting?	**0**	**A**
mentions seeing animals by boat?	**22**	
thinks it's best to go on an organised trip?	**23**	
says you will always remember seeing an animal?	**24**	
mentions being in quite a dangerous situation?	**25**	
is concerned about the fall in animal numbers?	**26**	**27**
recommends a place to see more than one species?	**28**	
comments on the way animals organise themselves?	**29**	
had only one sighting of an animal during a long period?	**30**	
came across an animal one evening?	**31**	
comments on animals being visually attractive?	**32**	
thinks animals could belong to another planet?	**33**	
thinks it's easy to see cheetahs and leopards?	**34**	
mentions controlling access to the animals?	**35**	

Tip Strip

Question 25: Look for a sentence that makes the situation clearly dangerous, even though the word itself isn't in the text.

Question 31: What other words do you know for 'evening'?

Question 33: How else can we refer to something belonging to another planet?

Cat-watching

A Julian

For thirty years I have followed the big cats of Africa, the lions, the leopards and the cheetahs and they have never lost their magic for me. They are such mysterious creatures, and in their comings and goings they are like spirits from another world.

Cheetahs are easy to find because they hunt in daylight. They are also the fastest animal on Earth with powerful, long limbs. They cannot fight lions but they can run away or hide.

Leopards are much harder to find as they are very shy. But it is lions that I find most exciting of all, and many years ago it was the lions of the Masai Mara in Kenya that first caught my imagination.

Lions are the only truly social cats, increasing their strength by living in groups, called prides. A typical pride might include about six females and two or three mature males. Most females remain in the same pride all their lives, but young males are forced to leave after two or three years to wander until they become strong enough to form their own pride.

If you're hoping to see all three big cats in action, there is nowhere better than the Masai Mara.

B Ruth

It's not easy to see a tiger, but when you do, you'll never forget it. I saw my first one at dusk in Nepal. Half the tigers in the world live in India, but in western Nepal, on the Kanali River, which is famous for its dolphins, you can see tigers as well.

When I first saw the tiger it was sitting far away on a forest road, but it had disappeared when we reached the spot. I searched the bushes without success, until I realised a huge male tiger was staring out at me from among the leaves. I backed away and it sprang across the road and vanished.

Tigers are so beautiful, orange and stripy, and with cuddly white spots behind their ears. There are probably fewer than 7,000 left in the whole world and sightings of tigers are rare.

If you want to see tigers, it's worth visiting a Project Tiger Reserve in India. You can stay in government-run rest houses, which are quite cheap. However, you then have to hire your own transport with a driver and a guide. You are also likely to be given a fixed route by the warden which you must keep to. This is one way of making sure that not everybody goes to the same place at the same time and it reduces the amount of disturbance.

C William

For me, the jaguar is the most impressive of all the big cats. Why? Its beauty? Its status in South American folk tales? Its power? All these and more.

The jaguar is a rare animal, hard to see, and it deliberately avoids humans. Almost everyone who goes on safari in Africa will see a lion and many people will see cheetahs and leopards. But you have to be very lucky to see a jaguar.

The jaguar is the world's third largest cat after the lion and the tiger. It is most often found in the tropical rainforest in Brazil, but if you really want to see one, you have to keep to the rivers and the beaches. In the dry season between May and September you may be lucky and see a jaguar sunbathing on the river banks, but you can increase your chances of seeing one if you go on a river cruise.

In Central America there are thought to be only a few hundred, while in Amazonia they are still widespread. I spent eight months in South America and only saw a jaguar once during the whole time I was there.

P A R T   1   You **must** answer this question.

1   You recently joined an international friendship club. You are not satisfied with the service you have received. Read the advertisement, together with the notes you have made, and write a letter to the director of the club asking for an explanation.

> ## International Friendship Club
>
> *Would you like to make friends with people
> from all over the world?*
>
> Just send us your name, age and address, brief
> details about yourself, your family and your hobbies,
> together with a recent photograph.
> The photograph will be returned directly.   — *sent photo
> a month ago*
>
> Choose 6 countries where you would like
> to have a friend. We will then send you the names
> and addresses of the people who will correspond
> with you.   — *2 only so far*
>
> Within 2 weeks you will receive letters from your   — *have heard
> nothing*
> 6 new friends.
>
> This service is free for all students!   — *Why did I get
> a bill, then?*

Write a **letter** of between **120** and **180** words in an appropriate style. Do not write any addresses.

Write an answer to **one** of the Questions **2–5** in this part. Write your answer in **120–180** words in an appropriate style.

Tip Strip

Question 2:
• Choose a place which you have some ideas about. It could be a specific place (i.e. Sydney, Australia) or an unspecified place (i.e. a skiing resort).
• Make sure you include reasons for your choice.

Question 3:
• The tone of your letter should communicate pleasure at the opportunity to see your friend.
• Clearly suggest a meeting place, as your friend is a stranger.
• Don't be too ambitious in your plans as you only have one day!

Question 4:
• Don't choose this question if you don't like sport!
• The question allows you to be either a player or a spectator, but your answer should convey enthusiasm.

Question 5(a):
• Say whether you agree or not with the statement, and give reasons (with clear reference to the ending of the book) for your opinions.
• Use a formal or neutral style.

Question 5(b):
• Remember to begin and end the letter appropriately.
• Give a reason for writing to your friend. Tell them briefly about the story.
• Give some examples from the book to explain why you like and dislike the two characters you have chosen.
• Use an informal style.

2 If you had to choose one place to spend a holiday, where would it be and why would you choose it?

Write your **composition.**

3 This is part of a letter you receive from an English-speaking friend who is coming on holiday to your country.

> *We will be spending a day in your town during our coach tour. Do you think we could meet? If so, what do you suggest we do? I've never been to your area and it would be great to see you.*

Write your **letter**, suggesting how you could both spend the day together. Do not write any addresses.

4 A magazine for young people called *Personal Opinions* has asked you to write about your favourite sport. Write an article, describing your favourite sport and what makes it so enjoyable for you.

Write your **article.**

5 Answer **one** of the following two questions based on your reading of **one** of the set books.

Either (a) 'A book must always have a happy ending.' With reference to the book you have read, write a **composition**, saying whether you agree or disagree with this statement, and why.

Or (b) Write a **letter** to an English friend telling them about the character you like most and the character you like least in the book you have read, and why.

PAPER 3 Use of English (1 hour 15 minutes)

For Questions **1–15**, read the text below and decide which answer **A, B, C** or **D** best fits each space. There is an example at the beginning (**0**).

Mark your answers **on the separate answer sheet.**

Tip Strip

Question 5: Which word means the same as 'be alive'?

Question 10: Which phrasal verb means 'find something by chance'?

Question 13: Which word has the same meaning as 'certain'?

Example:

0　**A** idea　　　　**B** subject　　　　**C** thing　　　　**D** object

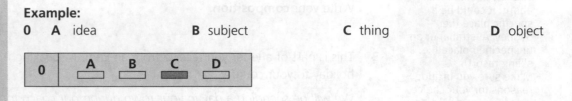

THE DODO LIVES ON

For many people the island of Mauritius in the Indian Ocean means one (**0**) ..... : a tropical paradise. But for scientists, it (**1**) ..... the heart of an age-old mystery: the mystery of the dodo. There are so many stories that (**2**) ..... this bird, which could not fly, that it is difficult to separate fact from (**3**) ..... .

The dodo was one of the most famous birds of all (**4**) ..... , yet we know very little about it. Within a few years of being discovered it had ceased to (**5**) ..... and there are not many good eye-witness reports that describe it. It (**6**) ..... in Mauritius, but after its discovery in the late sixteenth century, the dodo was (**7**) ..... around the world as a (**8**) ....., a flightless bird which attracted and fascinated everyone who saw it. But some birds occasionally suffered a worse (**9**) ..... . They were cooked and eaten by starving sailors who (**10**) ..... across dodos when they landed on the island.

There are (**11**) ..... from the seventeenth century which record (**12**) ..... of the bird in its island home and beyond. However, nobody can be really (**13**) ..... about the history of the dodo and (**14**) ..... the truth is never going to (**15**) ..... easy.

	A		**B**		**C**		**D**
1	represents		gives		makes		reproduces
2	create		treat		support		surround
3	literature		fiction		fairy tale		evidence
4	days		time		periods		history
5	exist		matter		happen		last
6	arrived		started		originated		born
7	packed		shipped		sailed		wrapped
8	speciality		puzzle		show		curiosity
9	event		fate		destruction		finish
10	fell		walked		came		tripped
11	indications		sheets		documents		prints
12	sightings		viewings		inspections		reflections
13	fixed		sure		particular		steady
14	uncovering		lifting		undoing		telling
15	come		feel		prove		suggest

For Questions **16–30,** read the text below and think of the word which best fits each space. Use only **one** word in each space. There is an example at the beginning (**0**).

Write your answers **on the separate answer sheet.**

Tip Strip

Question 18: This missing word introduces a contrasting idea.

Question 22: What tense is needed here?

Question 25: Remember that this common missing word is acting as an adjective in this sentence.

Example:

0	during

NAPPING IS GOOD FOR YOU

Napping, or taking short periods of sleep (**0**) .....during..... the day, is a basic human need. According (**16**) .... numerous studies, napping decreases tiredness and increases energy levels. Napping is based on common sense and (**17**) .... animal on the planet naps. (**18**) .... many people prefer to fight against tiredness rather (**19**) .... take a short sleep during the day.

For the (**20**) .... of workers a nap in the afternoon increases productivity, creativity and problem-solving skills. One expert (**21**) .... called for a new part to the work day, a period called 'nap time'. He argues that the modern work system (**22**) .... not designed around the actual physical needs of people's bodies. People have coffee breaks, (**23**) .... what they really need is nap breaks.

Chronobiologists, scientists (**24**) .... study sleep patterns, say that 'morning' people can benefit from a twenty (**25**) .... nap around noon, while 'night owls' need a nap around three or four in (**26**) .... afternoon. The key is to (**27**) .... out what kind of nap you need and for (**28**) .... long. It has been established that even very short breaks reduce errors and accidents and are (**29**) .... useful if taken about eight or nine hours (**30**) .... you wake up.

Tip Strip

Question 34: Which preposition follows 'blame'?

Question 40: This is a very informal way of making a suggestion.

For Questions **31–40,** complete the second sentence so that it has a similar meaning to the first sentence, using the word given. **Do not change the word given.** You must use between two and five words, including the word given. Here is an example (**0**).

Example: **0**   The bag is not big enough for all my luggage.

small

The bag .... for all my luggage.

The gap can be filled by the words 'is too small' so you write:

0	is too small

Write **only the missing words** on the separate answer sheet.

31 You can still get a ticket for tonight's concert if you haven't got one already.
unless
You can still get a ticket for tonight's concert ....
already.

32 'My mother doesn't work in the factory any more,' said Vera.
no
Vera said that .... in the factory.

33 They say that the President is thinking of calling an election.
said
The President .... of calling an election.

34 Joe said it was my fault that he missed his bus.
blamed
Joe .... his bus.

35 I could never have won the writing competition without your advice.
you
I could never have won the writing competition, ...
me.

36 I haven't seen my grandparents since Christmas.
time
The .... grandparents was Christmas.

37 A second-hand car is cheaper than a new one.
expensive
A second-hand car .... a new one.

38 To my astonishment the stranger knew my name.
find
I .... the stranger knew my name.

39 Although he had hurt his hand, Don still did his violin practice.
his
Despite ...., Don still did his violin practice.

40 Let's visit my parents tomorrow.
go
Why .... see my parents tomorrow?

For Questions **41–55**, read the text below and look carefully at each line. Some of the lines are correct, and some have a word which should not be there.

If a line is correct, put a tick (✔) by the number **on the separate answer sheet.** If a line has a word which should not be there, write the word **on the separate answer sheet.** There are two examples at the beginning (**0** and **00**).

Example:

0	✔
00	*too*

0	....	Mongolia lies in the heart of Asia, between China and Russia.
00	....	It has a rich collection of ancient folk tales which are too
41	....	popular with Mongolian people, especially one about a very
42	....	foolish fellow. One night this man went to fetch a water from
43	....	his well. Gazing down into the well he quite saw the moon
44	....	reflected in the distant water at its own bottom. He immediately
45	....	thought the moon had fallen down the well, so went to fetch up
46	....	a large iron hook which he attached to a long rope. He let the
47	....	rope down carefully and tried to catch the moon so he could pull
48	....	it to the safety. He heard the hook splash into the water and so
49	....	he started out pulling. But the hook had caught on some weeds
50	....	and no matter how hard he tried it wouldn't move. Eventually he
51	....	pulled with all his strength. The rope been broke and he was thrown
52	....	flat onto his back. Looking up he saw the moon shining down at him
53	....	from the night sky. With a such satisfied smile he thought that
54	....	although it was the heaviest thing he had ever had to be move,
55	....	at least the moon was back where it belonged.

Tip Strip

Question 56: What kind of word is required here?

Question 61: Watch your spelling!

Question 62: Will you need a negative or positive word here?

For Questions **56–65,** read the text below. Use the word given in capitals at the end of each line to form a word that fits the space in the same line. There is an example at the beginning (**0**).

Example:

0	memorable

Write your answers **on the separate answer sheet.**

THE OXFORD AND CAMBRIDGE UNIVERSITY BOAT RACE

The first Boat Race was a (**0**) memorable occasion and took place   **MEMORY**
in 1829. One of the (**56**) .... of the race was Charles   **FOUND**
Wordsworth, who had (**57**) .... established the university   **SUCCESS**
cricket match in 1827. Today, almost two centuries later, one of the most
(**58**) .... things about the Race is its   **AMAZE**
(**59**) .... worldwide. In fact, there is even a Boat Race society **POPULAR**
which is responsible for the annual (**60**) .... of videos of the **DISTRIBUTE**
Race to all its members.

The Race is rowed on the River Thames in London over a
(**61**) .... of about four miles. Thousands stand on the banks to   **LONG**
watch, however (**62**) .... and cold the weather might be. Just   **PLEASE**
(**63**) .... if the weather is very windy, a boat may fill with   **OCCASION**
water and sink, a (**64**) .... sight and obviously a great   **DRAMA**
(**65**) .... to the boat's crew.   **EMBARRASS**

PAPER 4

PART 1

Listening (approximately 40 minutes)

You'll hear people talking in eight different situations. For Questions **1–8**, choose the best answer, **A, B** or **C**.

Tip Strip

Question 1: Listen for another way of saying what you 'like most' about something.

Question 3: The tone of voice the speakers use is a further clue to choosing the right option.

Question 5: The speaker is giving instructions; some of the vocabulary can only refer to one of the options.

1   You hear a young woman talking about starting a new job.
    What does she like most about it?
    A   the salary
    B   the people
    C   the hours

    [1]

2   You hear a taxi driver talking about a passenger.
    What did the passenger do?
    A   He objected to the cost.
    B   He forgot his luggage.
    C   He lost an address.

    [2]

3   You hear two women talking about magazines.
    What is their attitude towards the magazines?
    A   They refuse to buy them.
    B   They dislike the free offers.
    C   They disapprove of them.

    [3]

4   You hear a man talking about a local exhibition.
    What did he find interesting?
    A   the oil paintings
    B   the old photographs
    C   the advertisements

    [4]

5   You hear a woman explaining something to a child.
    What is she talking about?
    A   how to make a paper boat
    B   how to build a model plane
    C   how to draw a a motor car

    [5]

6   You hear two people discussing a friend.
    What has happened to their friend?
    A   He has broken his arm.
    B   He fell while out walking.
    C   He had a skiing accident.

    [6]

7   You hear a man talking about a book he has read.
    Why does he recommend reading it?
    A   because it deals well with a boring subject
    B   because it treats buildings seriously
    C   because it is such an impressive book

    [7]

8   You hear a woman talking about a journey.
    What is she complaining about?
    A   the lack of information
    B   the delay to the flight
    C   the standard of the hotel

    [8]

You will hear part of a local radio programme in which a man is talking about a new college which has recently opened. For Questions **9–18,** complete the notes.

Tip Strip

Another task in Part 2 can ask you to complete notes.

• Before you listen, read the questions. Think about the type of information that is missing.
• Look carefully at the layout of the questions. The words you need to write are on the tape.
• Write one to three words in each space.
• Check your spelling.

Question 10: You should be able to predict the kind of answer; listen carefully to see if you are right.

Question 14: Look carefully at the punctuation to help you understand what is required to fill the gap.

Question 15: Do you expect a noun or verb will be needed to fill the gap?

HARDACRE COLLEGE

College buildings surround a [_____ **9**]

Students are expected to travel by [_____ **10**]

Buildings are separated by [_____ **11**] and flowerbeds

[_____ **12**] and students can use college nursery

Disabled students can use [_____ **13**] to reach top floors

Banks and post office: open; [_____ **14**] will open later

Students interested in drama and music can use [_____ **15**]

Laboratories and lecture rooms have [_____ **16**] and interactive video

Total number of students will be [_____ **17**]

Another chance to visit college on [_____ **18**] next Saturday

You will hear five different people talking about their memory. For Questions **19–23,** choose from the list **A–F** what each speaker says. Use the letters only once. There is one extra letter which you do not need to use.

Tip Strip

A: What would you expect the person to refer to if their memory is 'visual'?
C: This is not the same as never being able to remember anything!
F: Listen for the person who says that despite trying hard they never seem able to remember things.

A   I have a very visual memory.

B   A good memory can be a disadvantage.

C   I forget where I put things.

D   I can't remember what matters.

E   I've learnt to train my memory.

F   I've got a hopeless memory.

Speaker 1 [**19**]

Speaker 2 [**20**]

Speaker 3 [**21**]

Speaker 4 [**22**]

Speaker 5 [**23**]

You will hear part of a radio interview with a woman called Susan who runs a city farm. For Questions **24–30,** choose the best answer **A**, **B** or **C**.

Tip Strip

Question 24: The speaker's intonation will give you a further clue to the correct answer.

Question 25: The speaker and the interviewer laugh but is it because Susan has told a joke?

Question 30: Listen for the speaker to say 'but what is really special' to help you focus on the right answer.

24 How do people react when Susan says what she does?
   A   They are shocked.
   B   They are upset.
   C   They are puzzled.

24

25 Why did the school teacher write to a newspaper?
   A   to advertise for farmers to visit her school
   B   to express alarm at the children's response
   C   to share a good joke with the readers

25

26 What was the feeling about the first city farm?
   A   Children loved it.
   B   Parents were annoyed.
   C   Local people disliked it.

26

27 Why did Susan get involved in the city farm scheme?
   A   She was attracted by the children's reaction.
   B   She had always taught young children.
   C   She had once been married to a farmer.

27

28 How did the children treat the animals?
   A   They were too afraid to touch them.
   B   They were unsure what to do with them.
   C   They were very kind towards them.

28

29 How did people react when Susan set up her city farm?
   A   The shopkeepers offered to buy her produce.
   B   People were interested and very helpful.
   C   Some people thought it was a waste of money.

29

30 What does Susan find most rewarding?
   A   the fact that some children want to be farmers
   B   the children's involvement outside school hours
   C   the way the children want to look after the lambs

30

PAPER 5

Speaking (14 minutes)

PART 1 (3 minutes)

Answer these questions:

What are your hobbies or interests?
What kind of music do you most enjoy listening to?
Do you like playing sport?
Are you interested in reading? What sort of things do you read?

PART 2 (4 minutes)

World of work (compare, contrast and speculate)

Turn to pictures 1 and 2 on page 163 which show people at work.

Candidate A, compare and contrast these photographs and say how easy or difficult these jobs might be. You have a minute to do this.

Candidate B, would you like to do one of these jobs?

Shopping (compare, contrast and speculate)

Turn to pictures 1 and 2 on page 164 which show people shopping.

Candidate B, compare and contrast these photographs and say what people find enjoyable or otherwise about shopping. You have a minute to do this.

Candidate A, do you like shopping for certain things?

PART 3 (3 minutes)

Choosing a decoration (discuss and evaluate)

Turn to the pictures on page 165 which show ideas for what to put in the entrance hall of a school or college. Look at the suggestions and decide what would be the most suitable thing to display.

PART 4 (4 minutes)

Answer these questions:

How important is it to provide works of art in public places?
Do you agree with people who think money could be better spent?
How important is it to decorate your own room or bedroom?
If you could choose anything at all to put in your own school/college/office, what would you choose and why?

TEST 6

PART 1

You are going to read an article about an English woman called Ellen MacArthur, the fastest and youngest person to sail around the world in a single-handed sailing race. Choose the most suitable heading **A–H** for each part (**1–6**) of the article. There is one extra heading which you do not need to use. There is an example at the beginning (**0**).

Mark your answers **on the separate answer sheet**.

A Unbelievable hardships and difficulties

B Disapproval of reporting style

C Success for someone so young

D Braver than a man

E Ellen MacArthur makes no fuss

F Unknown sailor beats competition

G She's so tiny!

H Huge welcome home

---

0 — **F**

Ellen MacArthur became front page news when, in 2001, she came second in the Vendée Globe round-the-world yacht race. Up until that point most people had never heard of her, even though at one stage during the race it had looked as if she might win.

1

The Vendée is the toughest race in the sailing world; others have died trying to complete the 26,000-mile course around Antarctica, but Ellen MacArthur spent three months at sea on her own and succeeded at the age of twenty-four where many others, far older and more experienced, had failed.

2

She sailed alone in a yacht which would usually require an 11-strong crew. She changed sails twice her weight many times a day; she climbed 30 metre-high poles to carry out repairs to the sails in storm force winds; she lived on dried food and slept for no more than 10 minutes at a time; she escaped icebergs and stared death in the face more than once.

3

As her damaged yacht limped back to civilisation, thousands of people gathered on the shore to cheer her on. Her parents were flown out in a helicopter when she was 120 miles from the finishing line and were able to wave to their daughter before greeting her in an emotional reunion once she had arrived on dry land.

4

It was an extraordinary adventure story, but what made it all the more interesting for the media was the fact that the hero was a woman – and a small woman at that! Some newspapers presented her as 'brave little Ellen' and referred to her by her first name as if she were a child. Indeed, in many newspapers she was called a 'girl', and the reports described how she cried when she finally stepped off her yacht.

5

Ellen MacArthur has been recognised as the best ocean-going sailor that Britain has ever produced, so this kind of reporting seems particularly insulting and depressing. It is hard to imagine that a man who had achieved the same success would be referred to as a 'sweet little thing' or 'Little Fairy of the Oceans'.

6

Ellen MacArthur's courage and determination were amazing but she herself has remained modest about her achievement. For her it was all in a day's work. In 1995 she had been judged Young Sailor of the Year and in 1998 Yachtsman of the Year, so taking on the Vendée Globe was the next natural step in her sailing career.

You are going to read a part of a story about a girl called Maria who is going on holiday with her parents. For Questions **7–13**, choose the correct answer **A**, **B**, **C** or **D**.

Mark your answers **on the separate answer sheet**.

'All right, back there?' said Maria's father.

'Not much longer now,' said Maria's mother.

3   Neither of them turned round. The backs of their heads rode smoothly forward between the landscapes that unrolled at either side of the car; hedges, trees, fields, houses came and went before there was time to examine them.

Back behind her parents' travelling heads, with the countryside unrolling tidily at each side of her, Maria hoped there would be something to talk to at this holiday house her parents had rented for the month. You can always talk to people, of course. It is usual, indeed. The trouble with people is that they expect you to say particular things, and so you end up saying what they expect, or want. And they usually end up saying what you expected them to. Grown-ups, Maria had noticed spent much time telling each other what the weather was like, or wondering aloud if one thing would happen, or another. She herself quite liked to talk to her mother, but somehow her mother was always about to go out, or into another room, and by the time Maria had got to the point of the conversation, she had gone. Her father when she talked to him would listen

16 with distant kindliness, but not as though what she said were of any great importance. Which, of course, it might not be. Except, she thought, to me.

And so for real conversation, Maria considered, things were infinitely preferable. Animals, frequently. Trees and plants, from time to time. Sometimes what they said

20 was consoling, and sometimes **it** was uncomfortable, but at least you were having a conversation. For a real heart-to-heart you couldn't do much better than a clock. For a casual chat almost anything would do.

'Here we are,' said Mrs Foster.

Maria and her parents got out of the car and stood in front of the house, considering it. At least Maria considered it. Her mother said, 'How pretty. I like the white walls,' and her father began to take the suitcases from the car. Maria went on considering.

It was a tidy house. It stood neat and square – or rather, rectangular, for it was longer than it was high – with a regular number of green-shuttered windows upstairs and down, on either side of a black front door.

'Well, Maria,' said Mr Foster. 'Is it anything like you imagined?'

'No,' said Maria.

'Built around 1820, I should think,' said Mr Foster in his instructing voice.

And Maria thought, never mind about that, because somewhere there is a swing. It is blowing in the wind – I can hear the squeaking noise it makes. Good, I shall like having my own swing. And someone's got a little dog that keeps yapping. She walked round the corner of the house into the garden, to see where the swing might be, but there was nothing to be seen except a large square lawn and a good many trees.

Tip Strip

This text is taken from a modern novel; the style is descriptive and the writer focuses on how Maria feels and reacts to things around her.

Question 7: Read the first few lines carefully. If Maria's parents really wanted to talk to their daughter they would probably turn to look at her – at least her mother would and her father would repeat his question if he needed an answer.

Question 10: Read the text carefully and think how Maria must feel when her mother disappears as soon as she wants to talk to her.

Question 13: Why does Maria say 'Good'?

7 What do we learn about Maria's parents when they speak to her without turning round (lines 1–3)?

   A They would rather ignore her.
   B They are too busy talking together.
   C They do not expect an answer.
   D They think she may be asleep.

8 Why does Maria hope there will be something to talk to at the house?

   A She says she often feels bored and lonely.
   B She can't rely on people to talk to her.
   C She dislikes being with other children.
   D She feels people have fixed ideas.

9 What does the writer suggest about Maria's opinion of adult conversation?

   A It is too difficult to follow.
   B It can often be quite dull.
   C The topics are unexpected.
   D The topics are interesting.

10 Which word best describes Maria's feelings when she tries to talk to her mother?

   A disappointed
   B worried
   C angry
   D impatient

11 What do you think the writer means by Maria's father listening with 'distant kindliness'? (line 16)

   A He cannot always hear what she says.
   B He tries very hard to understand her.
   C He is not really involved in what she says.
   D He pretends to know what she means.

12 What does 'it' in line 20 refer to?

   A what things say to Maria
   B Maria talking to herself
   C what people say to Maria
   D the attitude of Maria's father

13 What is Maria most interested in when she arrives at the holiday house?

   A there is a dog she can talk to
   B the fact that the house is very old
   C the fact that she can hear a swing
   D the surprising appearance of the house

You are going to read an article about a team of gardeners from England who went to India. Eight sentences have been removed from the article. Choose from the sentences **A–I** the one which fits each gap (**14–20**). There is one extra sentence which you do not need to use. There is an example at the beginning (**0**).

Mark your answers **on the separate answer sheet.**

A GARDEN FOR PALNA CHILDREN'S HOME

Palna Children's Home is in Delhi, in India. The word *palna* means 'cradle' in Hindi and the staff at the home look after helpless and often very sick children. The children receive a high standard of medical care as they are nursed back to health. | **0** | **E** |

Every three years The British Council, which is a charitable organisation, gives the Palna Children's Home about £50,000. | **14** | *Groundforce*, the team of people responsible for developing the garden, are best known for their gardening programme on BBC television. | **15** |

In setting out to transform the grounds of the children's home in Delhi, *Groundforce* visited the Taj Mahal palace. | **16** | Not only the buildings, but also the gardens of the Taj Mahal were a source of inspiration to *Groundforce* when it came to designing the children's garden in Delhi.

Before starting work, the team looked carefully at the existing grounds in order to design a garden which would be culturally appropriate and at the same time provide fun and pleasure for the children. | **17** | Natural substances from this tree can be used for medicinal purposes.

The garden at Palna was much larger than the typical British gardens that the team were used to working on. | **18** | They created a central circle around the Neem tree which was connected to other parts of the garden by long, formal avenues of palm trees, called bottle palms. The pathways were made out of local stone and the overall effect of the pathways radiating out from a central point resembled the rising sun. The walls were painted a deep rich red, and peaceful seating areas in the shade for staff to relax were carved by a local stonemason using stone from Rajasthan.

Groundforce used huge concrete drainage pipes for the children to run through. | **19** | One of the tunnels was designed with a water feature. This was made by creating a constant fountain-like spray of water at the tunnel entrance using shower heads fixed into the ground. Shower heads normally spray water downwards but these shower heads point upwards. The tunnel is known as The Terror Run; the slower the children run through it, the wetter they get!

When the garden was finished there was a grand opening ceremony at which everyone who had been involved in the project was present. | **20** | The team of gardeners, who said it was the most complicated garden they had ever created, were delighted by the looks on the children's faces when they saw their new garden for the first time.

Tip Strip

Sentence B: What is The Terror Run?
Sentence F: Which paragraph mentions a structure that can be referred to as a 'monument'?
Sentence H: Why was the assignment unusual?

A Before getting down to work the team decided to visit the local shops and markets.

B Also present were lots of children, the bravest of whom thoroughly enjoyed testing The Terror Run.

C In 2001 this money was used to create a garden for the children.

D In the centre of the garden was a large Neem tree which is common in many gardens in India.

E Many children live at the home, whereas others come on a daily basis.

F This white marble monument was built in the seventeenth century and is regarded as one of the most beautiful buildings in the world.

G The pipes were dug into the ground and made secure by piling up earth and building simple dry stone walls on either side of each tunnel.

H So for gardeners used to working in a very different environment and climate this assignment was unusual, to say the least.

I However, *Groundforce* came up with a design that made the most of the space, using the existing Neem tree at the centre.

PART 4

You are going to read a magazine article in which four young people talk about running their own business. For Questions **21–35**, choose from the people **A–D**. The people may be chosen more than once. When more than one answer is required, these may be given in any order. There is an example at the beginning (**0**).

Mark your answers **on the separate answer sheet**.

Who

went directly from studying into business? | **0** | **D**

was refused a bank loan? | **21** |

was unemployed for a while? | **22** |

is thinking of expanding their business? | **23** |

borrowed money from their family? | **24** |

has a small staff of people working for them? | **25** | | **26** |

gave their original work away as gifts? | **27** |

discovered the factory by reading about it? | **28** |

works on other designers' products? | **29** |

mentions the amount of time their work takes? | **30** | | **31** |

has already expanded their working space? | **32** |

chose their career while learning something else? | **33** |

doesn't mention the cost of their product? | **34** |

sells their product to the theatrical world? | **35** |

Tip Strip

Question 23: Look for the person who has new ideas for developing their business.

Question 32: 'expanded' is used here to indicate an increase in working space.

Question 34: One person makes no mention of whether or not their product is expensive.

young BUSINESSES

An old factory was empty for 30 years until young people started moving in and setting up their own businesses.

A Stuart

I started up my own business basically because I was out of work. I was fed up with applying for jobs and not even making it to the interview stage. Anyway, I saw an article in the local newspaper about renting work space in an old factory. You could get a loan for any equipment and you only needed to repay the money once your business was making a profit. Added to which the rent was very low.

So that's exactly what I did. I borrowed some money and bought a computer and a colour printer. I've always been interested in art and design and I love music and watching videos. I set about designing covers for music CDs and videos and sent off some of my work to various music companies, entertainment magazines and so on and within a year I had more orders than I could cope with by myself. Now, two years down the line, I employ a staff of three and we've branched out into designing the covers for computer games. I've been incredibly lucky and my business has really taken off.

B Sonya

My parents told me about the factory when I was looking for a studio to set up my own business. I had left art college full of ideas as to what I was going to do. But I was horrified when I saw the cost of renting even a tiny studio.

I produce hand-made gift boxes and wrapping paper. Each box is individually designed and decorated with gold flowers and butterflies. The wrapping paper is made to match and I will also take customers' requests if they want something very special. So, because everything is hand-made my products are quite expensive. But you can't buy them in shops or supermarkets so they really are special.

Actually as the demand for my work has increased, I've now got someone working for me and I'm thinking of setting up a mail order business, probably using the internet.

If it hadn't been for the opportunity to rent a space in the factory, I would still be waiting and hoping!

C Euan

I tried to get a loan from a bank in order to start up my business. I spent hours producing a business plan, but the manager turned me down because she thought it would take years for me to make any kind of profit. Well, how wrong she was! My parents lent me the money for the first year's rent and I started work in one of the factory's smallest rooms. Now, my business has grown to such an extent that I actually rent three rooms. I make wigs for people in show business. It's not that these people are bald, they've all got their own hair. It's just that most of them are on stage night after night and they don't always have time to look after their hair or get to a hairdresser. So they rely on being able to wear a wig that exactly matches their own hair colour.

A wig is very expensive – anything from £1000 upwards for just a small hairpiece. The raw material to make a wig is very costly and then every hair has to be threaded by hand so it's hours of work. And then you have to look after a wig very carefully; it needs to be repaired quite often which takes time. For that reason a lot of people actually have two.

D Meryl

I moved into the factory straight after leaving university. I studied history but ever since I was a small child I've been interested in sewing. And halfway through my degree course I realised that although I was enjoying the subject, what I really wanted to do as a career was embroidery – that's stitching with silk and threads and suchlike. I used to embroider scarves for friends for birthday presents and people loved them. So I sent some scarves to a couple of top London stores and they placed orders almost straightaway. They send me the scarves made by their own design team and I embroider and decorate each scarf so that it's completely unique and individual. As it's a very expensive decorative technique and takes hours to do, the scarves are only found at the top end of the fashion market. Recently, I've been asked to embroider the necklines of jackets and the bottom edges of trousers and skirts, so business continues to expand.

You **must** answer this question.

1   You have seen an advertisement asking for young people to support an environmental programme. You would like to join the team but you want to know more. Using the notes you have made, write to *Caring for our Forests*, giving necessary details and asking for further information.

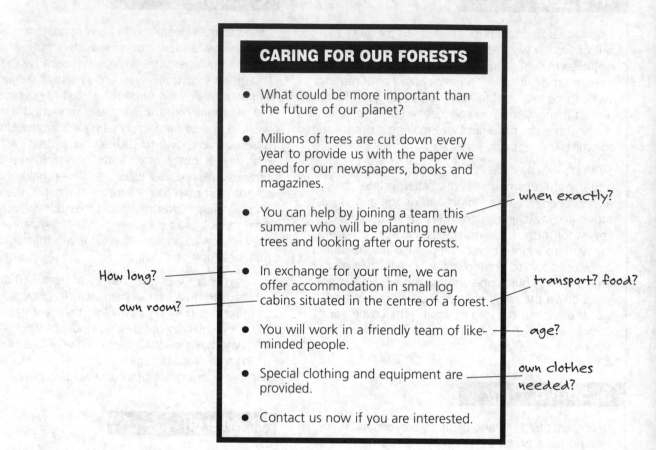

CARING FOR OUR FORESTS

- What could be more important than the future of our planet?

- Millions of trees are cut down every year to provide us with the paper we need for our newspapers, books and magazines.

- You can help by joining a team this summer who will be planting new trees and looking after our forests.   *when exactly?*

- In exchange for your time, we can offer accommodation in small log cabins situated in the centre of a forest.   *How long?*   *own room?*   *transport? food?*

- You will work in a friendly team of like-minded people.   *age?*

- Special clothing and equipment are provided.   *own clothes needed?*

- Contact us now if you are interested.

Write a **letter** of between **120** and **180** words in an appropriate style. Do not write any addresses.

Write an answer to **one** of the Questions **2–5** in this part. Write your answer in **120–180** words in an appropriate style.

Tip Strip

Question 2:
• Plan your story before you start writing.
• Make quite sure that you know how you are going to include the sentence which you have to end with. Your story must lead naturally to this conclusion and make complete sense in the context of the whole story.

Question 3:
• Read the question carefully as it provides clear paragraphs for your report: where the concert took place, the programme, what you liked about the music and whether you would recommend a concert like this to your class.

Question 4:
• This question asks you to discuss the topic; you may agree or disagree or you may think that there are arguments both in favour and against this statement.
• Make sure you support your opinion with some facts. (You may have had experience yourself which is relevant.)

Question 5(a):
• If you agree with this statement, it may be because you think the book is boring, or too difficult.
• If you disagree, you may think the book is exciting and has a theme or a message which appeals to young people.
• Use a formal or neutral style.

Question 5(b):
• Think about the aspects of the book which might make a good film, e.g. visual interest because the story takes place in different locations, strong and interesting characters, fast and exciting plot.
• Use a formal or neutral style.

2 You have been asked to write a story for your student magazine which **ends** with these words:

A day which had begun with tears ended in smiles.

Write your **story**.

3 You have been to a concert which you enjoyed very much. Your teacher has asked you to write a report of the concert saying what you enjoyed about the music and whether a similar concert would appeal to other students.

Write your **report**.

4 After discussing the topic in class, your teacher has asked you to write a composition with the following title:

Living with a family abroad is the only way to learn a foreign language.

Write your **composition.**

5 Answer **one** of the following two questions based on your reading of **one** of the set books.

Either **(a)** *'This book is not really suitable for young people.'* Write a **composition** saying whether you agree or disagree with this statement and why.

Or **(b)** A magazine has asked readers to recommend a book which they think would make a good film. With reference to the book you have read, write an **article** saying why you think it is suitable material for a film.

Use of English (1 hour 15 minutes)

For Questions **1–15**, read the text below and decide which answer **A, B, C** or **D** best fits each space. There is an example at the beginning (**0**).

Mark your answers **on the separate answer sheet.**

Tip Strip

Question 3: This is a fixed phrase - only one word can be right.

Question 5: Which of these words collocates with 'work'?

Question 9: Which of these phrases means to be in contact with someone?

Example:

0   **A**   goes   **B**   makes   **C**   sets   **D**   does

CIRCUS CHILDREN

When the Moscow State Circus (**0**) ..... on its annual tour of Europe, the younger members of the circus are still expected to (**1**) ..... with their education. The circus usually (**2**) ..... for a few days in each town, so how do the young performers manage?

One twelve-year-old gets up at the crack of (**3**) ..... to practise her act before (**4**) ..... off to school. She returns at lunchtime to her family's caravan and more practice. Not only does she work (**5**) ....., but she also has to make a whole new (**6**) ..... of friends each time she moves on. 'It's exhausting work but I like the circus (**7**) .....,' she says. 'The worst (**8**) ..... is when I make new friends and have to leave them, although I try to (**9**) ..... by letter.'

The Russian who runs the circus makes (**10**) ..... that all the children get a proper education. When the circus first arrives in Britain, he (**11**) ..... the traveller education service and gives them the (**12**) ..... of all the children, and when they will be in certain towns and cities. 'It's a fantastic (**13**) .....,' he says. 'I receive a (**14**) ..... when we reach the next town telling us where to meet. We are then accompanied to the school and introduced to the head teacher. It works like (**15**) ..... .'

1	**A**	progress	**B**	maintain	**C**	continue	**D**	further
2	**A**	slows	**B**	stops	**C**	places	**D**	moves
3	**A**	dawn	**B**	morning	**C**	day	**D**	light
4	**A**	following	**B**	leaving	**C**	heading	**D**	directing
5	**A**	strict	**B**	difficult	**C**	strong	**D**	hard
6	**A**	form	**B**	gathering	**C**	set	**D**	collection
7	**A**	life	**B**	way	**C**	living	**D**	type
8	**A**	section	**B**	piece	**C**	part	**D**	side
9	**A**	keep in view	**B**	keep in touch	**C**	keep in line	**D**	keep in mind
10	**A**	sure	**B**	definite	**C**	important	**D**	time
11	**A**	connects	**B**	notices	**C**	reaches	**D**	contacts
12	**A**	facts	**B**	details	**C**	quantities	**D**	demands
13	**A**	system	**B**	habit	**C**	plan	**D**	order
14	**A**	sign	**B**	signal	**C**	message	**D**	word
15	**A**	lightning	**B**	clockwork	**C**	new	**D**	wildfire

PART 2

For Questions **16–30**, read the text below and think of the word which best fits each space. Use only **one** word in each space. There is an example at the beginning (**0**).

Write your answers **on the separate answer sheet.**

Example:

0	*who*

PETER BENCHLEY LIKES SHARKS

Peter Benchley, the author (**0**) ....*who*........ wrote the novel *Jaws*, thinks it may be partly his fault that people don't like sharks. The movie, (**16**) .... on his book, involved a terrifying monster fish (**17**) .... main purpose was to attack anyone (**18**) .... everyone in the ocean.

In (**19**) ...., sharks kill approximately 12 people a year. In (**20**) ...., people kill millions of sharks every year and (**21**) .... to 90 per cent of great white sharks have been (**22**) .... out. Peter Benchley admits, 'I created something that doesn't exist.' He hopes to set (**23**) .... record straight with a new documentary film he has made. The film focuses (**24**) .... some of the more attractive aspects of great white sharks. For (**25**) .... , one extremely brave diver demonstrates that when you touch a shark on the nose, (**26**) .... goes very still.

Benchley grew up in Massachusetts in the US and (**27**) .... a large part of his childhood swimming in the ocean. He got the idea for *Jaws* (**28**) .... a newspaper article about a man who caught a shark which (**29**) .... about 2,000 kilos. When the movie was made, Benchley had the opportunity to appear (**30**) .... an actor, playing the reporter on the beach just before the shark attacks for the first time.

Tip Strip

Question 17: The missing word is a possessive relative pronoun – take care with the spelling.
Question 20: This phrase introduces a contrast to the previous sentence.
Question 23: This word is part of a fixed phrase.

For Questions **31–40,** complete the second sentence so that it has a similar meaning to the first sentence, using the word given. **Do not change the word given.** You must use between two and five words, including the word given. Here is an example at the (**0**).

Example: **0**   The bag is not big enough for all my luggage.

   small

   The bag .... for all my luggage.

The gap can be filled by the words 'is too small' so you write:

0	is too small

Write **only the missing words** on the separate answer sheet.

---

31 I offered to lend Lisa money for a holiday but she refused.
turned
Lisa .... to lend her money for a holiday.

32 If you are not satisfied with the hotel service, you should say so.
make
You should .... if you are not satisfied with the hotel service.

33 The gardens are open each day for visitors to enjoy the flower displays.
that
The gardens are open each day .... the flower displays.

34 Could you carry my case for me, please?
mind
Would .... my case for me, please?

35 I wish I hadn't missed your birthday party.
regret
I .... your birthday party.

36 'Have you bought a new bicycle?' Ben asked Katy.
whether
Ben asked Katy .... a new bicycle.

37 The flight to the islands took fifteen hours.
was
It .... flight to the islands.

38 John's spelling is so bad I can hardly read his letters.
such
John is .... I can hardly read his letters.

39 The cold wet weather depresses me and I feel homesick.
gets
The cold wet weather .... and I feel homesick.

40 How long have you been a doctor?
become
When .... a doctor?

PART 4

For Questions **41–55**, read the text below and look carefully at each line. Some of the lines are correct, and some have a word which should not be there.

If a line is correct, put a tick (✔) by the number **on the separate answer sheet.** If a line has a word which should not be there, write the word **on the separate answer sheet.** There are two examples at the beginning (**0** and **00**).

Tip Strip

Line 48: Make sure you read to the end of the sentence on the next line.

Line 50: Which word in this line is unnecessary but would be correct if the word 'make' was in the same line?

Line 55: Is there a comparison in this last sentence?

Example:	0	✔
	00	*outside*

0	....	I had a terrible rail journey home last week when I went to see
00	....	my parents. They live in the country, outside miles from the
41	....	nearest station, so they usually pick me up by their car.
42	....	The train was late at leaving London, so I rang home on my
43	....	mobile to have let my parents know what was happening.
44	....	There was just one delay after the another. First of all, there
45	....	was a signal failure, then the train in front of ours broke down.
46	....	After that there was a problem with the engine, so we had to
47	....	wait for ages long at a station while a mechanic checked things.
48	....	When I finally tried to ring home, my phone battery was gone
49	....	flat. The guard offered to lend me his mobile but still by this
50	....	time my parents had left home, so I couldn't contact with them.
51	....	When we eventually arrived almost three hours late, the platform
52	....	was in complete darkness. I couldn't see my parents much anywhere
53	....	and I was really worried. I made my way carefully down the steps
54	....	and headed for the car park. There, so fast asleep inside the car
55	....	were my poor parents, more exhausted with waiting for me.

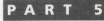

PART 5

For questions **56–65,** read the text below. Use the word given in capitals at the end of each line to form a word that fits the space in the same line. There is an example at the beginning (**0**).

Example:

0	*difference*

Write your answers **on the separate answer sheet.**

ANGEL OF MERCY

Vicky Smith is a paramedic with a (**0**) *difference*, her business is saving   **DIFFER**

lives by flying to accidents in a helicopter. She flies three or four times

(**56**) .... with the paramedic team, which can be on the scene   **DAY**

(**57**) .... ten minutes.   **WITH**

Her job clearly brings huge (**58**) .... but Vicky finds it very   **RESPONSIBLE**

rewarding. After leaving school she (**59**) .... as a medical   **QUALIFY**

technician, learned to drive an ambulance and completed her

(**60**) .... to become a paramedic. Her job has a great deal of   **TRAIN**

(**61**) ...., and she has received an award for her   **VARY**

(**62**) .... in rescuing a woman trapped in a house fire.   **BRAVE**

Air ambulances provide an essential (**63**) .... that helps save   **SERVE**

hundreds of lives in countries throughout the world. (**64**) ....,   **USUAL**

people who receive (**65**) .... immediately after an accident,   **TREAT**

especially in the first sixteen minutes, have a higher chance of survival.

Tip Strip

Question 56: Take care with spelling.
Question 57: You need to add a short suffix to this word.
Question 62: What kind of word is needed here?

Listening (approximately 40 minutes)

You'll hear people talking in eight different situations. For Questions **1–8**, choose the best answer, **A**, **B** or **C**.

Tip Strip

Question 3: Listen carefully to the disagreement between the two speakers. What was the main problem?

Question 5: What point does the speaker make about families?

Question 8: The girl summarises what she likes **after** making her choice.

1 You hear a man talking about his new car.
Why did he buy it?
- **A** He wanted another colour.
- **B** He needed to replace his previous car.
- **C** He received an attractive offer.

1

2 You hear a woman talking about having her purse stolen.
Where did she always keep her bag?
- **A** beside her chair
- **B** on a shelf
- **C** under her desk

2

3 You hear a woman talking on the phone to her friend.
What has happened?
- **A** Her friend waited outside the wrong cinema.
- **B** The woman misunderstood the time.
- **C** They have both missed the film.

3

4 You hear a doctor talking about a baby's first year.
What point is he making?
- **A** It is a difficult subject to investigate.
- **B** Parents are the most important influence.
- **C** The experiments include grandparents.

4

5 You hear a radio announcement about a new health and fitness centre.
Who is it designed for?
- **A** students
- **B** workers
- **C** families

5

6 You hear a woman telling her friend that she is giving up her job as a banker.
What is her reason for leaving?
- **A** She wants to earn more.
- **B** She needs a change.
- **C** She dislikes the stress.

6

7 You hear a man talking about an evening picnic.
What was the disadvantage?
- **A** the food
- **B** the weather
- **C** the insects

7

8 You hear a girl talking about a new hotel for young people.
What does she particularly like about it?
- **A** the security arrangements
- **B** the fact that it is on the beach
- **C** the low prices and good food

8

PART 2

Tip Strip

Question 10: Can you predict what might be frightening in this context?

Question 12: What are you likely to be listening for to answer this question?

Question 16: Do you expect a noun or verb will be needed to complete this sentence?

You will hear part of a radio programme in which a man called David North talks about an animal called the bay cat. For Questions **9–18,** complete the sentences.

David North was in Borneo to make a

[_____ **9**] about the island's geography.

He wanted to run away when he thought he heard

[_____ **10**] in the grass.

There may be intervals of [_____ **11**] between people seeing bay cats.

The bay cat was first seen in 1874 but not recorded

again until [_____ **12**]

The animal's long tail is [_____ **13**] at its end.

In 2000 a [_____ **14**] photographer managed

to take photos of the animal.

The fact that a bay cat was caught indicated

the environmental [_____ **15**] on the animal.

A [_____ **16**] had forced the bay cat into the open.

The world's [_____ **17**] did not find out about the

bay cat until it was back in the jungle.

Scientists hope the bay cat will continue to live

in the hill [_____ **18**] in Borneo.

You will hear five different people talking about what puts them in a good mood. For Questions **19–23,** choose from the list **A–F** what each speaker says. Use the letters only once. There is one extra letter which you do not need to use.

Tip Strip

C: Speakers 2 and 5 both mention e-mails. Which one finds that e-mails benefit their mood?

E: Speakers 1 and 5 both mention food or drink. Whose mood is changed by these things?

F: Speakers 1 and 3 both mention music. Who says it puts them in a good mood?

A   Talking to friends makes me feel good.

Speaker 1 ☐ 19

B   Taking exercise works for me.

Speaker 2 ☐ 20

C   Receiving e-mails cheers me up.

Speaker 3 ☐ 21

D   I have to go shopping.

Speaker 4 ☐ 22

E   I need to eat something sweet.

Speaker 5 ☐ 23

F   I rely on music.

You will hear a radio interview with a young man called Ollie Smart, who is an artist. For each of the Questions **24–30,** decide which of the statements are True and which are False. Write **T** for **True** or **F** for **False** in the boxes provided.

Tip Strip

Question 25: Ollie says 'I was convinced ...' Is this reflected in the statement?

Question 26: What did Ollie expect? How does 'but what is really nice ...' help you to focus on the key information?

Question 30: What does Ollie say about his father's behaviour in the kitchen that links with this statement?

24   Ollie had expected a large number of replies from children.

☐ 24

25   Ollie was sure that painting attracted many young people.

☐ 25

26   Ollie is surprised that children paint for their families.

☐ 26

27   Ollie thinks allowing children into a kitchen can be a problem.

☐ 27

28   Ollie's mother always encouraged him to experiment.

☐ 28

29   Ollie wants children to run their own TV show.

☐ 29

30   Ollie used to get annoyed when his father helped him.

☐ 30

PAPER 5

Speaking (14 minutes)

 **PART 1** (3 minutes)

Answer these questions:

What is the most popular food in your country?
Do people normally go out to eat or do they prefer to eat at home?
What do you enjoy doing at weekends?
What did you do last weekend?

 **PART 2** (4 minutes)

Old and new (compare, contrast and speculate)

Turn to pictures 1 and 2 on page 166 which show different combinations of things old and new.

Candidate A, compare and contrast these photographs and say whether you think it is important to keep some things from the past. You have a minute to do this.

Candidate B, did you enjoy studying History when you were at school?

Education (compare, contrast and speculate)

Turn to pictures 1 and 2 on page 167 which show people in classrooms.

Candidate B, compare and contrast these photographs and say whether you think it is important to spend as much time as possible studying before going out to work. You have a minute to do this.

Candidate A, do you enjoy studying?

 **PART 3** (3 minutes)

Holiday job (discuss and evaluate)

Turn to the pictures on page 168 which show the different ways students can work in their holidays. Which jobs do you think would provide really useful experience and why?

PART 4 (4 minutes)

Answer these questions:

What sorts of jobs would you be willing to do in your holidays?
Do you think earning a lot of money is more important than the job?
Would you like to do one or many different jobs in the future?
Do you think work is more important than leisure? Why (not)?

TEST 7

PART 1

You are going to read a magazine article about a woman who made a special train journey. Choose the most suitable heading from the list **A–I** for each part (**1–7**) of the article. There is one extra heading which you do not need to use. There is an example at the beginning (**0**).

Mark your answers **on the separate answer sheet.**

A The daily pattern	**D** Caring for the passengers	**G** The train acts like a market
B Difficulty with the plumbing	**E** A taste of each country	**H** Getting to know the locals
C A strong sense of absence	**F** A reminder of previous glory	**I** Slow progress

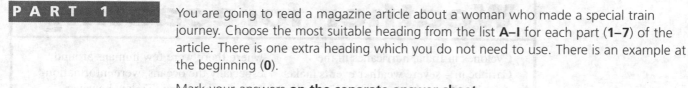

Slow train to China

0   *F*

We boarded the train in Moscow as the sun was setting. Our cabin was a vision of past grandeur: heavy mirrors, old light fittings and various pictures of different country scenes. I sat on my bed and drank tea as I watched Moscow slipping away. This was to be my home for the next four nights. The greatest train journey in the world was, so far, living up to my expectations.

1

'Hi guys,' said a voice from the next-door cabin. This turned out to be Rachel, from New Zealand and she, too, was travelling all the way to Beijing in China. We each had a luxury cabin and each day an attendant cleaned and dusted the tiny room and looked after us. This meant that whenever the train stopped he would make sure we were back on board on time.

2

On the first night I was puzzled over how to get any water from the taps, and ended up brushing my teeth in mineral water. I later discovered that there is a piece of metal sticking out behind the tap, and that this has to be pushed up in order for the water to appear.

3

This was proper train travel. There were no delays, no problems with the track or the signals and I fell asleep as the train chugged gently through western Russia, and woke up with the train still chugging through western Russia. Outside, smoke curled from the chimneys of little houses surrounded by birch trees.

4

I sat with Rachel in the restaurant car and discovered that the food was provided by the country you happen to be passing through at the time. This meant that in Mongolia the meals were quite small and simple and in China they were like a feast with lots of different dishes to choose from.

5

During the first and longest part of the journey, 5,191 kilometres between Moscow and Siberia, we moved officially from Europe into Asia. At each station we got out to stretch our legs and settled into a peaceful train life, broken only by the occasional energetic walk along a platform in a distant town where we smiled at the local people. By the time we reached Irkutsk we had crossed five time zones in four days, resulting in the unusual experience of train lag.

6

The train moved onward to Mongolia and stopped in Ulan Baatar, where the platform was crowded with people. They had come to buy from the traders who had piled their boxes onto the train when it left Siberia.

7

The final train which took us to China, stopped, considerably, at a station situated within the Great Wall, so we could take photos. That left two days in Beijing before we flew home. The whole trip lasted just over a week but we came back feeling we had been away for months.

PART 2

You are going to read an article about weather forecasting. For Questions **8–14,** choose the correct answer **A, B, C** or **D.**

Mark your answers **on the separate answer sheet.**

Weather forecasting

Cyclones in India, hurricanes in the Caribbean – severe weather events make news headlines almost weekly. Yet even in Britain, which has comparatively few climate extremes, the country is still governed by the weather. If it's pouring with rain the British might stay indoors or go to the cinema; if it's fine they'll have a picnic.

Most people nervously study the weather forecast the evening before if they've got an important appointment the following day. Even if they have nothing planned, the weather often affects their mood.

For individuals, the worst that can usually happen if the weather catches them on the hop is that they get wet. For business, the effects are far more serious. Airlines and shipping companies need to avoid severe weather and storm-force conditions. Power companies need to make sure they can supply the demand for electricity in cold weather; farmers plan their harvests around the forecast and food manufacturers increase their production of salads and other summer foods when fine weather is promised.

So who or what do meteorologists – weather forecasters as they are more commonly known – rely on when it comes to producing a forecast? Ninety percent of the information comes from weather satellites, the first of which was launched into space nearly forty years ago and was a minor revolution in the science of forecasting. Up until then, forecasters had relied on human observers to provide details of developing weather systems. As a result, many parts of the world where there were few humans around, especially the oceans, were information-free weather areas. Today, however, satellites can watch weather patterns developing everywhere.

In the UK meteorologists have also relied on releasing four weather balloons a day from eight fixed sites. These balloons measure wind, temperature and humidity as they rise upwards to a height of about 26,000 metres.

Some commercial aircraft can also be fitted with a range of forecasting instruments although this system has certain disadvantages. For example, it can provide a great deal of information about the weather on popular routes, such as London to New York, but little about the weather on more out-of-the way routes.

Instruments aboard ships can also supply basic weather information as well as important data on wave height. Generally, the range of these instruments is fairly limited but they can indicate which direction rain is coming from, how low the cloud is and give an idea of when the weather system will reach land.

One forecaster who has made a name for himself is a man called Piers Corbyn, who bases his forecasts on watching the Sun. Most forecasters will offer forecasts for only 10 days ahead, but Corbyn's forecasts are for 11 months. Although most meteorologists believe that there is no scientific basis for his work, Corbyn's forecasts are used by insurance companies who want to plan months in advance.

Tip Strip

Question 9: People get wet if they have not got a raincoat or umbrella with them; did they expect it to rain?

Question 10: How many different businesses are listed?

Question 11: Read to the end of the paragraph to discover why it was a 'revolution'.

8 The weather system affects people's lives in Britain

    A despite being fairly moderate.
    B because it is so changeable.
    C because it is always raining.
    D despite being very seasonal

9 What does the writer mean by the phrase 'catches them on the hop' in lines 16/17?

    A People run for shelter.
    B People are too busy to notice.
    C People are far from home.
    D People are unprepared.

10 Why does the writer list so many different businesses in paragraph 3?

    A to give examples of ordinary people's lives
    B to show the extent of the weather's influence
    C to describe the recent effects of the bad weather
    D to explain how people manage in bad weather

11 Why is the first weather satellite described as a 'minor revolution' in line 35?

    A It watched the human observers.
    B It replaced human observers.
    C It provided extra forecasts.
    D It forecast the weather in space.

12 Using airplanes to help forecast the weather is

    A very popular.
    B not expensive.
    C quite new.
    D not ideal.

13 What does 'it' in line 54 refer to?

    A using balloons
    B using satellites
    C using aircraft
    D using ships

14 Corbyn's forecasts using the Sun are considered

    A useless and unscientific.
    B helpful but short-term.
    C useful by some people.
    D unhelpful in the long-term.

You are going to read a newspaper article about a man who works in the kitchens of a fast food restaurant. Eight sentences have been removed from the article. Choose from the sentences **A–I** the one which fits each gap (**15–21**). There is one extra sentence which you do not need to use. There is an example at the beginning (**0**).

Mark your answers **on the separate answer sheet.**

FAST WORK FOR FAST FOOD

When I graduated from cookery school, I could have applied for jobs in ski chalets or on board ships sailing around the Caribbean. Instead, I applied to work in a fashionable fast-food restaurant and suddenly found myself working very long hours in hot, sweaty kitchens full of completely crazy characters.

I thought that starting at the bottom of the food chain, as opposed to the high life of skiing and sailing, would be good training. **0** **H**

At 7.45 each morning I stagger into the kitchen with all the other cooks, exhausted from working a 10-hour shift the night before. **15** Nothing is where it should be. Vegetables have been left on the floor and raw fish has been left uncovered in the fridge. A couple of dustbins have not been emptied and everything has to be cleaned before we can begin the day's work.

16 I fill a sink with water, throw in several box loads of the stuff and wash each leaf separately. My hands are so cold I can hardly feel them.

Between 9 and 10, the line chefs start arriving. **17** They swan around the kitchens shouting orders at the poor cooks like me whose job it is to prepare all the ingredients.

But if anything goes wrong once the customers' orders start coming in, you can guess who gets the blame. If they run out of sauce, then it's the cook's fault for not preparing enough in the first place. **18**

The chefs are only under pressure at particular points in the day. The cooks are under pressure all the time.

19 This is when the waiters get told what the day's special menus are. Then, no sooner are we back in the kitchen to start the lunch service than three deliveries of food and drink arrive all at the same time. **20** I am faced with carrying boxes of frozen chips or bottles of fruit juice from the lorries down two flights of stairs to the store rooms.

By mid-afternoon, the lunchtime rush is dying down. **21** Then I am allowed to have my free staff 'lunch', by which time I'm too tired to eat.

A This means I get sent to sort them out.

B These are the people who get all the glory.

C Before we open at midday, all the staff meet in the restaurant.

D I arrive home twelve hours after I left.

E My first job of the day is shopping, and shredding leaves and lettuces for salads.

F However, I don't get anything to eat until the end of my working day, at 6 that evening.

G There's been a break of just about four hours and the kitchen has not been tidied from last night.

H I couldn't have been more wrong.

I If the chicken goes cold, then it's the cook's fault for not keeping it in the oven longer.

Tip Strip

Sentence B: Can you find a verb + preposition which is associated with the idea of behaving proudly?

Sentence C: Why do you think the staff meet?

Sentence E: What has to happen before the lettuce is shredded?

You are going to read a magazine article in which four young people from different countries talk about falling in love. For Questions **22–35**, choose from the people **A–D**. The people may be chosen more than once. When more than one answer is required, these may be given in any order. There is an example at the beginning (**0**).

Mark your answers **on the separate answer sheet**.

Who

fell in love while on holiday?   **0**   C

was speechless when the relationship ended?   **22**

seems to have made a mistake by being generous?   **23**

was the younger person in the relationship?   **24**

finds it difficult to forget about the other person?   **25**

thinks most people experience disappointment?   **26**

planned to meet up later in the year?   **27**

fell in love at university?   **28**

is still unsure about what went wrong with the relationship?   **29**   **30**

fell in love in an instant?   **31**

didn't agree with what was said?   **32**

says they took the lead in the relationship?   **33**

thinks they were told a lie?   **34**

went away with other people during the relationship?   **35**

Tip Strip

Question 22: Look for another way of saying 'speechless'.
Question 31: Look for another way of saying 'in an instant'.
Question 33: What does it mean to 'take the lead' in a situation?

Who Broke Your Heart?

A Pablo (20)

Mexico

Everybody my age has had their heart broken. A girl called Maria broke my heart when I first went to university. I hadn't had many girlfriends and I thought Maria was the love of my life. She was a beautiful girl with lovely eyes, and I still don't really understand why she finished with me. We had been out for the evening with some friends and on the way back my car broke down. Our friends decided they would walk back to town but Maria didn't want to. I tried to fix the car myself but it was dark and I couldn't see what I was doing. Anyway, in the end I had to leave her alone in the car while I walked to the nearest phone. When the car was eventually mended and we drove back to her flat she told me she didn't want to see me again. I mean it's not as if it was my fault that the car broke down – these things happen.

B Heidi (17)

Switzerland

After leaving school, my boyfriend worked in the local supermarket. It wasn't very well paid, but he wasn't sure he wanted to go to university. I got a job as a trainee in a large bank and so I was earning more than him.

We decided we'd go on holiday with a group of friends and my parents agreed as we would all be staying in a youth hostel. I paid for my boyfriend and we all had a fantastic time. However, when we got back he started behaving strangely and said he felt depressed and wanted to be alone. I did everything I could to support him but he said: 'I'm not good enough to be your boyfriend any more.' I tried to persuade him to change his mind, but he wouldn't and I was really upset for ages after we stopped going out together.

C Steve (18)

South Africa

I went to Germany with my parents for a holiday a couple of years ago. And it was while we were there that I met Sonya. She was Swedish and the same age as me. We had a great time together and when the holiday came to an end we decided we'd keep in touch and she'd come to South Africa at Christmas. We wrote, e-mailed and telephoned each other, sometimes two or three times a day. I missed her dreadfully and the three months until Christmas seemed ages away. I guess it must've been some time during November when I didn't hear from her for a couple of days. I rang her home and in the end her mother answered the phone. She said Sonya didn't want to speak to me as she was too busy. I didn't believe her so I wrote a long letter asking Sonya to explain what was going on. I never heard back and of course she never came to South Africa. I still think about her and wonder what she's doing.

D Miranda (17)

Australia

I was 16 when I met Scott. He was a really good-looking guy and he was new to our college as his parents had emigrated from England. For me it was love at first sight. The second I saw him it was like a shot of electricity.

My parents told me not to be silly, but when there was a college disco I went up to him and asked him to dance. After that we started going out once or twice a week, but looking back it was probably more to do with me asking him than the other way round. I didn't mind so long as we could be together. He was so cool: tall, blond, sporty and, most impressively of all, he had a big motorbike. He was a year older than me and very popular with everyone. Then one day, after about three months, he just said: 'It's finished. It's all over.' I was very sad and quite angry. I just stood there not knowing what to say and he turned around and walked off. It was ages before I could get through a day without thinking about him.

PAPER 2   Writing (1 hour 30 minutes)

PART 1

You **must** answer this question.

1   You and a friend want to arrange an end-of-term entertainment for your English class. Your friend has found an advertisement. Read his/her notes together with the advertisement and write a letter asking for more information.

> What do you think about this place? I'm away with my parents this weekend, so can you contact the Centre for more information? I've added everything I can think of, but you will probably think of something else.
>
> See you next week.

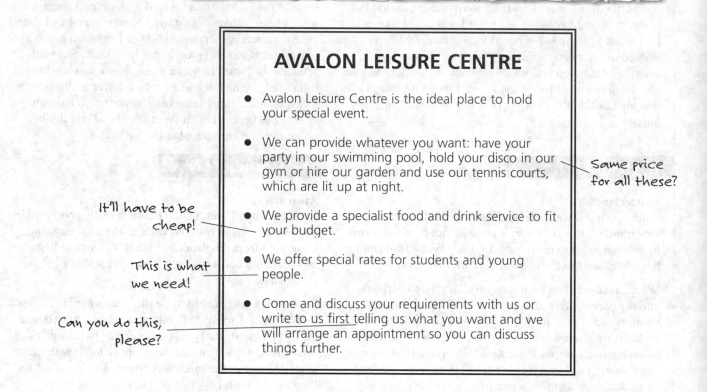

AVALON LEISURE CENTRE

- Avalon Leisure Centre is the ideal place to hold your special event.

- We can provide whatever you want: have your party in our swimming pool, hold your disco in our gym or hire our garden and use our tennis courts, which are lit up at night.

  Same price for all these?

- We provide a specialist food and drink service to fit your budget.

  It'll have to be cheap!

- We offer special rates for students and young people.

  This is what we need!

- Come and discuss your requirements with us or write to us first telling us what you want and we will arrange an appointment so you can discuss things further.

  Can you do this, please?

Write a **letter** of between **120** and **180** words in an appropriate style. Do not write any addresses.

Write an answer to **one** of the Questions **2–5** in this part. Write your answer in **120–180** words in an appropriate style.

Tip Strip

Question 2:
Think carefully as to whether you can write about an experience and make it sound amusing. Don't exaggerate things but try to describe the experience in as lively a way as possible.

Question 3:
Mention some of your country's traditional food. You will need to know the names for the ingredients and give clear instructions on how to make the dish. Don't forget to include an appropriate opening and ending to your letter.

Question 4:
This question asks you to discuss the topic; you may agree or disagree with this statement. Make sure you support your opinion with some examples.

Question 5(a):
Think about how the plot develops because of a relationship between two of the characters. If these two people were not part of the story, what difference would it make? Use a formal style.

Question 5(b):
Say whether you agree or disagree with the statement. In order to support your opinion you will also need to mention other parts of the story, e.g. the middle and the ending. Use a formal or neutral style.

2   Your school magazine has asked for articles about readers' amusing experiences. Write an article describing an experience which you have had and why it was amusing.

Write your **article.**

3   Your pen friend has asked you about the typical food in your country so that he/she can try and make a traditional dish at home. Write a letter telling your friend about your country's traditional food, giving details about how to cook one special dish.

Write your **letter.**

4   You have been discussing fashion and the clothing industry in your English lesson. Your homework is to write a composition with the following title:

The fashion industry is only interested in young people.

Write your **composition.**

5   Answer **one** of the following two questions based on your reading of **one** of the set books.

Either   (a)   A student magazine is publishing articles about relationships in fiction. With reference to the book you have read, write an **article** about the most important relationship in the book and the way that relationship affects the story.

Or   (b)   *'The best part of the story was the beginning.'* Write a **composition** saying whether you agree or disagree with this statement.

PART 1

Use of English (1 hour 15 minutes)

For Questions **1–15**, read the text below and decide which answer **A, B, C** or **D** best fits each space. There is an example at the beginning (**0**).

Mark your answers **on the separate answer sheet.**

Tip Strip

Question 2: Only one world collocates with 'money' and also has the correct meaning in this context.

Question 6: A, B and C collocate with 'hold' but only one of them is right in this context.

Question 15: Which word collocates with 'growth area'?

Example:

0 **A** ought   **B** should   **C** will   **D** may

0	A	B	C	D

FUN AND GAMES

Do you think computer games are just for kids? Then you (**0**) ..... think again. You might be (**1**) ..... to learn that the games industry now (**2**) ..... more money than Hollywood. (**3**) ..... a family buys a new PC, all they really want to do is to play games.

It is hardly surprising that video gaming has (**4**) ..... one of the most popular (**5**) ..... of entertainment today. A good game is like a good film; it will hold your (**6**) ..... , capture your imagination and play with your emotions.

The big (**7**) ....., however, is that watching a movie is a passive (**8**) ..... . You have no say in how the plot (**9**) ..... or which characters dominate the story. With computer games, you direct the (**10**) ..... and that is what makes them so exciting. Finding the (**11**) ..... game is likely to signal the beginning of a lasting love (**12**) ..... with the interactive (**13**) ..... of make-believe.

It is (**14**) ..... to think of gaming as something simply for children and teenagers. In fact, the (**15**) ..... growth area of the market is the 25–35 age group.

1	**A** concerned	**B** admired	**C** surprised	**D** startled
2	**A** has	**B** makes	**C** does	**D** gains
3	**A** As soon as	**B** As well as	**C** As far as	**D** As long as
4	**A** begun	**B** grown	**C** sounded	**D** become
5	**A** makes	**B** branches	**C** shapes	**D** forms
6	**A** gaze	**B** attention	**C** breath	**D** control
7	**A** gap	**B** variety	**C** difference	**D** direction
8	**A** pastime	**B** task	**C** routine	**D** employment
9	**A** becomes	**B** develops	**C** turns	**D** produces
10	**A** movement	**B** change	**C** action	**D** performance
11	**A** accurate	**B** right	**C** complete	**D** proper
12	**A** match	**B** story	**C** secret	**D** affair
13	**A** region	**B** area	**C** society	**D** world
14	**A** immoral	**B** wrong	**C** false	**D** dishonest
15	**A** longest	**B** widest	**C** biggest	**D** deepest

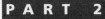

PART 2

Tip Strip

Question 18: Which negative word is often used before 'only'?

Question 20: What kind of word fits the meaning here?

Question 21: What verb + 'over' makes a phrasal verb that fits the meaning here?

For Questions **16–30,** read the text below and think of the word which best fits each space. Use only **one** word in each space. There is an example at the beginning (**0**).

Write your answers **on the separate answer sheet.**

Example:

0	*do*

FUNCTIONAL FOODS

In the 21st century food will (**0**) ......*do*........ more than just feed you. A new range of products appearing (**16**) .... shelves in shops and supermarkets (**17**) .... designed to give you specific health benefits. The demands of modern life make these foods very attractive. (**18**) .... only do they provide proven ways to improve health, but they are also very attractive (**19**) .... a quick and convenient way of making sure we enjoy a healthy diet.

In some countries it is already possible to buy crisps that make you feel (**20**) .... depressed, chewing gum that increases your brain power and tea that helps you (**21**) .... over the tiredness associated (**22**) .... long-distance air travel. (**23**) .... the future, experts promise biscuits that will keep your heart healthy, and a hot chocolate drink to give you strong bones.

(**24**) .... the fact that these 'functional' foods cannot replace a balanced diet and regular exercise, they can help the body perform at (**25**) .... best a lot of the time. At (**26**) .... , these foods are more expensive than other foods, but that is due to the ingredients they (**27**) .... of and the way they are made. All the foods contain probiotics (**28**) .... increase the number of 'good' bacteria in your stomach, helping to keep your digestive system healthy.

There may even (**29**) .... a functional food to protect eyesight, so keep an eye out as you never know (**30**) .... you might be eating tomorrow!

Tip Strip

Question 32: What preposition must come after 'accused'?

Question 36: Don't overlook the need to include the reference to the person.

Question 39: This sentence needs a phrasal verb.

For Questions **31–40,** complete the second sentence so that it has a similar meaning to the first sentence, using the word given. **Do not change the word given.** You must use between two and five words, including the word given. Here is an example (**0**).

Example: 0   The bag is not big enough for all my luggage.

small

The bag .... for all my luggage.

The gap can be filled by the words 'is too small' so you write:

0	is too small

Write **only the missing words** on the separate answer sheet.

---

31   My father says he's too old to learn another language.

young

My father says .... to learn another language.

32   'You borrowed my watch, didn't you?' Donna's sister said.

accused

Donna's sister .... her watch.

33   Most people hope they will have enough money to buy a house or a flat.

afford

Most people hope they .... to buy a house or a flat.

34   Do you know who this pen belongs to?

know

Do you .... is?

35   I wish I had not lied to my parents.

truth

If only .... to my parents.

36   I can't possibly get to work if the buses are on strike.

impossible

It .... to get to work if the buses are on strike.

37   The students are raising the money for charity.

raised

The money .... the students for charity.

38   It's unusual for Zoe to be rude.

hardly

Zoe .... rude.

39   There's no milk left, so can you buy some?

run

We .... , so can you buy some?

40   My shoes need to be repaired next week.

must

I .... next week.

PART 4

For Questions **41–55,** read the text below and look carefully at each line. Some of the lines are correct, and some have a word which should not be there.

If a line is correct, put a tick (✔) by the number **on the separate answer sheet.** If a line has a word which should not be there, write the word **on the separate answer sheet.** There are two examples at the beginning (**0** and **00**).

Tip Strip

Line 42: There is a fixed expression in this line. Which word should not be there?

Line 44: Does Josef Nesladek turn into his wife and children?

Line 47: Can 'play' be reflexive here?

Example:

0	✔
00	*on*

0	....	Josef Nesladek is a street musician who works in an office during
00	....	the week and plays on the trumpet in a jazz band at weekends.
41	....	He feels that this combination suits to him very well as it allows
42	....	him the best of both the worlds. Monday to Friday he leads a
43	....	regular life, getting up early, travelling to work, and returning home
44	....	in the evening to be his wife and children. He regards playing in
45	....	the street as a way of advertising the jazz band. People stop to
46	....	listen and often ask it if the band is for hire. They get asked to play
47	....	themselves at private parties, weddings and clubs; in this way
48	....	they can earn up enough money to pay for their street licence,
49	....	which costs quite a lot. In the summer months, however, when
50	....	there are more than tourists around, the band does quite well
51	....	financially. According to Josef, sunshine makes people more
52	....	generous, especially that if the band can play in a town square
53	....	where people are sitting and outside enjoying a drink or a meal.
54	....	On those occasions people do like to sit for ages, listening to
55	....	good music, eating, drinking and chatting to their most friends.

PART 5

For Questions **56–65,** read the text below. Use the word given in capitals at the end of each line to form a word that fits the space in the same line. There is an example at the beginning (**0**).

Example:

| **0** | conversations |

Write your answers **on the separate answer sheet.**

THE RECIPE FOR GOOD COMMUNICATION

Research shows that more than half of our (**0**) .conversations. **CONVERSE**
end in some sort of (**56**) .... While it's easy to blame **UNDERSTAND**
the listener for the problem, we are also to blame if we don't
(**57**) .... what we mean in the first place. **CLEAR**

Accurate listening requires (**58**) .... and effort, and if you try to **CONCENTRATE**
do something else at the same time, you won't listen (**59**) .... **EFFECT**
There's a (**60**) .... for people to think they know what a **TEND**
speaker is going to say, instead of hearing them out,
or to criticise too (**61**) .... before a person has **READY**
(**62**) .... made their point. It's when people feel they are being **FULL**
undervalued and are not being treated with (**63**) .... that **POLITE**
problems begin and (**64**) .... can break down. Treating others **RELATION**
as you want to be treated is an (**65**) .... rule for good **ESSENCE**
communication.

Tip Strip

Question 56: Read the next sentence carefully so you know whether you are looking for a positive or negative word.

Question 59: What kind of word is needed here?

Question 64: You need to think of an abstract noun to fill this gap.

PAPER 4

PART 1

Listening (approximately 40 minutes)

You'll hear people talking in eight different situations. For Questions **1–8**, choose the best answer, **A, B** or **C**.

Tip Strip

Question 2: Listen for how the girl's feelings reveal what she says about her experience.

Question 3: Who behaved more rudely – the audience or the politician?

Question 7: Make sure you know the difference between 'happy' and 'relieved' before you listen.

1 You hear a radio advertisement for a music shop in London.
What is special about the shop?
A the well-informed staff
B the range of music
C the live performances

`1`

2 You overhear a student talking about working in a hospital.
What does she say about her experience?
A She learnt to look after the patients.
B She felt sorry for some of the patients.
C She liked working with the doctors.

`2`

3 You hear two people talking about a politician.
What do we learn about the politician?
A He was irritated by the audience.
B He behaved in a charming way.
C He ignored some of the questions.

`3`

4 You hear a man talking about camping.
Why is he so keen on camping?
A He likes modern tents.
B He loves wet weather.
C He enjoys the fresh air.

`4`

5 You hear a woman talking about her personal trainer.
What does she say about herself?
A She regrets having a personal trainer.
B She's glad the trainer keeps her fit.
C She's not so lazy now she has a trainer.

`5`

6 You hear two people discussing a film course they have been on.
What do they agree about the film industry?
A People are well paid for not much work.
B People have to accept idleness at times.
C People enjoy working in a fun industry.

`6`

7 You hear a woman talking about a dream she has had.
How has the dream made her feel?
A sad
B happy
C relieved

`7`

8 You hear a woman talking on the phone to her friend.
What is she offering to do for her friend?
A look after her children
B go to the conference
C organise her work

`8`

You will hear a radio programme in which a film critic discusses three new films. For Questions **9–18**, complete the notes.

Tip Strip

Question 9: You'll hear two titles mentioned - be careful!

Question 14: Don't overlook the preposition 'in' in the question prompt which will help you with the correct answer.

Question 18: What does 'theft' mean?

1 **Film title**: [_____ **9**] – a thriller

Film set in both [_____ **10**] and on the moon.

Takes place in year [_____ **11**]

Special feature: people travel between

[_____ **12**] using their minds

2 **Film title**: [_____ **13**] – a love story

Film set in [_____ **14**] in New Zealand

Special feature: part of action filmed among [_____ **15**]

3 **Film title**: [_____ **16**] – a comedy

Film set in [_____ **17**]

Special feature: based on theft of [_____ **18**]

You will hear five different people talking about their first day at work. For Questions **19–23,** choose from the list **A–F** what each speaker says. Use the letters only once. There is one extra letter which you do not need to use.

Tip Strip

B: Which speaker comments on the contrast between the way she was treated at her interview and her first day?

E: Listen for a speaker who starts her day feeling very excited.

F: What does the speaker say to explain how helpful people were?

A I was very bored.

B I found the atmosphere unfriendly.

C I didn't understand things.

D I received a useful introduction.

E I felt very disappointed.

F I found everyone was very helpful.

Speaker 1 [**19**]

Speaker 2 [**20**]

Speaker 3 [**21**]

Speaker 4 [**22**]

Speaker 5 [**23**]

You will hear part of a radio interview with a woman called Christine who lives on a houseboat. For Questions **24–30**, choose the best answer **A, B** or **C.**

Tip Strip

Question 24: Christine understands why people think a houseboat is romantic but what does she go on to say?

Question 25: Listen to what Christine says about people being curious.

Question 30: Christine is not sure what will happen but she suggests something.

24 Christine thinks that life on a houseboat is
   A especially romantic in the summer.
   B not as romantic as people think.
   C romantic if you have a nice boat.

    24

25 The family's social life has got better
   A thanks to having a huge kitchen.
   B because the boat is so large.
   C as they have so many visitors.

    25

26 When it was stormy
   A the children were afraid.
   B they all left the boat.
   C nothing got broken.

    26

27 Things on the boat feel damp
   A unless you light the oven.
   B if the weather gets cold.
   C as there is a slight leak.

    27

28 Why does Benny get paid double to grind flour?
   A because he works twice as fast as his brothers
   B because he's the eldest of the three boys
   C because he finds it harder than the others

    28

29 Other parents don't mind their children staying on the houseboat because
   A they always wear life jackets.
   B they are always with Christine.
   C they know how much they love it.

    29

30 What does Christine say about the future?
   A She'd like to move to a proper house.
   B It'll be easier when the boys leave home.
   C They might use the boat for travelling.

    30

PAPER 5   Speaking (14 minutes)

PART 1   (3 minutes)

Answer these questions:

Do you enjoy watching television? What is your favourite programme?
How often do you go to the cinema?
What kind of films do you enjoy?
Who is your favourite film star? Why?

PART 2   (4 minutes)

Free time (compare, contrast and speculate)

Turn to pictures 1 and 2 on page 169 which show children enjoying themselves.

Candidate A, compare and contrast these photographs and say how you think these children are feeling. You have a minute to do this.

Candidate B, what do you do in your free time?

Indoor sport (compare, contrast and speculate)

Turn to pictures 1 and 2 on page 170 which show people doing sporting activities indoors.

Candidate B, compare and contrast these photographs and say how important it is to keep fit. You have a minute to do this.

Candidate A, what do you do to keep fit?

PART 3   (3 minutes)

Looking after people and things (discuss and evaluate)

Turn to the pictures on page 171 which show teenagers looking after other people and different things. How easy or difficult is it to look after others?

PART 4   (4 minutes)

Answer these questions:

Have you ever had to look after younger brothers or sisters?
What are the problems in looking after elderly people?
Are you attracted to a job like nursing?
How good are you at looking after your own personal possessions?

TEST 8

PAPER 1   Reading (1 hour 15 minutes)

PART 1

You are going to read a magazine article about cyber cafes. Choose the most suitable heading from the list **A–H** for each part (**1–6**) of the article. There is one extra heading which you do not need to use. There is an example at the beginning (**0**).

Mark your answers **on the separate answer sheet.**

A Staying in contact

B E-mail keeps costs down

C The cyber cafe is here to stay

D The cyber cafe may replace the office

E Costs vary during the day

F Internet use is now widespread

G Office workers like the cyber cafe

H The original attraction of the cyber cafe

CYBER CAFES

0   **H**

In the early nineties in Great Britain going for a coffee and surfing the Net were new and exciting things to do. The cyber cafe was a successful mixture of two things: coffee and the Internet. Not even cold coffee and slow connections put people off from going to these cafes.

1

Ten years later the picture has changed and in the 21st century millions of people can use the Internet from home, work, school or university. In many ways the Internet has become a personal playground and as for the coffee, well, there's a lot more choice of different coffee shops serving every kind of coffee you can wish for.

2

So who's using the cyber cafes now that surfing the Net is as ordinary as waking up every morning? Some people say that if their computer goes wrong at home they don't bother to get it fixed. They will rely on the cyber cafe to find out what is happening in the world and to check their e-mail; they feel that there is nothing special about cyber cafes any more. These cafes are part of the cultural scene in the same way that cinemas and supermarkets are.

3

One man, who is the director of a chain of Internet shops, says that although consumer demand for using the Internet has risen, home computers are no good if you are out and about or happen to be on holiday somewhere. The cyber cafe is the obvious place to go if you want to keep in touch with friends and family.

4

'Most of our users are backpackers and international students checking their e-mail,' he says. 'We also operate a price structure which is good for those students who get up early. This means that the cheapest time of day is six in the morning and as the cafe fills up, the price goes up. Early evening is one of the most expensive times.'

5

Cyber cafes are also popular with foreign students studying abroad. These students feel it's important to keep in touch with everyone at home and e-mail is cheaper than the telephone. Some students use the cyber cafe for as much as four hours a week and like the fact that the cafes are clean and friendly places.

6

In the future it is likely that the cyber cafes will also attract people who are self-employed. With mobile phones and e-mail there's less need for traditional offices, and as more and more people in the UK choose to work for themselves the cyber cafes could become communication centres for these workers by providing the electronic support for people who neither have nor want traditional office space.

You are going to read an article by an actress called Josie Lawerence, in which she writes about her holidays. For Questions **7–14,** choose the correct answer **A, B, C** or **D.**

Mark your answers **on the separate answer sheet.**

My Holidays

On New Year's Eve a few years ago, I decided to go skiing for the first time, with two friends. They are the complete opposite of me in that they're really brave and fearless – they've been skiing and diving all their lives, whereas I'm a bit of a coward. Surprisingly, however, I
8 enjoyed it very much and the second time we went I felt much more confident and decided to move away from skiing on the nursery slopes. I was doing really well and skiing down quite a steep slope when I heard one of my friends say, 'Wow, Barbara, you're moving fast!' I thought 'Yes, I am, aren't I – but how do I stop?' Suddenly all my confidence left me and I fell very badly. I didn't break anything but I twisted my knee. The rest of the holiday was spent sitting on top of the mountain, looking after everybody's bags and coats.

If I'm honest, I prefer going somewhere hot and sunny for a holiday. I love going to Thailand, for example, and staying in one of the beautiful resorts on the coast. The people are extremely friendly and in one hotel we stayed at we got to know the chef quite well and he would take us round the market with him. And one of the waiters took us to visit his uncle who owns a coconut farm. It's only in ways
32 like this that you begin to get a feel for the country and its people, as these kinds of opportunities are not available for the average tourist.

I'm not a rough-it kind of person: I did enough of that when I was younger. The trouble with me is that I have a genuine problem with mosquitoes – they absolutely adore me! If I get bitten, the bites turn into mini-balloons all over my body. Once when we were travelling by jeep during the monsoon season, the rain was so heavy that we stopped in a village. A young Thai boy noticed this huge bite on my arm, which was going a funny colour, and looked as if it might be infected. He picked some leaves off a tree and made a mixture of them using some salt and a little alcohol and then rubbed the mixture into my arm. You could see the infection disappear: it was amazing, it was like letting the air out of a balloon.

Generally, after I've finished a run of performances in a play, I feel exhausted. Pleasantly exhausted, but not too weary to escape! All I want to do is find a hotel with a fantastic view, a beach, a good book and a mosquito net. My needs are very simple, really, and I just want the opportunity to refresh myself. Sometimes I might consider a holiday in a completely different environment, like visiting a friend in a country cottage or staying in a small bed and breakfast place and walking in the surrounding hills. It's good for my soul.

Tip Strip

Question 8: Read the first sentence of the first paragraph.

Question 10: What kinds of experience are not available for the average tourist?

Question 12: What effect did the boy's mixture have on Barbara's arm?

7 How did Josie feel about going away with her friends for the first time?

   A very surprised
   B rather afraid
   C not bothered
   D really terrified

8 What does 'it' in line 8 refer to?

   A New Year's Eve
   B diving
   C skiing
   D being a coward

9 How was Barbara's confidence destroyed?

   A She broke her leg.
   B She started to think.
   C Her friend embarrassed her.
   D Her friend criticised her.

10 What does 'to get a feel for' in lines 32/33 mean?

   A to experience
   B to develop
   C to visit
   D to understand

11 What personal problem does Barbara mention?

   A She hates mosquitoes.
   B She enjoys travelling by jeep.
   C She prefers living rough.
   D She dislikes very bad weather.

12 What effect did the mixture have on Barbara's arm?

   A It changed colour.
   B It became better.
   C It became infectious.
   D It turned into a balloon.

13 How does Barbara feel when a play finishes?

   A completely worn out
   B desperate to get away
   C pleased that she's free
   D very tired but satisfied

14 What does Barbara mainly want from a holiday?

   A the chance to her build up her energy
   B the chance to visit somewhere fresh
   C the possibility of relaxing on a beach
   D the opportunity to stay with friends

You are going to read a magazine article about the kinds of fear which people can experience. Seven sentences have been removed from the article. Choose from the sentences **A–H** the one which fits each gap (**15–20**). There is one extra sentence which you do not need to use. There is an example at the beginning (**0**).

Mark your answers **on the separate answer sheet.**

FEARS AND PHOBIAS

It's not easy trying to cope with fear. Most people at some stage in their lives feel afraid of something; fear of the dark as children, afraid of spiders or flying. **0** **B**

However, some people are afraid of something to such an extent that it prevents them from leading a normal life. **15** It means that you cannot open a fridge door in case you get an electric shock, you cannot go into a brightly lit clothing store, you cannot go near any electrical equipment.

In fact, you can be afraid of anything and there is almost certainly a name for it. **16** Apparently, the list of phobias gets longer every day but for people who have a real terror of something, help is at hand.

Researchers are making enormous progress in understanding what a phobia is and what causes it. **17**

It is surprising how many people think they suffer from a phobia when actually all they are really experiencing is a strong dislike or distaste for something. **18** But that's not the same as being really 'mechanophobic', suffering from a racing heart and being short of breath at the mere sight of a computer.

19 If you can't run away from whatever is causing the fear, you feel that death is inevitable. On the other hand, it's natural for most people to feel afraid if they're aboard an aeroplane which is flying into a storm.

Most psychologists agree that phobias can be described in three main ways. **20** Then there are panic disorders in which the person is terrified temporarily for no apparent reason and thirdly, specific phobias – the fear of snakes, mice, heights and suchlike.

A Progress in treating anxiety is providing help for many people.

B For the most part, these fears are normal and do not interfere with our ability to get on with our lives.

C You may think you are computer phobic and want to throw your machine out of the nearest window.

D For example, 'electrophobia' – being afraid of electricity – makes life in today's world extremely difficult.

E Experts say that you can't mistake a true phobia as it affects the whole of your central nervous system.

F With this understanding has come a range of treatments which can completely cure a person's phobia or gradually reduce a person's fear.

G There are social phobias in which the sufferer is afraid of any kind of social or professional occasion.

H You can be afraid of clouds, certain colours, bicycles, rain, mushrooms and even sitting down.

Tip Strip

Sentence C: Can you guess what 'phobic' means from the context?
Sentence E: What happens if a person's central nervous system is so seriously affected?
Sentence H: Where in the text does the writer suggest that anything can cause a phobia?

PART 4

You are going to read four advertisements for summer schools in the UK. For Questions **21–35,** choose from the advertisements **A–D**. The advertisements may be chosen more than once. When more than one answer is required, these may be given in any order. There is an example at the beginning (**0**).

Mark your answers **on the separate answer sheet**.

Which school

offers the most organised day?	**0**	*A*
emphasises the fact that it is unique?	**21**	
has the best equipped student rooms?	**22**	
puts you with one teacher responsible for you throughout your course?	**23**	
offers daily trips?	**24**	
has an upper age limit?	**25**	
does not provide on-site accommodation?	**26**	
says it doesn't have many places?	**27**	**28**
is situated on the coast?	**29**	
allows you to do what you want after classes have finished each day?	**30**	
guarantees your own room?	**31**	
provides a library?	**32**	
caters for individual food preferences?	**33**	
gives most information about its afternoon programme?	**34**	
includes a weekly trip for everyone?	**35**	

Tip Strip

Question 26: If accommodation is not 'on-site', where else could it be?
Question 28: Look for another way of saying 'on the coast'.
Question 34: Look for a word which means the same as 'acting'?

SUMMER SCHOOLS

Thousands of young people from all over the world attend summer holiday courses in Britain.

A Jolyon International

Jolyon International having been running summer school programmes for over twenty years. We offer a variety of courses designed to meet the needs of individuals. There is no upper age limit and we cater for students from the ages of 16 upwards.

The school day is divided into three sessions. In the morning you are expected to attend intensive language classes at one of three levels: beginners, intermediate or advanced. In the afternoon you are free to choose from a range of optional activities including sport, drama, music or excursions. In the evening our staff provide a programme of entertainment in which students are invited to take part.

Our courses last a minimum of two weeks and are fully residential. The school is situated in beautiful countryside and occupies an historic building set in its own gardens. Student accommodation consists of individual study bedrooms equipped with private bathroom, TV and computer. There is a student dining room, swimming pool, TV and video lounge.

You are advised to make early application as places are limited.

B Polydor in Summer

Polydor is a popular language school in the heart of a bustling and exciting city. Its summer courses focus on providing fun and entertainment for young teenagers aged between 13 and 17.

Each day starts with a 2-hour language class covering a range of different skills. This is followed by afternoon activities which develop from the morning class and students are encouraged to work on group projects which focus on speaking and listening skills. This means that each afternoon students will find themselves working in small groups in and around the city, carrying out surveys, interviewing local people and visiting the library to investigate different topics.

At the end of every day there is a short presentation session where students come together to tell each other what they have been doing and exchange ideas.
Evenings are free although the school remains open for students who want to spend the evenings relaxing in the student common rooms. There is a weekly disco each Friday organised by the school staff.

Accommodation is provided with local families. Some families provide single rooms but most students can expect to share a room. Breakfast and evening meals are provided by the host family, and the school operates a snack bar serving popular fast food at lunch time.

C Excelsis UK

The Excelsis UK schools are located in popular seaside towns, close to attractive countryside, where we can offer the best of all worlds. Our courses are based in leading boarding schools and therefore provide all the facilities you would expect.

We employ well-qualified and experienced teachers and for the duration of your course you will be placed in a small tutor group with an experienced member of staff. We believe this is the best way for you to feel well-looked after and for your individual interests and needs to be catered for.

Our classes are small, with a maximum of 8 students per class. In this way you get as much attention as possible from your class teacher. You will also be expected to do a small amount of homework each evening in preparation for the next day's lessons.

As we take over established boarding schools, all our courses provide sporting and other facilities on site: swimming pool, tennis courts, volleyball, indoor climbing walls, gymnasium, computers, art rooms and snooker.

Accommodation is in three or four-bedded dormitories, all comfortably furnished with individual desks, armchairs and cupboards.

Students are expected to take all their meals in the student dining room; we make every effort to cater for individual dietary requirements if you let us know in advance.

D Plumtree Academy

Plumtree Academy is a summer school with a difference: there is no other school like ours. Throughout the year Plumtree Academy is based in a small market town in central England. In July and August each year, Plumtree Academy becomes mobile by transferring its classrooms to a train!

The school has its own carriages which have been converted into fully equipped classrooms, with desks, whiteboards, video and TV. There is also a large library on board as well as internet access. Accommodation is in *couchettes,* twin sleeping compartments each equipped with its own bathroom and plenty of storage space. All meals are taken in the dining car and the school employs its own chef for the entire summer season.

Our weekly courses end with a day's excursion by train giving you an opportunity to stop off to shop, sightsee or just relax in one of England's famous spa towns.
We provide a novel approach to studying English and there is always a big demand for places on our summer schools. If you are interested in coming on board, don't leave it too late to contact us or you may find you've missed the train!

PAPER 2 Writing (1 hour 30 minutes)

PART 1

You **must** answer this question.

1 You would like to persuade some friends to join the local help scheme in your town. You have seen the advertisement below but your friends need to know more about the scheme. Using their comments, write a letter to the scheme giving relevant details and asking for more information.

WE NEED YOUNG PEOPLE

- Are you aged between 14 and 20?   *how many?*
- Can you spare a few hours every week?   *same day?*

We run a scheme in the town to help the elderly with things like:

- shopping   *I would have to go after school*
- cleaning   *I hate cleaning!*
- gardening   *I don't mind doing this*
- decorating   *inside or out? Isn't this too difficult?*
- jobs around the home   *such as?*

Or if you prefer, just call in for a chat with someone who lives alone.   *Can we go with a friend?*

If you drive a car you might like to take someone out for a short trip at the weekend.   *Who pays for the petrol?*

Please let us know if you can help.

Write a **letter** of between **120** and **180** words in an appropriate style. Do not write any addresses.

PART 2

Write an answer to **one** of the Questions **2–5** in this part. Write your answer in **120–180** words in an appropriate style.

Tip Strip

Question 2:
- You have a choice as to whether you begin or end your story with these words.
- Don't start writing until you have a clear idea of how to develop your story.
- Think about verb sequences e.g. Past simple and Past perfect.

Question 3:
- What are the things that help you in learning a language? Do you make lists of new words? Do you use the internet? Do you like to write everything down? Is there one particular thing you do to help you learn the grammar?
- Organise your idea and make suggestions based on your own experience.

Question 4:
- Remember that you are writing this report for other readers. Avoid being too critical.
- Concentrate on positive things; include one or two negative points if you think they are important for people to know e.g. the prices are expensive, it's small and you have to book in advance etc.

Question 5(a):
- Whether you agree or disagree, you will need to include some concrete facts to support your opinion.
- Think about the plot, the language, the vocabulary, the cultural background etc.
- Use a formal style.

Question 5(b):
- Whether you agree or disagree, you will need to support your feelings about the book by referring to concrete facts: was the plot full of suspense, did each chapter end with a 'cliff-hanger', were you impatient to find out what was going to happen to the different characters etc.?
- Use a formal style.

2 You want to enter a competition for a story to be included in the next edition of your school magazine. The story must begin **or** end with the words:

There was nothing else I could do and nobody I could ask.

Write your **story**.

3 An international magazine is offering a prize for the best article on suggestions for ways to help learn a language. In your article you should write about your own experience of learning a foreign language, and the different things which help you.

Write your **article**.

4 A local newspaper has asked readers to send in reports on local restaurants which they would recommend to other people. Your report should include comments on the food, the service, the size and decoration of the restaurant and whether it is suitable for a particular kind of customer.

Write your **report**.

5 Answer **one** of the following two questions based on your reading of **one** of the set books

Either **(a)** *'This is not a book to take on holiday – it's much too difficult and complicated.'* Write a **composition** saying whether you agree or disagree with this statement and why.

Or **(b)** *'I couldn't put it down – it was so exciting.'* Write a **composition** saying whether this was how you felt when you were reading the book, giving reasons for your opinions.

PAPER 3 — Use of English (1 hour 15 minutes)

Tip Strip

Question 1: Only one of these verbs collocates with 'choice'.

Question 6: This word forms part of a fixed expression.

For Questions **1–15**, read the text below and decide which answer **A, B, C** or **D** best fits each space. There is an example at the beginning (**0**).

Mark your answers **on the separate answer sheet.**

Example:

0   A like   **B** get   **C** bring   **D** choose

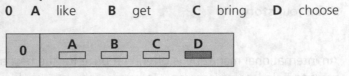

SHADES OF MEANING

When we decide to (**0**) ..... a colour for anything – whether it's a T-shirt or a cover for a mobile phone – our brains have to work really hard. In order for us to (**1**) ..... a choice that feels right, the brain has to (**2**) ..... various bits of information.

There are various (**3**) ..... which make each of us like or dislike certain colours. Firstly, our brains consider (**4**) ..... associations. These are completely (**5**) ..... and are a result of our individual experiences. Particular colours call to (**6**) ..... certain memories which may be connected to a place, a person or an experience. For example, we may associate red with the (**7**) ..... of a fire or a (**8**) ..... childhood sweater. Blue and green may (**9**) ..... us of holidays and peaceful weekends in the country.

Secondly, there is evidence to show that different colours (**10**) ..... our nervous system in different ways. Red can actually (**11**) ..... the level of adrenaline in our body. This is why energetic people are drawn to red and also why sports cars are (**12**) ..... this colour. On the other (**13**) ..... , blues and greens are passive colours which have a relaxing (**14**) ..... on the nervous system and (**15**) ..... people who like to feel completely at ease.

1	A	keep	B	do	C	set	D	make
2	A	produce	B	process	C	run	D	manufacture
3	A	methods	B	ways	C	factors	D	aspects
4	A	complete	B	trusted	C	past	D	forgotten
5	A	personal	B	hidden	C	private	D	secret
6	A	mind	B	heart	C	thought	D	feeling
7	A	heater	B	warmth	C	burning	D	temperature
8	A	favourite	B	popular	C	preferable	D	likeable
9	A	refer	B	remember	C	recall	D	remind
10	A	cause	B	create	C	affect	D	reflect
11	A	rise	B	lift	C	raise	D	hold
12	A	traditionally	B	knowingly	C	fashionably	D	recognisably
13	A	side	B	hand	C	foot	D	part
14	A	result	B	note	C	message	D	effect
15	A	attract	B	pull	C	gather	D	favour

PART 2

Tip Strip

Question 21: Which verb makes sense here if children are learning to manage money?

Question 24: Which words collocate with 'of money'?

For Questions **16–30,** read the text below and think of the word which best fits each space. Use only **one** word in each space. There is an example at the beginning (**0**).

Write your answers **on the separate answer sheet.**

Example:

0	been

CREDIT CARDS FOR CHILDREN

Children as young as twelve have (**0**) ......*been*...... offered credit cards by certain companies. They encourage the children to load (**16**) .... plastic cards with money (at terminals in the high street) and use (**17**) .... to shop on the Internet. The companies aim to open up the market to young people (**18**) .... are not allowed to use the Internet for shopping, as they are (**19**) .... young to get credit cards. (**20**) .... a credit card, the child's card has numbers on the front of it and a magnetic strip on the back (**21**) .... the children (**22**) .... to sign. This serves only to add to its 'grown up' feel, as signatures are (**23**) .... necessary for Internet shopping.

Some people are concerned that the teenagers could get into debt at an early age. Others argue that the cards will be limited to a fixed (**24**) .... of money and that children will therefore only be able to spend as (**25**) .... as they have on the card. They believe that the cards will help children to manage (**26**) .... own money at an early age, and not to (**27**) .... it.

The cards have been advertised (**28**) .... teenage magazines and research shows that children like the independence of (**29**) .... able to shop with plastic and the fact that they are not tied (**30**) .... their parents.

PART 3

Tip Strip

Question 32: What preposition is used with 'keen'?

Question 38: This is an impersonal structure and you need to put a noun after 'There is ...'.

Question 40: What verb must you use with 'tendency'?

For Questions **31–40,** complete the second sentence so that it has a similar meaning to the first sentence, using the word given. **Do not change the word given.** You must use between two and five words, including the word given. Here is an example (**0**).

Example: **0**   The bag is not big enough for all my luggage.

small

The bag .... for all my luggage.

The gap can be filled by the words 'is too small' so you write:

0	is too small

Write **only the missing words** on the separate answer sheet.

31   We pack our chocolates in small silver boxes.
are
Our .... in small silver boxes.

32   I would love to learn different languages.
keen
I .... different languages.

33   Mike has never flown in a plane before.
first
This .... Mike has flown in a plane.

34   Barbara always has a shower before going to work.
until
Barbara never goes to work .... a shower.

35   My holiday plans had been cancelled at the last minute.
fallen
My holiday plans .... at the last minute.

36   Please don't forget to switch off the light.
turn
Please remember .... the light.

37   Can you tell me the population of India?
what
Do .... population of India is?

38   Some people believe that there must be life on other planets.
exists
There is .... on other planets.

39   I'm sorry I was late for the meeting.
apology
Please .... late for the meeting.

40   Silvia tends to be quite shy.
tendency
Silvia .... to be quite shy.

PART 4

For Questions **41–55**, read the text below and look carefully at each line. Some of the lines are correct, and some have a word which should not be there.

If a line is correct, put a tick (✔) by the number **on the separate answer sheet**. If a line has a word which should not be there, write the word **on the separate answer sheet**. There are examples at the beginning (**0** and **00**).

Tip Strip

Line 43: Which preposition is wrong here?

Line 50: Is 'feel' reflexive in this context?

Line 53: Can 'to' ever be used after 'would'?

Example:

0	✔
00	have

0	....	I must tell you what I did last weekend when I went out with a
00	....	group of friends. You will feel really jealous when I have tell
41	....	you that we went to a chocolate factory! Although I've always
42	....	known about the factory, I've never of thought to visit it.
43	....	Anyway, last weekend they held out an open day for the public
44	....	so we had decided to have a look at what goes on there. It
45	....	was fascinating and we very thoroughly enjoyed ourselves.
46	....	We were allowed to watch chocolate for being made and
47	....	we were told that we could help ourselves if we wanted to taste
48	....	anything. Well, of course, we couldn't wait enough to try everything.
49	....	As the chocolate was straight off the production line, it was still warm
50	....	and quite delicious. But after a while I began to feel myself rather
51	....	sick. The factory was hot, anyway, because of all the machinery
52	....	and there were crowds of people who standing around watching.
53	....	I thought I would to faint so I made my way very quickly towards the exit.
54	....	Just as yet I got to the door, one of the employees stopped me and
55	....	handed me a free gift – a bag filled with a range of their chocolates!

PART 5

For Questions **56–65,** read the text below. Use the word given in capitals at the end of each line to form a word that fits the space in the same line. There is an example at the beginning (**0**).

Example:

0	foreigners

Write your answers **on the separate answer sheet.**

GOING TO SCHOOL IN WEST AFRICA

Africa has more languages than any other continent.
Although (**0**) foreigners have been responsible for the   **FOREIGN**
(**56**) .... of some languages, there are hundreds of local   **INTRODUCE**
languages.

It is important that (**57**) .... for children begins in the local   **TEACH**
language to avoid unnecessary (**58**) .... In West Africa,   **CONFUSE**
despite (**59**) .... efforts, it is not always possible for every child **GOVERN**
to receive and (**60**) .... and for many families the fees for   **EDUCATE**
children to attend school are very (**61**) .... However,   **EXPENSE**
although a family will usually have to contribute towards the school fees,
(**62**) .... can be put off until the harvest is finished.   **PAY**

The (**63**) .... small number of Africans reaching university,   **RELATIVE**
therefore, find themselves in (**64**) .... of a great deal of power   **POSSESS**
and influence, as they are always in a (**65**) ....   **MINOR**

Tip Strip

Question 57: Read the next sentence carefully and look at the verb which comes after this gap.
Question 59: Be careful when spelling this word.
Question 63: What kind of word is needed here?

Listening (approximately 40 minutes)

You'll hear people talking in eight different situations. For Questions **1–8**, choose the best answer, **A**, **B** or **C**.

Tip Strip

Question 1: Where do you think the man is as he speaks?

Question 4: Why does the lecturer want the student to 'pull up a chair'? Listen carefully.

Question 5: The speaker is unsure about her choice but she emphasises one thing in particular.

1   You hear a man talking about his past life.
What is he describing?
A   his house
B   his family
C   his school

| | 1 |

2   You hear a jewellery designer talking about his customers.
What annoys him about some customers?
A   They want to use their own designs.
B   They expect his work to be cheap.
C   They dislike what is on display.

| | 2 |

3   You hear an announcement at an airport.
What has happened to the plane the passengers are waiting for?
A   It is not at the airport yet.
B   It has not left North Africa.
C   It has a mechanical fault.

| | 3 |

4   You hear a lecturer talking to a student about his essay.
What point is the lecturer making?
A   It's important to introduce ideas clearly.
B   It's necessary to check through an essay.
C   It's essential to end an essay effectively.

| | 4 |

5   You hear a woman explaining about some furniture she wants.
What is she concerned about?
A   the colour of the wood
B   the choice of material
C   the size of the chairs

| | 5 |

6   You overhear two people talking about a party they've been to.
Where was the party held?
A   in a village hall
B   in someone's house
C   in an empty flat

| | 6 |

7   You hear a man talking about children and what interests them.
What does he consider to be of lasting interest?
A   computers
B   toys
C   animals

| | 7 |

8   You hear a woman giving a talk on flags.
What makes flags so important?
A   They advertise a country.
B   They represent strength.
C   They are very decorative.

| | 8 |

You will hear part of a radio programme in which a woman called Helena Smith talks about her life as a weather presenter on TV. For Questions **9–18,** complete the sentences.

Tip Strip

Question 9: Listen carefully because Helena mentions quite a lot of figures.

Question 11: What kind of word will you need to complete the sentence?

Question 17: Read the question carefully as you have to fill in the first word of the sentence.

Helena's working day consists of [9] shifts.

Her first job is to read the [10] from the previous shift.

At 11.30am there is a meeting in the weather [11] for everyone.

The team decides which maps and [12] to use.

Radio, as well as TV, makes use of the [13] which are written.

The lights and microphone are worked by pressing a [14]

The presenters can hear the [15] through their ear-piece.

Helena is frequently asked about the presenters' [16]

[17] must not be tight as presenters have to raise their arms.

Some viewers complained that Helena wore the same [18] for too long.

You will hear five different musicians talking about their job. For Questions **19–23,** choose from the list **A–F** what each speaker says. Use the letters only once. There is one extra letter which you do not need to use.

Tip Strip

A: What expression does the musician use to suggest change?

C: Which musician has to take more care than most?

E: Which musician feels his work is undervalued because people don't understand it?

A I could do with a change.

B It awakens my sense of history.

C I have to look after myself.

D It gives me a sense of adventure.

E I do a very difficult job.

F It's good to know about the individual learner.

Speaker 1 [19]

Speaker 2 [20]

Speaker 3 [21]

Speaker 4 [22]

Speaker 5 [23]

PART 4

You will hear part of a radio interview with a photographer called Peter White. For Questions **24–30**, choose the best answer **A, B** or **C.**

Tip Strip

Question 24: Peter's answer is unexpected so listen carefully!

Question 26: Does Peter agree with this opinion?

Question 29: Does Peter say the same thing about his wife as he does about his children?

24 Peter's favourite holiday is
   A   on a beach.
   B   by a lake.
   C   at home.

                                                   24

25 Peter earns his living by
   A   making advertising films.
   B   supplying picture libraries.
   C   selling photos to his agents.

                                                   25

26 The photo of the woman standing in the sea is
   A   Peter's favourite.
   B   highly regarded.
   C   very famous.

                                                   26

27 What does Peter say is the disadvantage of his job?
   A   Someone might steal his equipment.
   B   Customs officers keep his equipment.
   C   He has lost quite a lot of his equipment.

                                                   27

28 What does Peter say about his trips?
   A   He makes lists to remember things.
   B   His agents pay all his expenses.
   C   There is always a risk to his work.

                                                   28

29 How does Peter's family feel about his job?
   A   They all miss him when he's away.
   B   His wife is very understanding.
   C   His children don't mind his absence.

                                                   29

30 What does Peter say about taking photos of his own family?
   A   He probably tries too hard.
   B   He has taken some good ones.
   C   He likes taking his children.

                                                   30

PAPER 5   Speaking (14 minutes)

 **PART 1**   (3 minutes)

Answer these questions:

Why did you decide to learn English?
How important will English be for you in the future?
What do you enjoy most about learning another language?
Do you plan to learn another language in the future?

PART 2   (4 minutes)

Holidays (compare, contrast and speculate)

Turn to pictures 1 and 2 on page 172 which show people on holiday.

Candidate A, compare and contrast these photographs and say how important you think it is to have a holiday. You have a minute to do this.

Candidate B, where do you like to go on holiday?

Visiting famous places (compare, contrast and speculate)

Turn to pictures 1 and 2 on page 173 which show people visiting famous places.

Candidate B, compare and contrast these photographs and say how important you think it is to visit famous places. You have a minute to do this.

Candidate A, do you like visiting museums?

PART 3   (3 minutes)

 **Importance of water** (discuss and evaluate)

Turn to the pictures on page 174 which show the many ways water is essential in our lives. Imagine there is a global water shortage and you have to put these uses in order of their importance so as to save water.

PART 4   (4 minutes)

Answer these questions:

What would you miss most if there was a serious water shortage?
In what ways do some people waste water?
Do you think we need to take better care of our environment? In what way(s)?
Did you learn about looking after the environment when you were at school?

TEST 1, PART 2

Candidate A

Useful phrases

Candidate A

Well, there are people having something to eat in both photos.

In the first photo some people are having a meal in a restaurant

In the second photo there are people sitting outside at a café and a couple sitting on a wall eating ice creams.

The people eating ice cream could be on holiday.

They look very relaxed sitting in the street.

I can't see any traffic so perhaps they're watching a musician or a street entertainer.

It looks as if the people are having a Chinese meal.

They *could be* celebrating a birthday or something special.

Candidate B

Useful phrases

Candidate B

Both these photos show people being filmed, or perhaps they are making a programme for TV.

I think the children in the first photograph look a little puzzled.

But I also think they are interested in what is happening as they have stopped to watch.

The man on the mobile phone does not seem to notice them.

In the second photo the man is smiling and talking to the camera.

I think he looks quite happy and relaxed, but the man who is interviewing him is frowning.

He has probably asked a question and does not agree with what the man is saying.

Candidates A and B

Useful phrases

Candidates A and B

Well, I think different things are popular with different people. It depends on their lifestyle. *What do you think?*

Yes, I agree in general. For example, if you want to go on holiday, you probably fly. But if you have a baby like these people, I'm not sure. What do you think is best for them?

My feeling is that it's easier for them to travel by car because they can pack everything they need.

Yes, that's a good point.

But which form of transport is popular with young people? I think the train is, but *what's your opinion?*

Candidate A

Useful phrases

Candidate A

I think the people in the first photo could be at an airport because they are wheeling a lot of luggage.

And in the other photo the men could be at a station. Perhaps they are getting out of a taxi.

In the first photo the people *are probably* feeling stressed with all their bags and suitcases.

In the second photo the men do not have as many suitcases, but they are probably feeling stressed as well because their suitcases look heavy.

I think people can feel exhausted when they travel because everywhere is so busy, and they have to carry all their things with them. It's not much fun.

Candidate B

Useful phrases

Candidate B

Well, both these photos show people playing music.

In the first photo I think they are students and they look quite concentrated.

Perhaps they are feeling tired but they look very serious.

And in the second photo there is a man playing an instrument.

I don't know what it is but it only has two strings.

I think he comes from Asia or the Far East

He could be singing as well because his mouth is open.

I think he must be feeling quite lonely and the lady watching him does not look as if she is enjoying the music.

Candidates A and B

Useful phrases

Candidates A and B

Right. Let's discuss each one in turn. What do you think about newspapers and magazines?

Well, they're good because you can find out about what's happening in the world. They're probably the best.

I don't agree. It's much quicker if you check things on the internet. And it's more up-to-date.

Yes, but not everyone can do that. What about radio and television? I like radio.

Yes, *I would agree with you*.

So do you think radio is the best?

It's not as good as the internet, though.

Candidate A

Useful phrases

Candidate A

Both these photos show people sitting by themselves.

In the first photo the man looks as if he's travelling somewhere.

From the way he is dressed I think he is feeling very comfortable and enjoying being by himself.

He can choose where to go and what to do when he wants.

And in the second photo I think the man is sitting on his motorbike.

He is feeling very contented, reading a magazine and smoking his pipe.

When you are alone you can please yourself how you spend your time.

Candidate B

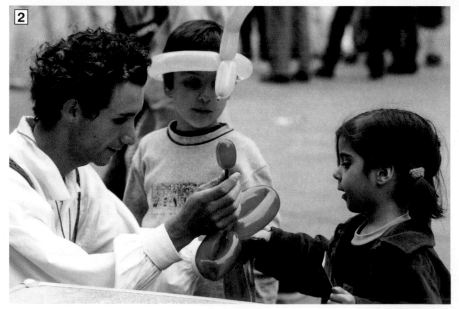

Candidate B

These people are making things, creating things.

In the top photo the people are artists.

They are drawing plants and flowers and I think people get a lot of fun when they do this.

It doesn't matter if you only do it for yourself, you have the feeling of producing something beautiful.

In the second photo the man is getting enjoyment from what he does because he is making things for children.

I think the children love wearing the balloons he is making for them.

They all get a lot of fun from what he does, and perhaps he is teaching them how to make things as well.

Candidates A and B

Useful phrases

Candidates A and B

OK, which club would you like to join?

Shall we discuss the different clubs and then decide? *Are you interested in* computers? I think that would be quite a good club.

I disagree. We have computer lessons at school. What about a museum club? That would be something different.

Yes, you're right. But it would depend on the kind of museum. *Is that your first choice?*

I don't know yet. What about the other five which we haven't mentioned. Like the sports club and the theatre club? I like acting and I think it would be a great opportunity to be in a play or a musical.

Candidate A

Useful phrases

Candidate A

The young children in the first photo appear to be enjoying themselves on a boat.

The boy who is standing looks very happy.

They don't look like brother and sister, so perhaps they are making friends with each other.

In the other photo there is a baby sitting in a pram.

I don't know whether it's a boy or a girl. Probably a girl. I think she's eating a piece of toast.

And I think she must be feeling contented being pushed around in her pram, watching everything that happens around her.

Candidate B

Useful phrases

Candidate B

The people sitting on some steps are looking at a map.

I think the people in the other photo are asking for directions or information.

It's quite hard if you are in a foreign country like the women in the first photo.

Even if you have a map, it's not always easy to find where you are. If you can speak the language, it's easier to ask for help like the old people are doing in the second photo.

Candidates A and B

Useful phrases

Candidates A and B

Right. *What shall we talk about* first?

A minibus is quite expensive so we have to think about best way to get a lot of money. *What's your opinion about* washing cars?

I don't think that's very good idea. You can't earn much money doing that. *What about* a concert?

I think that's a good idea. If you can arrange a really good concert, then you can sell hundreds of tickets and that would bring in lots of money.

I agree. It would involve a lot of work, though. You could use the school hall but the performers would not be able to charge, otherwise you would not make much profit. And it might be quite difficult to persuade people that they must perform for free.

You're right. What about this other picture where ... ?

Candidate A

Useful phrases

Candidate A

Both these photos show people working outdoors.

I think the work they are doing is quite hard, physically, that is.

If the weather is fine, then the men mending the road might like being outside.

The woman in the photo is cutting vegetables.

I can't see what they are, perhaps they are green beans but it must be quite a difficult life and very tiring if you are standing all day.

And when the weather's cold it must be unpleasant because your hands will get very cold.

Candidate B

Useful phrases

Candidate B

One of these photos shows people waiting in a cake shop *and the other one shows* an old woman buying things in a market.

I think shopping is quite enjoyable if you have enough money to buy what you want.

I know some people don't like shopping because they find it boring.

But choosing something nice to eat like these pastries is enjoyable.

But carrying heavy bags of vegetables is not so enjoyable.

Candidates A and B

Useful phrases

Candidates A and B

Okay. What do you like?

I think they are all quite nice. *What shall we choose first*? *Do you like* the picture?

It's all right but it's a bit boring. *I prefer the* fountain.

Yes. That's really original. *But I think* the students might jump in it or throw things in it.

And it would make the floor wet, *which would not be a good idea* in an entrance hall.

You're right. What about …?

Have we decided then?

Yes, let's agree to choose …

Candidate A

Useful phrases

Candidate A

Well, both these photos have things that are old and things that are new.

Yes, I do think it's important to try and keep some things from the past.

For example, like the bridge in this photo, which looks really old.

And the buildings in the background look very modern.

And in the other photo there's a modern bus driving behind some people who are riding in a carriage.

And there are two horses pulling the carriage. It looks very strange to see the bus and horses together.

I suppose the carriage is more for tourists.

But it is important because it tells you about the history of this place, and how people used to travel around in the past.

Candidate B

Useful phrases

Candidate B

Both these photos appear to have been taken in a classroom.

In one of them the student is smiling and looks very happy.

It could be a geography lesson because there is a map on the wall.

And in the other photo all the students are using computers. Perhaps they're on the internet.

Yes, I think it's very *important* to study for as long as possible.

It's not necessary to go to university but I think everyone should get a qualification like a diploma and then it's easier to get a good job.

Candidates A and B

Useful phrases

Candidates A and B

So, which of these jobs gives you really useful experience?

I don't think working in a café would be useful.

Why not? I don't agree. You learn to work with other people and you know it is only for a short time.

Maybe. But I think working with small children is more useful.

Only if you want to be a teacher!

No. In my opinion it's good experience, especially if you want a family of your own one day.

What about working in a supermarket? *Do we agree on that one*?

Candidate A

Useful phrases

Candidate A

All the people in these photos seem to be enjoying themselves.

The boy who is dancing on his hands must be very strong.

I think the children who are in a boat are learning to row. And that makes them feel grown up.

I think it's good to do things like this in your free time.

Candidate B

Useful phrases

Candidate B

These photos look very interesting.

I think it's good to do sport and if you don't live in a country where the weather is very good, you can do things inside like these people.

It looks quite hard for that little girl climbing the wall.

And running like these boys is an excellent way to keep fit. It's good for your heart.

For me it's very important to keep fit.

Candidates A and B

Useful phrases

Candidates A and B

Which picture shall we choose first? What about this one with the goldfish? It's not too difficult to look after a goldfish, is it?

No, but you still have to feed it! *Let's compare it with* looking after a house. That's far more difficult. You have to check that everywhere is locked when you go out.

Yes, *of course*. You have to switch off lights and things. That's a big responsibility. But, *what's your opinion about* looking after a baby? Isn't that the most difficult of all?

I don't know. I suppose looking after things is easier than looking after old people or children.

Yes, *that's what I think, too*.

Candidate A

Useful phrases

Candidate A

In the first photo the little girl is sitting on her father's back and they must be at an airport. I think it's really important for parents and children to enjoy holidays together. *Like the family in the second photo who look as if* they are on a cycling holiday. When the children are older you can do more things together like cycling.

You come back feeling fresh and relaxed. I don't know anyone who doesn't like holidays and for people who lead very busy lives, holidays are essential.

I think holidays are great whatever age you are!

Candidate B

Useful phrases

Candidate B

In the top photo it looks like a Kindergarten class.

I don't know how much these little children will remember if they go to a famous place.

In the other photo I don't know where these people are, but I imagine it's a famous museum.

Or perhaps it's a palace or a castle where you can see modern paintings.

I do think it's important to see as many famous places as possible. In that way you learn about your culture.

Candidates A and B

Useful phrases

Candidates A and B

This is interesting. *Where shall we begin?*

Well, I think water for drinking is the most important, don't you?

Absolutely. So that comes first. And water for washing is important as well.

Agreed. But you don't need to wash your car. People waste a lot of water doing that.

OK. And you can save water if you don't water the garden. And I think fountains are the least important.

I'm not sure because they keep using the same water. What about swimming pools? *Would you agree* that they're not essential?

Yes. They use huge amounts of water. *So we are in agreement?*

1 7 5

Answer Sheet 1 (FCE paper 4 Listening)

UNIVERSITY *of* CAMBRIDGE
Local Examinations Syndicate

SAMPLE

Candidate Name
If not already printed, write name in CAPITALS and complete the Candidate No. grid (in pencil).
Candidate's signature

Examination Title

Centre

Supervisor:
☒ If the candidate is ABSENT or has WITHDRAWN shade here ▭

Centre No.

Candidate No.

Examination Details

Candidate Answer Sheet: FCE paper 4 Listening

Mark test version below

A	B	C	D	E

Special arrangements S H

Use a pencil

For **Parts 1** and **3**:
Mark ONE letter for each question.

For example, if you think **B** is the right answer to the question, mark your answer sheet like this:

0   A B̶ C

For **Parts 2** and **4**:
Write your answers in the spaces next to the numbers like this:

0 EXAMPLE

Part 1

	A	B	C
1			
2			
3			
4			
5			
6			
7			
8			

Part 3

	A	B	C	D	E	F
19						
20						
21						
22						
23						

Part 2

	Do not write here
9	9
10	10
11	11
12	12
13	13
14	14
15	15
16	16
17	17
18	18

Part 4

	Do not write here
24	24
25	25
26	26
27	27
28	28
29	29
30	30

FCE-4

DP320/94

Answer Sheet 2 (FCE paper 1 Reading)

UNIVERSITY *of* CAMBRIDGE
Local Examinations Syndicate

SAMPLE

Candidate Name
If not already printed, write name in CAPITALS and complete the Candidate No. grid (in pencil).
Candidate's signature

Examination Title

Centre

Supervisor:
☒ If the candidate is ABSENT or has WITHDRAWN shade here ▭

Centre No.

Candidate No.

Examination Details

Candidate Answer Sheet: FCE paper 1 Reading

Use a pencil

Mark ONE letter for each question.

For example, if you think **B** is the right answer to the question, mark your answer sheet like this:

0   A B̶ C D

Change your answer like this:

0   A B C D

	A B C D E F G H I
1	A B C D E F G H I
2	A B C D E F G H I
3	A B C D E F G H I
4	A B C D E F G H I
5	A B C D E F G H I
6	A B C D E F G H I
7	A B C D E F G H I
8	A B C D E F G H I
9	A B C D E F G H I
10	A B C D E F G H I
11	A B C D E F G H I
12	A B C D E F G H I
13	A B C D E F G H I
14	A B C D E F G H I
15	A B C D E F G H I
16	A B C D E F G H I
17	A B C D E F G H I
18	A B C D E F G H I
19	A B C D E F G H I
20	A B C D E F G H I
21	A B C D E F G H I
22	A B C D E F G H I
23	A B C D E F G H I
24	A B C D E F G H I
25	A B C D E F G H I
26	A B C D E F G H I
27	A B C D E F G H I
28	A B C D E F G H I
29	A B C D E F G H I
30	A B C D E F G H I
31	A B C D E F G H I
32	A B C D E F G H I
33	A B C D E F G H I
34	A B C D E F G H I
35	A B C D E F G H I

FCE-1

DP318/92

UNIVERSITY of CAMBRIDGE
Local Examinations Syndicate

Centre No.

Candidate Name
If not already printed, write name
in CAPITALS and complete the
Candidate No. grid (in pencil).

Candidate's signature

Candidate No.

Examination Title

Examination Details

Centre

Supervisor:
☒ If the candidate is ABSENT or has WITHDRAWN shade here

Candidate Answer Sheet: FCE paper 3 Use of English

Use a pencil

For **Part 1**: Mark ONE letter for each question.

For example, if you think **C** is the right answer to the question, mark your answer sheet like this:

0	A	B	C	D

For **Parts 2, 3, 4** and **5**: Write your answers in the spaces next to the numbers like this:

0	

Part 1

	A	B	C	D
1	A	B	C	D
2	A	B	C	D
3	A	B	C	D
4	A	B	C	D
5	A	B	C	D
6	A	B	C	D
7	A	B	C	D
8	A	B	C	D
9	A	B	C	D
10	A	B	C	D
11	A	B	C	D
12	A	B	C	D
13	A	B	C	D
14	A	B	C	D
15	A	B	C	D

Part 2

		Do not write here
16		16
17		17
18		18
19		19
20		20
21		21
22		22
23		23
24		24
25		25
26		26
27		27
28		28
29		29
30		30

Turn over for Parts 3 - 5 →

DP319/93

FCE-3

Part 3

		Do not write here
31		31 0 1 2
32		32 0 1 2
33		33 0 1 2
34		34 0 1 2
35		35 0 1 2
36		36 0 1 2
37		37 0 1 2
38		38 0 1 2
39		39 0 1 2
40		40 0 1 2

Part 4

		Do not write here
41		41
42		42
43		43
44		44
45		45
46		46
47		47
48		48
49		49
50		50
51		51
52		52
53		53
54		54
55		55

Part 5

		Do not write here
56		56
57		57
58		58
59		59
60		60
61		61
62		62
63		63
64		64
65		65

KEY

Test 1

PAPER 1 Reading

Part 1: The history of surfing

1 E: Hawaii has the best surf in the world
2 I: the force can be life-threatening
3 A: Nature's way of saying: stay away (i.e. a warning)
4 F: one man in particular was responsible for fresh enthusiasm
5 H: he came across a substance ... he created a wetsuit
6 D: the first ever snowboarding world cup event
7 B: now wants to surf a wave called Jaws

Part 2: Hungry pop stars

8 A: Incorrect: She does not say people are fussy.
8 B: Incorrect: There is no reference to restaurants.
8 C: Correct: 'She has to cater for many different tastes'.
8 D: Incorrect: Only some people are on a special diet.
9 A: Incorrect: The stars are not worried about their personal safety.
9 B: Correct: 'no one is bothering them for autographs'.
9 C: Incorrect: The managers may be more trouble than the stars.
9 D: Incorrect: We don't know whether or not this is true.
10 A: Correct: 'her own particular mixture ...'.
10 B: Incorrect: They simply like herbal tea.
10 C: Incorrect: They take the special mixture on stage.
10 D: Incorrect: They no longer drink as much alcohol.
11 A: Incorrect: 'rich' is the opposite of 'plain'.
11 B: Incorrect: There is only a reference to how much Valerie spends.
11 C: Incorrect: The emphasis is on providing nutritious food.
11 D: Correct: 'they're not used to expensive food, so Valerie prepares plain food'.
12 A: Incorrect: There is no reference to people wanting more expensive food.
12 B: Incorrect: She doesn't keep the list 'just in case'; she uses it.
12 C: Correct: This refers back to 'a stock of people's requirements'.
12 D: Incorrect: She has made use of the list so that things are there if necessary.
13 A: Incorrect: Having a lot of money does not make you an expert.
13 B: Correct: She has learnt to buy what people need quickly.
13 C: Incorrect: There is no mention of a budget.
13 D: Incorrect: She is not under pressure to shop quickly.
14 A: Correct: They won't eat before a concert because they're too nervous.
14 B: Incorrect: There is food available whenever they want it.
14 C: Incorrect: They don't eat at all before a concert.
14 D: Incorrect: There is no mention of this.
15 A: Incorrect: Bands are mad but Valerie does not say 'completely mad'.
15 B: Correct: She is amazed at the change in their behaviour.
15 C: Incorrect: Valerie does not say they are actually rude on stage.
15 D: Incorrect: They can be really quiet off stage.

Part 3: Why the United Nations Went to School

16 G: Explanation of 'Model United Nations'.
17 H: Link with reference to 'other countries'.
18 A: Link with 'other roles'.
19 F: Link with students arriving: 'Once they are all together'.
20 C: Link with students deciding who will speak after the committee stage.
21 B: Link between students being nervous but also 'gaining in self-confidence'.

Part 4: An Actor's World

22 B: Laura Dyson is just 21 and already a box office name.
23 A: His father and mother are both actors ... his career path was inevitable.
24 C: in the afternoon I was told I would be on stage that evening
25 A: I had to learn ... the exact opposite.
26 D: Then one day ... and the next day I was on the film set.
27 B: I didn't have to say a single word!
28 D: has had no formal training
29 B: I used to feel quite desperate ... out of work
30 A: I find most of them very boring
31 C: it has not been an easy ride to stardom
32 D: But I'm quite choosy now and turn down more scripts than I accept!
33 B: I used to spend hours making up my face so that I'd look older.
34 C: my father refused to agree ... to pay my way
35 A: there was something fascinating ... other personalities

Questions **1–21** = 2 marks each
Questions **22–35** = 1 mark each
The total score is adjusted to give a mark out of 40.

PAPER 2 Writing

Part 1
Question 1

Style: Formal letter. Avoid informal expressions.
Content: 1 Give information about your interests, and say where and how you would like to travel.
2 Ask how long the courses are and whether you can do more than one activity on a course.
3 Ask about the furnished apartments.
4 Ask whether language tuition is individual or in groups.
5 Add a question of your own based on the information in the advertisement.

Part 2
Question 2

Style: Formal to neutral. Use clear paragraphs.
Content: 1 Introduce the topic.
2 Suggest a few examples of things people can do to look after their environment.
3 Explain why and how these examples would help the environment.
4 Conclude your composition with a general comment.

Question 3

Style: Informal
Content: 1 Introduce your letter with a welcoming sentence.
2 Tell your friends about two or three of the special tourist attractions in your area.
3 Suggest one or two things their children would enjoy. These may or may not be the same as the special tourist attractions.
4 Conclude the letter appropriately, e.g. that you are looking forward to their visit.

Question 4

Style: Neutral.
Content: 1 Choose a person and use their name as a heading or title.
2 Introduce the person and explain why their influence is important.
3 Give two or three examples of their influence and its effect.
4 Conclude with an appropriate comment.

Question 5(a)

Style: Formal or neutral. Do not use informal expressions.
Content: Briefly describe one of the events. Explain your reasons for choosing it and say why you find it interesting/enjoyable/effective etc. (i.e. memorable).

Question 5(b)

Style: Formal or neutral. Do not use informal expressions.
Content: Decide whether you think the book is more suitable for radio or television and say why. Choose two or three examples of scenes/events from the book which you think would make good radio or television supporting and explaining your decision.

The two parts of the Writing Paper have equal marks.
The total score is adjusted to give a mark out of 40.

PAPER 3   Use of English

Part 1: Øresund Bridge

1 A: Only 'longest' collocates with 'bridge'.
2 C: Only 'stretches' makes sense.
3 B: The expression is 'into the distance'. The other words do not collocate.
4 B: Only 'meets' collocates.
5 A: 'links' here means 'unites'; none of the others makes sense.
6 D: Building work is 'completed'.
7 D: Only 'separating' collocates.
8 B: 'turns into' means 'becomes'; all the other phrasal verbs have different meanings.
9 C: Only 'record' collocates with 'breaker'.
10 A: Although C and D work grammatically they do not make sense; B does not collocate.
11 C: Only 'structure' can be used with 'bridge'.
12 B: Only B works grammatically; A, C and D would all need another noun phrase to complete the structure.
13 D: Only 'jointly' has the right meaning for something done by two parties.
14 A: Only A collocates in this context; you can 'spare' and 'spend' 'time' but they mean something different.
15 B: Only 'benefit' collocates in this context.

Part 2: Artist Development Manager

16 responsible (adjective): collocates with 'for'
17 of (preposition): indicates belonging
18 all (determiner): collocates in the expression 'all that it involves'

19 wears (verb in Present simple): collocates with 'clothes'
20 a (indefinite article): refers to any one day
21 During (preposition): indicates length of time
22 sent (verb in Past simple): used to show that tapes have been received
23 be/become (verb): collocates with 'hoping to' and 'famous'
24 what (pronoun): subject of 'makes'
25 able (adjective): completes phrase 'be able to'
26 spite (noun): part of the prepositional phrase 'in spite of'
27 worth (preposition): forms part of the expression 'it is worth it'
28 doing (present participle): follows 'by' and collocates with 'work experience'.
29 as (conjunction): part of the fixed phrase 'as well as'
30 found (verb in Past simple): part of phrasal verb 'find out' meaning 'discover'

Part 3

31 was unaware ∎ of Rona's: 'unaware' must be followed by 'of'
32 (been) months ∎ since I saw: 'since' + Past simple (from Present perfect)
33 took ∎ my advice: 'advice' collocates with 'take'
34 put up ∎ with: phrasal verb with two particles
35 were prevented ∎ from running by: passive construction? prevent + from + -ing
36 you ∎ lend me: 'lend' without 'to' meaning 'allow to borrow'
37 his horror ∎ Jim found: possessive adjective + noun + Past simple
38 do ∎ you want: auxiliary verb used to form question
39 wish ∎ I could speak: 'I wish' must be followed by a pronoun
40 is grown ∎ by: passive construction in the Present simple + by preceding agent 'farmers'

Part 4: Red Nose Day

41 together: 'collected' does not need 'together'
42 ✓
43 like: 'such as' cannot be followed by 'like'
44 because: grammatically incorrect within the sentence
45 ✓
46 for: wrong to put a preposition here – 'health care' is a noun phrase
47 ✓
48 being: 'by' is followed directly here with the main verb in its participle form
49 on: 'on' is used with 'put on a programme/show'
50 here: does not refer to any place, so it is meaningless
51 over: 'give' by itself is all that is needed here; 'over' can be used with 'hand' but not in this context
52 ✓
53 ✓
54 about: the expression 'for fun' cannot be preceded by 'about' in this context
55 had: you cannot use 'had' before Present simple 'buy'

Part 5: Aboriginal Stories

56 surroundings (verb to noun)
57 traditional (noun to adjective)
58 knowledge (verb to noun)
59 theatrical (noun to adjective)
60 lives (noun to noun, plural form)
61 believed (noun to verb, Past simple)
62 personality (adjective to noun)
63 importance (adjective to noun)
64 uncomfortable (noun to negative adjective by adding prefix)
65 possibility (adjective to noun)

Questions **1–30** and **41–65** = 1 mark each
Questions **31–40** = 2 marks each
The total score is adjusted to give a mark out of 40.

PAPER 4 Listening

There is a mark for each correct answer in parts 1–4.

Part 1

1 B 2 A 3 A 4 A 5 C 6 A 7 B 8 B

Part 2

9 25/twenty-five years
10 power
11 project
12 3/three days
13 cabins
14 to smoke
15 natural
16 water
17 job
18 fund

Part 3

19 F 20 E 21 D 22 B 23 C

Part 4

24 F 25 T 26 F 27 T 28 T 29 F 30 F

Questions **1–30** = 1 mark each
The total score is adjusted to give a mark out of 40.

Test 2

PAPER 1 Reading

Part 1: Dark days

1 G: Now life starts again.
2 H: The station is home to physicists ... and a chef.
3 D: they can start and finish work at whatever times suit them
4 I: small social groups develop within this isolated community
5 F: can open up a new road system
6 A: a way of having some personal and private space
7 B: they are isolated and imprisoned ... but for many months at a time no chance of leaving

Part 2: Into the Gap

8 A: Incorrect: He is not in a courtroom.
8 B: Incorrect: He hasn't yet begun to teach.
8 C: Incorrect: He is apprehensive.
8 D: Correct: He expects to be judged because 'They have never met a foreigner before'.
9 A: Incorrect: This is not mentioned.
9 B: Incorrect: This is not his decision.
9 C: Correct: This refers back to 'not been an easy choice to take the opportunity of doing a gap year'.
9 D: Incorrect: This is not his decision.
10 A: Incorrect: The students eye him nervously.
10 B: Correct: 'left me feeling exhausted, but rewarded'.
10 C: Incorrect: People are enthusiastic.
10 D: Incorrect: This is not mentioned.
11 A: Incorrect: This is not mentioned.
11 B: Incorrect: This is not mentioned.
11 C: Correct: 'I ... felt appreciated and welcomed ... everyone wants to be your friend'.
11 D: Incorrect: This is not mentioned.
12 A: Correct: The best nights were those he spent listening to stories and eating with the family, relatively simple pleasures.
12 B: Incorrect: He doesn't say this.
12 C: Incorrect: He doesn't mention missing Western entertainment.

12 D: Incorrect: He only mentions Mr Chow, not students in general.
13 A: Incorrect: We know that he isn't.
13 B: Correct: He says that 'you can feel like a cross between a celebrity and a creature from outer space'.
13 C: Incorrect: There is no evidence for this.
13 D: Incorrect: There is no evidence for this.
14 A: Incorrect: He doesn't say this.
14 B: Incorrect: This is part of his experience but not the end result.
14 C: Incorrect: This is also part of his teaching experience but not the end result.
14 D: Correct: 'and become more independent ... there's no faster way to grow up'.

Part 3: Rattling the Cage

15 C: Link between 'disliked having a clever young boss', 'two years' and 'first year'.
16 D: Link between 'conditions for animals' and 'heating in the animal houses'.
17 A: Link between 'heating', 'the keepers went on strike' and 'leaving all the heating turned on'.
18 E: Link between 'the zoo's animal hospital' and 'he was at last in charge of a proper clinic'.
19 B: Link between 'safari parks', 'cages' and 'to be fair to London Zoo'.
20 F: Link between 'cars' and 'they can go to the country'.
21 I: Link between 'he actually lived in the zoo grounds' and 'he had a flat'.

Part 4: My Own Personal Space

21 B: I share a flat with three others
22 D: I'd love to be able to go for a walk
23 C: I tell them it's nothing personal
24/5 C: It's important that I create space for myself at the beginning of each day
24/5 A: I have at least an hour to myself
26 B: It's hopeless to try and find any privacy in the flat, so I go out for a walk
27 B: it gives me the opportunity ... to think about what I have to do the next day
28/9 B: If I don't get time to myself, I'll be like a bear with a sore head
28/9 A: If I don't make this space for myself, I feel really tense and irritable.
30 C: I'm sure it must be the same for singers ... complete silence
31 D: when I get home it's wonderful to be able to relax
32 A: office bustle, phones, e-mail, do this, do that
33 C: If people try and talk to me before midday, I really snap at them.
34 A: Even if I'm away from home, I try to find the time just to be alone
35 D: The breaks are so short there's no time to do anything other than ...

Questions **1–21** = 2 marks each
Questions **22–35** = 1 mark each
The total score is adjusted to give a mark out of 40.

PAPER 2   Writing

Part 1
Question 1
Style: Formal letter. Avoid informal expressions.
Content: 1 Give information about your group (age, sex etc.) and ask for details about two countries.
2 Ask what is meant by 'large groups', and 'special prices'.
3 Ask about sporting activities and whether horse-riding is possible.
4 Ask about accommodation and food.
5 Ask about information packs.

Part 2
Question 2
Style: Neutral or informal because the readers will be young people.
Content: 1 Introduce the person.
2 Say why you have chosen him or her.
3 Explain what interests you about this person.

Question 3
Style: Semi-formal or neutral.
Content: 1 Make it clear why Joni had closed the door so quietly.
2 Explain what Joni is waiting for.
3 How does the story end? Who or what was behind the door?

Question 4
Style: Informal.
Content: 1 Explain how your decision to go camping was made at the last minute (good weather?) and that was why your friend didn't know.
2 Tell your friend who you went camping with.
3 Tell them what happened; mention two or three concrete details to do with camping.
4 Conclude appropriately.

Question 5(a)
Style: Formal or neutral. Do not use informal expressions.
Content: Say which character is your favourite. Give specific references from the book to explain why you like the character so much.

Question 5(b)
Style: Formal or neutral. Do not use informal expressions.
Content: Say whether you agree or disagree with the statement. Give reasons for your opinion and refer to specific examples from the book which make it clear why you enjoyed reading it.

The two parts of the Writing Paper have equal marks.
The total score is adjusted to give a mark out of 40.

PAPER 3   Use of English

Part 1: Coffee Culture
1 B: The world can only 'go by'.
2 A: Only 'queue' collocates; 'line' would be right if followed by 'of people'.
3 A: Only 'demand' makes sense here and has to be followed by 'for' in this context.
4 C: Read the complete paragraph carefully in order to understand the writer's scepticism and the fact that the attraction is the environment, not the coffee!

5 B: Only 'lies' collocates with 'attraction'.
6 C: Only 'join' fits the meaning here.
7 D: People 'gather'; moreover, A, B and C do not fit grammatically.
8 A: 'regular' collocates with 'times'; the others don't in this context.
9 B: 'exchange' collocates with 'news and gossip'.
10 B: 'issues of the day' is a fixed expression.
11 C: 'do business' is a fixed expression.
12 B: The phrasal verb can only be followed by 'transactions'.
13 A: 'it is estimated' is a fixed passive expression.
14 B: Only 'growing' collocates with 'number'.
15 C: Only 'attractions' collocates with 'tourist'.

Part 2: Sports Tourism
16 there (pronoun): there + verb 'to be' to indicate that something exists
17 No (adverb): part of negative adverbial expression 'no longer'
18 sit (verb): collocates with 'armchair'
19 where (adverb): adverb of place
20 so (conjunction): links people's desire with their action
21 addition (noun): part of the prepositional phrase 'in addition to'
22 every (determiner): collocates with 'number'
23 they (pronoun): refers back to 'Olympics'
24 have (verb): part of modal verb 'have to' used in the passive
25 but (conjunction): part of structure 'not just/only ... but also'
26 who (relative pronoun): refers to 'visitors'
27 as (conjunction): used here to mean 'because'
28 has (verb in Present simple): collocates with 'effect'
29 since (preposition): used to refer to a fixed point of time in the past
30 become (past participle): part of verb in the Present perfect

Part 3
31 asked John ❙ not to speak: 'asked' used as a reporting verb
32 wish ❙ I could: 'I wish' must be followed by a pronoun
33 in case ❙ it rains: in case + pronoun + verb in Present simple
34 even though ❙ he was feeling/felt: conjunction used to express contrast
35 told her son ❙ off: phrasal verb meaning 'scold/rebuke'
36 do not ❙ interest: auxiliary verb + infinitive
37 everyone's/our surprise ❙ Kitty came: 'surprise' used as noun
38 think that ❙ one of: passive to active
39 you mind ❙ if I borrow: auxiliary question form + if + Present simple
40 is not ❙ as/so cheap as: comparative structure

Part 4: Time Travel
41 the: no article before 'history'
42 ✓
43 is: grammatically wrong
44 ✓
45 since: a conjunction is not needed here
46 and: 'however' is the adverb which links the ideas correctly
47 far: you cannot put 'far' between 'so' and 'tiny'
48 ✓
49 so: if this word were used, it would have to be at the start of the sentence
50 there: no specific reference to a place, so it is wrong
51 ✓
52 or: 'stop' followed by participle
53 ✓
54 on: 'take on' is not used to talk about time
55 to: the verb 'reach' is not followed by the preposition 'to'

Part 5: Voices Foundation

56 passionately (noun to adverb)
57 musical (noun to adjective)
58 majority (adjective to noun)
59 inspiration (verb to noun)
60 development (verb to noun)
61 significant (verb to adjective)
62 mathematical (noun to adjective)
63 communication (verb to noun)
64 enjoyment (verb to noun)
65 willingly (noun to adverb)

Questions **1–30** and **41–65** = 1 mark each
Questions **31–40** = 2 marks each
The total score is adjusted to give a mark out of 40.

PAPER 4   Listening

There is a mark for each correct answer in parts 1–4.

Part 1
1 A   **2** C   **3** A   **4** B   **5** B   **6** C   **7** C   **8** C

Part 2

9 tin/metal roof   **14** sugar cane
10 tape   **15** rats
11 candles   **16** heaters
12 tracks   **17** 1000/1/one thousand kms/kilometres
13 plane   **18** inside

Part 3
19 C   **20** E   **21** A   **22** F   **23** D

Part 4
24 A   **25** C   **26** B   **27** B   **28** A   **29** C   **30** B

Questions **1–30** = 1 mark each
The total score is adjusted to give a mark out of 40.

Test 3

PAPER 1   Reading

Part 1: White Storks

1 G: So my initial job was to collect
2 B: It was a marvellous scene
3 D: The numbers of storks … The major cause for this
       decrease …
4 A: the birds adjusted to this loss by carrying their twigs
       even higher
5 F: If a stork can't find sufficient food … it will quite happily
       feed off what it can find in rubbish tips
6 H: the stork will no doubt find a way to ensure it will
       survive long into the future

Part 2: Unusual storytelling

7 C: It's gripping storytelling and not a single child has
       moved.
8 D: Women do not usually referee football matches.
9 C: who mainly sit at the back of classrooms and don't want
       to take part in lessons
10 D: The correct answer is expressed by the whole of
       the sixth paragraph.
11 A: 'strong male role models', 'grow up wanting …
       footballers' and 'they'll listen … teachers'

12 A: how relaxing with a book before a big game could
       improve their performance
13 D: Footballers have a fairly short career … and most of
       them move on to other jobs
14 B: I had almost no self-confidence but nowadays I'm quite
       happy standing up in front of 500 children

Part 3
15 G: Link between 'But writing a book … was one thing' and
       'Writing a book when … was quite another.'
16 D: Link between 'on arriving' and 'off I drove'.
17 F: Link between 'before I could open it' and 'once inside'.
18 B: Link with 'Every passer-by …'.
19 H: Link with 'children … sliding on ice … ' and 'children …
       sliding down the chute'.
20 I: Link with 'Have you heard?' and direct speech that
       follows.
21 A: Contrastive link between 'nothing to worry about' and
       'Some people did worry, however.'

Part 4: I Need My Computer
22 B: to remind me about meetings with other doctors
23 C: for finding out what other companies like mine are
       offering
24 A: moving from the notes I have made … to more
       developed pieces
25 D: Instead of having to draw pictures I can get them on the
       computer
26 A: I can work on trains and buses
27/8 B: to find out about the latest discoveries
27/8 E: and use the internet to research new music
29 C: everyone expects you to have a computer these days
30 E: My e-mail is like having a friend
31 C: it is not as personal as a phone call
32 E: it saves a lot of money
33 D: they let me have their old one
34 F: to send out information about myself
35 E: I owned one of the early laptops; My life … would be a
       real struggle without my computers.

Questions **1–21** = 2 marks each
Questions **22–35** = 1 mark each
The total score is adjusted to give a mark out of 40.

PAPER 2   Writing

Part 1
Question 1

Style: Formal letter. Avoid informal expressions.
Content: 1 Give information about yourself and your friend,
        ages and backgrounds.
        2 Ask where volunteers are sent and how old most
        people are.
        3 Ask about the skills that are needed.
        4 Ask about accommodation and whether food is
        included.
        5 Ask whether there are any extra costs.

Part 2
Question 2

Style: Formal to neutral. Use a heading or title.
Content: 1 Introduce the topic and refer to your own personal
        interests or hobbies.
        2 Develop the topic by dealing with each interest in
        turn.
        3 Summarise why you think what you do is a good
        way to spend your free time.

Question 3

Style: Semi-formal or neutral.

Content: 1 Explain what the 'secret' is.
2 Reason(s) why the matter must be kept secret.
3 What has happened/could happen that might make it difficult to keep the secret?

Question 4

Style: Formal; write clear paragraphs, perhaps using subheadings.

Content: 1 Recommend a televison programme.
2 Explain why it would be useful and helpful for foreign learners.
3 Give one or two examples of things from the programme that support your recommendation.

Question 5(a)

Style: Informal.

Content: Recommend the title of the book.
Say what you have especially enjoyed about the book (e.g. characters, storyline, level of language etc.).
Say why you think your friend would enjoy reading it.
Conclude appropriately.

Question 5(b)

Style: Formal.

Content: Briefly say what the book is about. Describe one event in the book that would interest people and possibly encourage them to read the book for themselves.

The two parts of the Writing Paper have equal marks.
The total score is adjusted to give a mark out of 40.

PAPER 3   Use of English

Part 1: Music – a Universal Language

1 D: Only 'arose' collocates with 'as a development'.
2 A: Only 'one' fits the meaning of the sentence.
3 A: In this context, the only word which collocates with 'languages'.
4 C: History was passed down the generations by being 'recorded' in music.
5 B: The phrasal verb 'pass on' is the only correct verb in this context; all the others mean something different.
6 D: Only correct word in context.
7 B: Only 'satisfy' collocates with 'the feel-good factor'.
8 A: Only word which collocates with the words on either side of the gap.
9 D: 'facts' would need a plural verb to be correct.
10 C: Only 'score' can be used in this context and collocates with 'test'.
11 D: Only word that forms a fixed expression.
12 A: 'supported' here means 'providing further evidence'.
13 B: Forms a phrasal verb meaning 'nurtured'.
14 D: Forms a fixed expression.
15 C: Forms a fixed phrase.

Part 2: Follow Your Nose

16 between (preposition): 'between' two things
17 takes (verb): collocates with 'two seconds'
18 enter (verb): collocates with 'nose'
19 which/that (relative pronoun): refers to 'brain'
20 how (adverb): refers to manner
21 not (adverb): used to negate the idea of 'understanding'
22 with (preposition): collocates with 'relationships' and 'other people'
23 fall (verb): part of fixed expression 'fall in love'
24 this (pronoun): refers to 'people tend to smell of what they eat'

25 part (noun): forms verb phrase 'take part'
26 likely (adverb): used after comparative 'more'
27 were (auxiliary verb): completes passive structure
28 used (past participle): collocates with 'knowledge'
29 level (noun): collocates with 'sub-conscious'
30 selling (gerund): relates to exploiting people's spending habits

Part 3

31 looked I up to: phrasal verb meaning 'respect'
32 apart from I Judith had: 'apart from' meaning 'with the exception of'
33 have difficulty I (in) learning: have difficulty + -ing
34 is not I worth asking: worth + -ing
35 would not have I been able: third conditional
36 are not allowed I to take: allowed + infinitive
37 never takes I any notice of   **or**
takes no I notice of: fixed phrase meaning 'ignore'
38 has gone I off: phrasal verb
39 ought to have I done
40 am having I my bedroom decorated: causative form

Part 4

41 ✓
42 ✓
43 then: there is no function for this word here
44 one: the fixed phrase is 'for example'
45 must: the writer is arguing that young people do things voluntarily
46 do: not a question, so the auxiliary is wrong
47 to: 'ask' cannot be followed by 'to'
48 ✓
49 by: there is no function for this word here
50 at: the preposition is unnecessary
51 even: wrong because there is no emphasis here
52 like: this often creeps into spoken English but is grammatically wrong here
53 ✓
54 having: the correct verb is 'we're chatting'
55 that: the fixed expression is 'you're only young once'

Part 5: Recognising a Liar

56 ability (adjective to noun)
57 truth (adjective to noun)
58 sixth (noun to adjective)
59 normally (adjective to adverb)
60 instance (adjective to noun)
61 different (verb to adjective)
62 alteration: (verb to noun)
63 realisation: (verb to noun)
64 judgement: (verb to noun)
65 unreliable (verb to negative noun by adding prefix)

Questions **1–30** and **41–65** = 1 mark each
Questions **31–40** = 2 marks each
The total score is adjusted to give a mark out of 40.

PAPER 4   Listening

There is a mark for each correct answer in parts 1–4.

Part 1

1 B   **2** B   **3** C   **4** A   **5** B   **6** A   **7** C   **8** A

Part 2

9 £19 million   14 season ticket
10 woolly scarf   15 filmed (for TV)
11 £80   16 competitions
12 world   17 products
13 dinner   18 wages

Part 3

19 D   20 B   21 E   22 A   23 C

Part 4

24 F   25 T   26 T   27 T   28 F   29 T   30 F

Questions **1–30** = 1 mark each
The total score is adjusted to give a mark out of 40.

Test 4

PAPER 1   Reading

Part 1: My Kind of Life

1 E: how photogenic the child would appear ... so each audition ... is watched on a monitor
2 I: The schedule was always very tight
3 A: when I first left university I worked as a personal assistant
4 H: you end up disappointing the vast majority of these kids
5 C: they've all worked and rehearsed enormously hard ... they may have travelled miles ... spent money on fares and new clothes
6 D: it is worth auditioning over and over again
7 G: some of these new young faces will go on to become big names in the years ahead

Part 2: Roamers

8 D: Matt Lassiter spotted a business opportunity
9 D: hostels that made young visitors feel at home
10 B: taking time off ... has quite a lot of money
11 A: like a kindly aunt or uncle looking after young people
12 C: offers a safe and secure form of accommodation
13 B: customers would all be familiar with the internet
14 A: knowing that backpackers want to feel like explorers

Part 3: Flying into the Record Books

15 A: Link between 'Polly's ... journey began' and 'it ended'.
16 F: Link between 'behind schedule' and 'the delay was the result of'.
17 C: Link between the past, Amelia Earhart and Polly's behaviour.
18 H: Link between the journey going well and the fact that Polly even had some free time.
19 B: Link between 'To her horror' and 'most dangerous kind of ice'.
20 D: Link between 'she had used more fuel than expected' and 'As a result the main tank had run dry'.
21 G: Link between 'warm welcome' and 'on one occasion'.

Part 4: Projects Abroad

22 C: ranging from well-equipped independent and state schools to much smaller ones
23 D: the French influence is still evident
24 A: you will be treated as an addition to any school or family that you join
25 B: children and their parents ... and children work hard at school

26 A: children as young as nursery age, and you may have the chance to work with them
27 C: walking and climbing, boating ... and white-water rafting
28 D: the best market in West Africa
29 B: bringing new investments and ideas with them
30 B: the main spoken languages are Ewe, Twi and Ga
31/2 C: Accommodation is either with host families or local hostels.
31/2 D: you can choose to stay with a host family or you may prefer to find your own room or apartment
33 A: and many people are vegetarians
34 A: It's an area with a special feel to it
35 B: teaching lively songs and rhymes is very popular

Questions **1–21** = 2 marks each
Questions **22–35** = 1 mark each
The total score is adjusted to give a mark out of 40.

PAPER 2   Writing

Part 1
Question 1

Style: Formal letter. Avoid informal expressions.
Content: 1 Give information about the event you are organising and say what you would like.
2 Ask about costs: food, drink and a private room.
3 Ask about the number of people that the restaurant can accommodate.
4 Ask about equipment for playing music and say you want to bring your own CDs etc.
5 Ask about special effects, lighting, decoration etc.
6 Ask about opening and closing times.

Part 2
Question 2

Style: Formal letter of application.
Content: 1 Say why you are interested in applying for the job.
2 Explain why you think you are a good person for the job (e.g. past experience, confident in dealing with people, available during the summer, good spoken English etc.).

Question 3

Style: Semi-formal or neutral.
Content: 1 Introduce yourself and your country.
2 Describe what you do on a typical day.

Question 4

Style: Formal; write clear paragraphs, perhaps using subheadings.
Content: 1 Explain where you took the group.
2 Describe what interested the visitors.

Question 5(a)

Style: Formal.
Content: Describe two characters from the book. Say what you find interesting about each of these characters and why you have chosen to meet them.

Question 5(b)

Style: Formal.
Content: Briefly describe the book, e.g. plot, setting, characters. Say why you think it is worth reading e.g. it's entertaining, interesting, exciting etc.

The two parts of the Writing Paper have equal marks.
The total score is adjusted to give a mark out of 40.

PAPER 3 Use of English

Part 1: The Early Days of Football

1 C: Only 'forms' collocates with 'game'.
2 A: 'An association' is 'formed'.
3 C: Only 'rules' is appropriate in this context.
4 A: Only 'grounds' collocates with 'football'.
5 D: 'meant' is used here with the sense of 'as a result'.
6 B: 'fans' are people who follow their team, or a pop group etc.
7 C: Forms a phrasal verb meaning 'established'.
8 B: 'preferred' is the only word which is grammatically correct here.
9 A: The choice was between football and rugby.
10 C: Only 'running' collocates with 'river'.
11 B: Only verb that makes sense in context.
12 B: The banks would have been built up (made) using earth.
13 C: Only 'proper' collocates with 'stands' in contrast to the 'earth banks'.
14 D: Only 'posts' collocates with 'wooden'.
15 A: The text indicates that nobody had thought of nets until 1891, so 'invented' is the right answer.

Part 2: Fast Track to Fluency

16 a (indefinite article): must follow 'such'
17 to (verb particle): part of the infinitive
18 grow (verb): part of phrasal verb 'grow up'
19 of (preposition): follows 'awareness'
20 for (preposition): follows 'ability' in this context
21 carried (past participle): part of phrasal verb
22 out (preposition): verb + particle + particle
23 were (verb): relates to state of being
24 whereas (conjuction): meaning 'on the other hand'
25 smaller (adjective): used in comparison with 'larger'
26 when (adverb): refers to time
27 same (adjective): collocates with 'way'
28 other (determiner): links to 'one language'
29 well (adverb): part of fixed expression 'as well as', meaning 'in addition to'
30 and (conjunction): links the two statements about children's skills

Part 3

31 should/ought to/must hang **I** on to: direct speech using a phrasal verb meaning 'to keep'
32 in spite of **I** never having: in spite of + -ing
33 is **I** not necessary: impersonal construction using 'it'
34 suggested (that) **I** we (should) go: reporting verb + (should +) infinitive without 'to'
35 would not **I** let him   **or**
did not **I** let him: let + object + infinitive without 'to'
36 had not **I** lost my mobile: third conditional
37 will be **I** met: active to passive
38 burst out **I** laughing: phrasal verb + -ing
39 objects to **I** people phoning: object + to + -ing
40 rather stay **I** in bed than: would rather + infinitive without 'to' + than

Part 4

41 this: no demonstrative adjective needed
42 ✓
43 for: not necessary
44 most: superlative form of 'old' is 'oldest'
45 grown: unnecessary and grammatically incorrect
46 in: cannot be used after 'believed' in this context
47 ✓
48 ✓
49 the: the definite article is not used before an abstract noun with general meaning
50 much: grammatically incorrect
51 well: cannot be used before 'useful'
52 ✓
53 kind: the correct structure would be 'a kind of flour'
54 a: the fixed expression is 'in fact'
55 ✓

Part 5: The Man who Furnished the World

56 hatred (verb to noun)
57 delivery (verb to noun)
58 shoppers (noun to noun)
59 choice (verb to noun)
60 addition (verb to noun)
61 throughout (preposition to preposition)
62 accusation [verb to noun]
63 argument (verb to noun)
64 products (verb to noun, plural form)
65 combinations (verb to noun, plural form)

Questions **1–30** and **41–65** = 1 mark each
Questions **31–40** = 2 marks each
The total score is adjusted to give a mark out of 40.

PAPER 4 Listening

There is a mark for each correct answer in parts 1–4.

Part 1

1 A **2** B **3** A **4** C **5** C **6** A **7** A **8** C

Part 2

9 2/two weeks
10 bucket
11 Bang with Style
12 22/twenty-two mins/minutes
13 6/six
14 hockey
15 builder
16 (the) drums
17 hammer
18 hard(-)line

Part 3

19 B **20** D **21** F **22** E **23** A

Part 4

24 B **25** B **26** C **27** B **28** C **29** A **30** A

Questions **1–30** = 1 mark each
The total score is adjusted to give a mark out of 40.

Test 5

PAPER 1 Reading

Part 1: Tweenagers

1 D: this group has become a clearly separate social and economic unit
2 F: pocket money has risen by 32%
3 B: From eight onwards other influences become important
4 I: they want to fit in with their peer group
5 A: not very likely to question what they see and hear
6 G: Most children of today get ... a lot more freedom of choice.
7 E: but they are still just children

Part 2: Design your own website

8 A: Incorrect: He makes reference to people as part of his job.

8 B: Incorrect: He deals with enquiries, but makes no mention of enjoyment.
8 C: Incorrect: He does not mention teaching.
8 D: Correct: 'loves the variety' and 'so many subjects'.
9 A: Incorrect: The option contradicts the phrase 'must-see'.
9 B: Correct: 'a destination' is somewhere people arrive at/go to.
9 C: Incorrect: The text does not say this about websites in general.
9 D: Incorrect: No details are given about the preparation.
10 A: Incorrect: 'He had no idea people shared his passion.'
10 B: Incorrect: It is not stated that he wanted to make money.
10 C: Incorrect: Pete Bennett is interested in flags, not the web advertiser.
10 D: Correct: 'He'd been fascinated by flags since boyhood'.
11 A: Incorrect: He already had 1.5 million hits a month, which was the problem.
11 B: Incorrect: The 'trebled fee' is mentioned but we don't know whether it was actually implemented.
11 C: Incorrect: No mention is made of this.
11 D: Correct: 'he couldn't afford to spend that amount of money on a hobby without any benefit to himself' and 'his hobby provides him with a small income'.
12 A: Correct: This refers back to 'selling products that people want' in the opening sentence of paragraph.
12 B: Incorrect: They are not mentioned in this context.
12 C: Incorrect: There is no reference made to them.
12 D: Incorrect: The woman who tells fortunes is the product advertiser.
13 A: Incorrect: There is no mention of addresses.
13 B: Incorrect: We are not told that this is the case.
13 C: Correct: 'has probably made a mistake in their programming'.
13 D: Incorrect: The reference is to people clicking on a site.
14 A: Incorrect: It appears straightforward but isn't.
14 B: Incorrect: There is no mention of the quality of instruction guides.
14 C: Correct: 'unless you're very skilled, you're likely to run into problems'.
14 D: Incorrect: This is not stated.
15 A: Correct: 'this is big business'.
15 B: Incorrect: This is not stated.
15 C: Incorrect: This is not stated.
15 D: Incorrect: This is not stated.

Part 3: She's the First Ever Professor of Pop

16 H: Link between 'having children' and 'her children had grown up'.
17 D: Link between 'The Open University … developing a course' and 'the course combined … '.
18 F: Link between 'number of women … is few' and 'it is a strongly male environment'.
19 B: Link between earlier sentences in this paragraph and concluding sentence in the same paragraph.
20 E: Contrastive link between Whiteley's youth and 'Now, however, …'.
21 G: Link between 'Popular Music Course' and 'This course is a mixture … '.

Part 4: Cat-watching

22 C: you can increase your chances of seeing one if you go on a river cruise
23 B: it's worth visiting a Project Tiger Reserve
24 B: you'll never forget it
25 B: I realised a huge male tiger was staring out at me
26/7 B: There are probably fewer than 7,000 left
26/7 C: In Central America there are thought to be only a few hundred
28 A: If you're hoping to see all three big cats

29 A: Lions are the only truly social cats … living in groups
30 C: I spent eight months … and only saw a jaguar once during the whole time
31 B: I saw my first one at dusk
32 B: Tigers are so beautiful, orange and stripy
33 A: they are like spirits from another world
34 C: and many people will see cheetahs and leopards
35 B: you are likely to be given a fixed route

Questions **1–21** = 2 marks each
Questions **22–35** = 1 mark each
The total score is adjusted to give a mark out of 40.

PAPER 2   Writing

Part 1
Question 1

Style: Formal letter. Avoid informal expressions.
Content: 1 Give information about the background to your complaint; point out that you sent all your personal details a month ago.
2 Ask what has happened to your photograph.
3 Ask why they only sent you two names and addresses and not six.
4 Point out that you have received no letters.
5 Ask why you were sent a bill if the service is free.

Part 2
Question 2

Style: Formal.
Content: 1 Describe where you would like to go on holiday
2 Explain reasons for choosing one particular place; give concrete examples of its attractions.

Question 3

Style: Informal.
Content: 1 Respond to your friend's suggestion.
2 Suggest an accessible place to meet so your friend will not get lost.
3 Suggest places you could see or things you could do together in a short time.
4 End your letter appropriately.

Question 4

Style: Semi-formal.
Content: 1 Describe your favourite sport.
2 Explain whether you enjoy it as a spectator or as a participant, or both of these.

Question 5(a)

Style: Formal or neutral.
Content: Say whether you agree or disagree with this statement. Explain the reasons for your opinion with reference to the ending of the book.

Question 5(b)

Style: Informal.
Content: Tell your friend about the book you have been reading. Describe the character you like most and why (e.g. attractive personality, role within the story, sympathetic person etc.) and give examples from the text. Describe the character you like least and why (e.g. unpleasant person, dishonest, selfish etc.) End your letter appropriately.

The two parts of the Writing Paper have equal marks.
The total score is adjusted to give a mark out of 40.

PAPER 3 Use of English

Part 1: The Dodo Lives On

1 A: Only word that makes sense in this context.
2 D: In the context of a mystery, the stories 'surround' the bird.
3 B: 'separate fact from fiction' is a fixed expression.
4 B: 'of all time' is a fixed expression.
5 A: A and B both collocate but only A makes sense in context.
6 C: Only 'originated' can apply to where the bird first developed.
7 B: This is used here to mean 'transported'.
8 D: The second part of this sentence clarifies how people regarded the dodo; 'curiosity' embodies 'attraction' and 'fascination'.
9 B: 'suffer a fate' is a fixed expression.
10 C: Forms phrasal verb 'come across', meaning 'find by accident'.
11 C: Only word that collocates with 'record'.
12 A: Only word correct in context.
13 B: Word with correct meaning.
14 A: Although 'telling' collocates with 'truth', it does not make sense in this context.
15 C: Only word that collocates with 'easy'.

Part 2: Napping Is Good for You

16 to (preposition): fixed phrase 'according to'
17 every (determiner): meaning 'all'
18 Yet/(But (conjunction): to contrast with idea expressed in previous sentence
19 than (conjunction): follows 'rather'
20 majority (noun): followed by 'of'
21 has (auxiliary verb): completes Present perfect
22 is (auxiliary verb): passive construction with the Present simple
23 although/but/whereas/while/when (conjunction): to contrast with idea expressed in first part of the sentence
24 who (relative pronoun): refers back to 'chronobiologists'
25 minute (noun, in combination here to form an adjective): make sure you don't add an 's'!
26 the (definite article): refers to a specific part of the day
27 find (verb): forms phrasal verb 'find out'
28 how (adverb)
29 most/very (adverb): + adjective
30 after (adverb): refers to a point later in time

Part 3

31 unless you have got **|** one: 'unless' means 'if not'
32 her mother **|** no longer worked: reported speech
33 is said **|** to be thinking: active to passive
34 blamed me for **|** having missed/missing: blame + for
35 without you **|** to advise: 'advice' (noun) to 'advise' (verb) **or** if you had not **|** advised: third conditional
36 last time **|** I saw my: Present perfect to Past simple
37 is less **|** expensive than: comparative to 'less' + adjective **or** is not so/as expensive **|** as: not/so + adjective + as
38 was astonished **|** to find: noun to adjective + infinitive
39 having hurt/hurting **|** his hand: despite + -ing
40 don't we **|** go to/and: why + auxiliary + verb

Part 4

41 ✓
42 a: the indefinite article cannot be used with 'water'
43 quite: cannot be use with 'saw', meaning 'look' as opposed to 'understand'
44 own: incorrect in terms of meaning
45 up: 'fetch' does not need a particle
46 ✓
47 ✓
48 the: the abstract noun 'safety' does not need the definite article
49 out: 'started' by itself is all that is needed
50 ✓
51 been: grammatically incorrect
52 ✓
53 such: 'such a' would be possible but not 'a such'
54 be: grammatically incorrect
55 ✓

Part 5: The Oxford and Cambridge University Boat Race

56 founders (verb to noun, plural form)
57 successfully (noun to adverb)
58 amazing (verb to adjective)
59 popularity (adjective to noun)
60 distribution (verb to noun)
61 length (adjective to noun)
62 unpleasant (verb to negative adjective by adding prefix)
63 occasionally (noun to adverb)
64 dramatic (noun to adjective)
65 embarrassment (verb to noun)

Questions **1–30** and **41–65** = 1 mark each
Questions **31–40** = 2 marks each
The total score is adjusted to give a mark out of 40.

PAPER 4 Listening

There is a mark for each correct answer in parts 1–4.

Part 1

1 A 2 A 3 C 4 B 5 B 6 B 7 C 8 A

Part 2: Hardacre College

9 (main) square
10 bus
11 trees
12 Staff
13 lifts
14 shops
15 (the) theatre
16 computers
17 8000/eight thousand
18 open day

Part 3

19 B 20 F 21 D 22 A 23 C

Part 4

24 C 25 B 26 A 27 A 28 C 29 B 30 B

Questions **1–30** = 1 mark each
The total score is adjusted to give a mark out of 40.

Test 6

PAPER 1 Reading

Part 1

1 C: succeeded at the age of twenty-four where many others have failed
2 A: and stared death in the face more than once
3 H: thousands of people gathered on the shore to cheer her on
4 G: a small woman ... brave little Ellen

5 B: this kind of reporting seems particularly insulting and depressing

6 E: she herself has remained modest

Part 2

7 A: Incorrect: We don't know that her parents would prefer to ignore her.

7 B: Incorrect: We are not told that they are chatting together.

7 C: Correct: Maria hears them but does not reply and they do not repeat their remarks.

7 D: Incorrect: Maria records what she sees and hears, so she is clearly not asleep.

8 A: Incorrect: There is no mention that this is how she feels.

8 B: Incorrect: People talk but 'expect you to say particular things'.

8 C: Incorrect: Other children are not mentioned

8 D: Correct: 'And they usually end up saying what you expected them to.'

9 A: Incorrect: Maria does not say this.

9 B: Correct: This is implied by 'Grown-ups ... spent much time telling each other what the weather was like, or wondering aloud if one thing would happen or another.'

9 C: Incorrect: Maria thinks the opposite.

9 D: Incorrect: She does not say this.

10 A: Correct: This is implied by 'but somehow her mother was always about to go out ... she had gone.'

10 B: Incorrect: This is not implied.

10 C: Incorrect: This is not implied.

10 D: Incorrect: This is not implied.

11 A: Incorrect: Her father can hear but doesn't think what she says is of any importance.

11 B: Incorrect: He is clearly not making any effort.

11 C: Correct: He is physically there, but removed from his daughter mentally although he means well.

11 D: Incorrect: He does not seem to respond.

12 A: Correct: 'it' refers back to 'what they said' in previous phrase.

12 B: Incorrect: There is no previous mention of this.

12 C: Incorrect: This is not referred to in the paragraph.

12 D: Incorrect: This is not referred to in the paragraph.

13 A: Incorrect: Maria does not say that is what interests her most.

13 B: Incorrect: 'never mind about that' indicates that she is not interested in what her father tells her about the house and its history.

13 C: Correct: 'Good, I shall like having my own swing.'

13 D: Incorrect: Even though the house is not what she was expecting it does not interest her more than the swing.

Part 3: A Garden for Palna Children's Home

14 C: Link between £50,000 and 'this money was used'.

15 H: Contrastive link between UK and India: 'different environment'.

16 F: Link between 'the Taj Mahal palace' and 'This white marble monument'.

17 D: Link between 'a large Neem tree' and 'substances from this tree'.

18 I: Link between the size of garden and the design they created.

19 G: Link between 'concrete drainage pipes' and 'The pipes were dug into the ground'.

20 B: Link with reference in previous paragraph to The Terror Run.

Part 4: Young Businesses

21 C: but the manager turned me down

22 A: because I was out of work

23 B: I'm thinking of setting up a mail order business

24 C: My parents lent me the money

25/6 A: I employ a staff of three

25/6 B: I've now got someone working for me

27 D: I used to embroider scarves for friends for birthday presents

28 A: I saw an article in the local newspaper

29 D: They send me the scarves made by their own design team

30/1 C: so it's hours of work

30/1 D: and takes hours to do

32 C: my business has grown to such an extent that I actually rent three rooms

33 D: And halfway through my degree course

34 A: B says 'my products are quite expensive'; C says 'A wig is very expensive'; D says 'it's a very expensive decorative technique'.

35 C: I make wigs for people in show business ... on stage night after night

Questions **1–20** = 2 marks each
Questions **21–35** = 1 mark each
The total score is adjusted to give a mark out of 40.

PAPER 2   Writing

Part 1
Question 1

Style: Formal letter. Avoid informal expressions.
Content: 1 Give information about yourself and why you are writing.
2 Ask about months, dates and how long you are expected to spend there.
3 Ask how you get to the centre of the forest.
4 Ask about accommodation, food and ages of other people.
5 Ask what the 'special clothing' is and whether you need to bring anything yourself.
6 Ask for further information, based on the advertisement.

Part 2
Question 2

Style: Neutral to formal.
Content: 1 What had happened at the beginning of the day to cause 'tears'?
2 How did things develop?
3 Justify the ending, i.e. that the day ended happily.

Question 3

Style: Formal; write clear paragraphs, perhaps using subheadings.
Content: 1 Describe where the concert took place
2 Mention the concert programme.
3 Say what you personally enjoyed.
4 Say whether you think other students would like such a concert.

Question 4

Style: Formal.
Content: 1 Say whether you agree or disagree with the statement.
2 Give reasons for your opinion and support your argument with some facts.

Question 5(a)

Style: Formal or neutral.
Content: Say whether you agree or disagree with this statement. Explain the reasons for your opinion with concrete examples.

Question 5(b)

Style: Formal or neutral.
Content: Say why you are recommending the book. Mention some things or events in the story that you think would make a good film.

The two parts of the Writing Paper have equal marks.
The total score is adjusted to give a mark out of 40.

PAPER 3   Use of English

Part 1: Circus Children

1 C **2** B **3** A **4** C **5** D **6** C **7** A **8** C **9** B **10** A
11 D **12** B **13** A **14** C **15** B

Part 2: Peter Benchley Likes Sharks

16 based
17 whose
18 and
19 fact
20 contrast
21 up
22 wiped
23 the
24 on
25 example/instance
26 it
27 spent
28 from
29 weighed
30 as

Part 3

31 turned down **|** my offer
32 make a **|** complaint
33 so that visitors **|** can enjoy
34 you mind **|** carrying
35 regret **|** having missed **or** regret **|** missing
36 whether she **|** had bought
37 was a **|** fifteen-hour
38 such a bad **|** speller (that)
39 gets me **|** down
40 did **|** you become

Part 4

41 their
42 at
43 have
44 the
45 ✓
46 ✓
47 long
48 gone
49 still
50 with
51 ✓
52 much
53 ✓
54 so
55 more

Part 5: Angel of Mercy

56 daily (noun to adjective)
57 within (preposition to preposition)
58 responsibility/responsibilities (adjective to noun)
59 qualified (verb to verb)
60 training (verb to noun)
61 variety (verb to noun)
62 bravery (adjective to noun)
63 service (verb to noun)
64 Usually (adjective to adverb)
65 treatment (verb to noun)

Questions **1–30** and **41–65** = 1 mark each
Questions **31–40** = 2 marks each
The total score is adjusted to give a mark out of 40.

PAPER 4   Listening

There is a mark for each correct answer in parts 1–4.

Part 1

1 C **2** C **3** B **4** A **5** B **6** B **7** C **8** A

Part 2

9 film
10 snakes
11 10/ten years
12 1950
13 white
14 wild life/wildlife
15 pressures
16 tire
17 (news)papers
18 forests

Part 3

19 E **20** C **21** F **22** B **23** A

Part 4

24 F **25** T **26** T **27** F **28** F **29** F **30** T

Questions **1–30** = 1 mark each
The total score is adjusted to give a mark out of 40.

Test 7

PAPER 1   Reading

Part 1: Slow train to China

1 D: an attendant ... looked after us
2 B: I was puzzled over how to get any water from the taps
3 I: the train chugged gently ... the train still chugging
4 E: food was provided by the country you happen to be passing through at the time
5 A: settled into a peaceful train life
6 G: They had come to buy from the traders
7 C: we came back feeling we had been away for months

Part 2: Weather forecasting

8 A: which has comparatively few climate extremes
9 D: the worst that can usually happen is that they get wet (because they have no warning)
10 B: For business, the effects are far more serious. (The list gives an idea of the range.)
11 B: up until then forecasters had relied on human observers ...
12 D: this system has certain disadvantages
13 C: Some commercial aircraft ...
14 C: Corbyn's forecasts are used by insurance companies who want to plan months in advance.

Part 3: Fast Work for Fast Food

15 G: Link between 'the night before' and 'last night' and 'Nothing is where it should be.'
16 E: Link between 'before we could begin the day's work' and 'My first job' and 'I fill a sink with water'.
17 B: Link between 'The chefs' and 'These are the people' and 'They swan around'.
18 I: Continues list of complaints by repeating structure 'If ... , then ...'.
19 C: Links with next sentence 'This is when ... '.
20 A: Link with 'deliveries of food and drink' and the writer having to 'sort them out'.

21 F: Link between 'the lunchtime rush is dying down' and 'However, I don't get anything to eat until 6 that evening' and 'I'm too tired to eat'.

Part 4: Who Broke Your Heart?

22 D: not knowing what to say
23 B: I paid for my boyfriend ... I'm not good enough to be your boyfriend any more.
24 D: He was a year older than me.
25 C: I still think about her and wonder what she's doing.
26 A: Everybody my age has had their heart broken.
27 C: she'd come to South Africa at Christmas
28 A: A girl called Maria broke my heart when I first went to university.
29/30 A: I still don't really understand why she finished with me
29/30 C: I wrote a long letter asking Sonya to explain what was going on. I never heard back
31 D: it was love at first sight
32 B: I tried to persuade him to change his mind
33 D: it was probably more to do with me asking him than the other way round
34 C: I didn't believe her
35 B: We decided we'd go on holiday with a group of friends

Questions **1–21** = 2 marks each
Questions **22–35** = 1 mark each
The total score is adjusted to give a mark out of 40.

PAPER 2   Writing

Part 1
Question 1
Style: Formal letter. Avoid informal expressions.
Content:　1 Give information about your class and why you are writing.
　　2 Ask for more details about the kind of event that you would like, based on their list.
　　3 Ask about special rates for students.
　　4 Ask about costs for supplying food and drink.
　　5 Ask for a time and date for an appointment to discuss things further.

Part 2
Question 2
Style: Semi-formal.
Content:　1 The experience must be amusing to the reader.
　　2 Explain why the experience was amusing.

Question 3
Style: Informal.
Content:　1 Describe your country's traditional food.
　　2 Focus on one particular speciality.
　　3 Explain how to make this speciality: necessary ingredients, preparation and cooking (if appropriate).

Question 4
Style: Formal.
Content:　1 Say whether you agree or disagree with the statement.
　　2 Give reasons for your opinion and support your argument with some facts, related to your own experience if appropriate.

Question 5(a)
Style: Formal.
Content: Discuss one relationship in the book. Explain the connection between the story and the relationship. Give some concrete examples from the text to show the connection.

Question 5(b)
Style: Formal or neutral.
Content: Say whether you agree or disagree with the statement. Discuss the beginning of the book and mention other parts of the story to support your opinion.

The two parts of the Writing Paper have equal marks.
The total score is adjusted to give a mark out of 40.

PAPER 3   Use of English

Part 1: Fun and Games
1 C　**2** B　**3** A　**4** D　**5** D　**6** B　**7** C　**8** A　**9** B　**10** C
11 B　**12** D　**13** D　**14** D　**15** C

Part 2: Functional Foods
16 on
17 is
18 Not
19 as
20 less
21 get
22 with
23 In
24 Despite
25 its
26 present
27 consist
28 which/that
29 be
30 what

Part 3
31 he is not **|** young enough
32 accused her **|** of borrowing
33 will be able **|** to afford
34 know whose **|** pen this
35 I had told **|** the truth
36 is/will be impossible **|** for me
37 is being **|** raised by
38 is **|** hardly ever
39 have run out of **|** milk
40 must get/have **|** my shoes repaired

Part 4
41 to
42 the
43 ✓
44 be
45 ✓
46 it
47 themselves
48 up
49 ✓
50 than
51 ✓
52 that
53 and
54 do
55 most

Part 5: The Recipe for Good Communication
56 misunderstanding (verb to negative noun by adding prefix)
57 clarify (adjective to verb)
58 concentration (verb to noun)
59 effectively (noun to adverb)

60 tendency (verb to noun)
61 readily (adjective to adverb)
62 fully (adjective to adverb)
63 politeness (adjective to noun)
64 relationships (noun to abstract noun, plural form)
65 essential (noun to adjective)

Questions **1–30** and **41–65** = 1 mark each
Questions **31–40** = 2 marks each
The total score is adjusted to give a mark out of 40.

PAPER 4   Listening

There is a mark for each correct answer in parts 1–4.

Part 1

1 C   **2** B   **3** B   **4** C   **5** A   **6** B   **7** C   **8** A

Part 2

9 Circle of Fear 2   **14** a small town
10 a small town   **15** hot water springs
11 3003   **16** Give it Back
12 planets   **17** mountains
13 Sometime, Never   **18** motorbike

Part 3

19 F   **20** E   **21** B   **22** A   **23** C

Part 4

24 B   **25** C   **26** C   **27** A   **28** C   **29** B   **30** C

Questions **1–30** = 1 mark each
The total score is adjusted to give a mark out of 40.

Test 8

PAPER 1   Reading

Part 1: Cyber Cafes

1 F: millions of people can use the internet
2 C: These cafes are part of the cultural scene
3 A: if you want to keep in touch with friends and family
4 E: as the cafe fills up, the price goes up
5 B: e-mail is cheaper than the telephone
6 D: become communication centres for these workers ... who neither have nor want traditional office space

Part 2: My Holidays

7 B: I'm a bit of a coward
8 C: I decided to go skiing for the first time
9 B: but how do I stop?
10 D: we got to know the chef quite well ... one of the waiters took us to visit his uncle
11 A: The trouble with me is that I have a genuine problem with mosquitoes – they absolutely adore me!
12 B: You could see the infection disappear
13 D: pleasantly exhausted
14 A: I just want the opportunity to refresh myself.

Part 3: Fears and Phobias

15 D: Link between being prevented 'from leading a normal life' and 'it means you cannot ...'.
16 H: Link between what you 'can be afraid of' and 'Apparently, the list of phobias gets longer every day'.
17 F: Link between 'understanding what a phobia is' and 'With this understanding'.

18 C: Link between 'You may think that you are computer phobic' and 'But that's not the same as being really 'mechanophobic'.
19 E: Introduces 'true phobia' compared with the previous paragraph.
20 G: Link between 'phobias can be described in three main ways', 'There are social phobias', 'Then there are panic disorders' and 'thirdly, specific phobias'.

Part 4: Summer Schools

21 D: there is no other school like ours; we provide a novel approach to studying English
22 A: individual study bedrooms equipped with private bathroom, TV and computer
23 C: for the duration of your course you will be ... with an experienced member of staff
24 A: In the afternoon you are free to choose from ... excursions
25 B. Teenagers aged between 13 and 17
26 B: Accommodation is provided with local families.
27 A: places are limited
28 C: located in popular seaside towns
29 B: Evenings are free
30 A: individual study bedrooms
31 D: There is also a large library on board
32 C: we make every effort to cater for individual dietary requirements
33 B: This is followed by afternoon activities
34 A: optional activities including ... drama
35 D: Our weekly courses end with a day's excursion by train

Questions **1–20** = 2 marks each
Questions **21–35** = 1 mark each
The total score is adjusted to give a mark out of 40.

PAPER 2   Writing

Part 1
Question 1

Style: Formal letter. Avoid informal expressions.
Content: 1 Give information about you and your friends, your ages and why you are writing.
2 Ask about days and times you are likely to be needed.
3 Suggest positive things you and your friends could do.
4 Ask for more information about 'jobs around the home'.
5 Ask for further information, e.g. money for petrol, visiting with a friend etc.

Part 2
Question 2

Style: Neutral to formal.
Content: 1 Story can either end or begin with the prompt sentence.
2 What has happened to create this situation?
3 Where are you if you cannot do anything else and you cannot speak to anyone?
4 How does the story end?

Question 3

Style: Semi-formal.
Content: 1 Describe your own language learning experience(s).
2 Recommend some of the things which you find helpful.

Question 4

Style: Formal; write clear paragraphs, perhaps using subheadings.
Content: 1 Refer to one specific restaurant.
2 Mention the kind of food served in the restaurant.
3 Comment on the good or bad aspects of the service etc.
4 Include a recommendation for a particular customer e.g. students, families with children etc.

Question 5(a)

Style: Formal.
Content: Say whether you agree or disagree with the statement. Discuss whether the plot and/or the language and vocabulary make the book straightforward or complicated.

Question 5(b)

Style: Formal.
Content: Say whether you agree or disagree with the statement. Say whether the plot was exciting or boring and give concrete examples from the text. Mention any other aspects which made you feel positive or negative about the book.

The two parts of the Writing Paper have equal marks.
The total score is adjusted to give a mark out of 40.

PAPER 3   Use of English

Part 1: Shades of Meaning

1 D   2 B   3 C   4 C   5 A   6 A   7 B   8 A   9 D   10 C
11 C   12 A   13 B   14 D   15 A

Part 2: Credit Cards for Children

16 up	23 not
17 them	24 amount/sum
18 who	25 much
19 too	26 their
20 Like	27 waste
21 which/that	28 in
22 have	29 being
	30 to

Part 3

31 chocolates are **|** packed
32 am keen **|** on learning
33 is the **|** first time (that)
34 until she **|** has had
35 had fallen **|** through
36 to turn **|** off
37 you know **|** what the
38 a belief that **|** life exists
39 accept my apology **|** for being
40 has **|** a tendency

Part 4

41 ✓
42 of
43 out
44 had
45 very
46 for
47 ✓
48 enough
49 ✓
50 myself
51 ✓
52 who
53 to
54 yet
55 ✓

Part 5: Going to School in Africa

56 introduction (verb to noun)
57 teaching (verb to noun)
58 confusion (verb to noun)
59 government (verb to noun)
60 education (verb to noun)
61 expensive (noun to adjective)
62 payment(s) (verb to noun)
63 relatively (adjective to adverb)
64 possession (verb to noun)
65 minority (adjective to noun)

Questions **1–30** and **41–65** = 1 mark each
Questions **31–40** = 2 marks each
The total score is adjusted to give a mark out of 40.

PAPER 4   Listening

There is a mark for each correct answer in parts 1–4.

Part 1

1 A   2 B   3 A   4 C   5 B   6 C   7 C   8 B

Part 2

9 12/twelve-hour	14 button
10 report	15 director
11 studio	16 clothes
12 charts	17 Sleeves
13 scripts	18 jacket

Part 3

19 F   20 A   21 D   22 E   23 C

Part 4

24 C   25 B   26 B   27 A   28 C   29 B   30 A

Questions **1–30** = 1 mark each
The total score is adjusted to give a mark out of 40.

TAPESCRIPTS

*answers to questions are underlined in each script

Test 1   PART 1

You will hear people talking in eight different situations. For Questions 1–8, choose the best answer, A, B or C.

1

Now if you're planning on making a quick getaway this weekend, you may want to rearrange your plans. As if it wasn't difficult enough last weekend with the train strike and the fog delaying flights midweek, <u>there are a number of motorway repairs being carried out over the next few days</u> which are bound to affect journey times, so for more detailed information phone the travel hot-line on ...

2

A: It's a number of years now, Lionel, since you brought out your illustrated book on garden plants but I know you're very busy with another project.

B: Yes, I am. When I was researching the book on flowers, I became quite interested in butterflies and my publisher suggested I should make them the subject of my next book. But I wasn't that keen.

A: So?

B: Well, I think it was wandering through the woods looking for plants when I first noticed how fascinating life on the <u>floor</u> of the woodland is. Quite amazing, another world in fact. <u>All kinds of tiny creatures crawling around</u>.

3

I mean, you know I wasn't looking forward to that meeting with the boss. He goes on and on and never knows when to stop, he never seems to realise that people get really bored when he starts lecturing them. Added to which of course, I was worrying over how I was going to explain that mistake I'd made. And then, would you believe it, his secretary rings to say he's been delayed and <u>he's decided not to go ahead after all so I can forget my</u> <u>appointment</u>!

4

Following on from last month's successful family concert which was a sell-out, National Promotions are pleased to announce their new series of concerts beginning in the autumn with a really exciting offer. Whatever price of ticket you purchase, <u>we will match it with a free ticket at the same price.</u> So bring along a friend or one of the family and enjoy a concert for <u>half the normal price.</u> Don't forget to book early if you want to enjoy a candle-lit supper before or after the concert in one of our restaurants. For further details, contact our booking office on ...

5

A: Can I help you, sir? Would you like the porter to take your suitcase to your room?

B: No, thank you. I'm afraid I can't get my case unlocked. <u>I usually carry two keys but I can't find either at the moment, so I wonder if you have one</u>. It's a standard lock, nothing special. I've tried to break it with my penknife without success even though it's only small. I suppose I could just cut into the top of it as it's fairly soft material but then I'll have ruined it and have to buy another one.

A: I'll see what I can do for you, sir, I know we have some. Just wait a few minutes and I'll have a look.

6

It's always exciting when a new exhibition opens. <u>Especially one where you know some of your own work is hanging.</u> There's also the opportunity to buy some of the work on display. I'm not so keen on meeting new people but I do like gossiping with friends about the new artists and what they're up to. No more painting in oils for this generation, they're far more adventurous. I love looking at those huge canvases covered with sand, bits of glass and metal, things that in my day we would've considered to be rubbish!

7

Hi, Celia, it's me. Yes I'm at the airport. No, no, I've got my passport – unlike last time when I forgot it. Look, <u>I'm afraid I've left my diary</u>. No, not the big desk one, <u>the one I keep in my handbag</u> – it's on top of my laptop computer. I know, I was going to bring my laptop but I just couldn't carry anything else. Well, if it's not there, it'll be in the top drawer of my desk. Yes? Brilliant. Can you get here in the next hour? I'll wait at check in – and thank you!

8

Hello. My name's Birch, Alan Birch, that's right, yes, from the studio. Yes, my usual please, no, hang on, I think I'd like a different topping. Can I have mushrooms instead of onion? I'm sorry this is bad line, I can hardly hear you, it's breaking up. What? I'm in my car, yes, stuck in a traffic jam. I'm absolutely starving. Look, <u>can you get the boy to go round to my office – opposite the studio</u> – and I'll pick it up from there? Sure, I'll be in my car. If he waits on the pavement outside, I'll pay him when I get there. Great. Thanks a lot.

Test 1   PART 2

You will hear part of a radio interview with a man who is the director of an Environmental Centre. For Questions 9–18, complete the sentences.

Interviewer: I have with me in the studio today Jeffrey Osland, who is the director of an Environmental Centre in mid Wales. Jeffrey, welcome.

Jeffrey Osland: Thank you.

Interviewer: Jeffrey, what exactly is an Environmental Centre?

Jeffrey Osland: Good question. Well, I suppose you could say that basically we're interested in protecting the environment and that means looking at alternative technologies to provide energy for the future.

Interviewer: I'm still not sure I understand. What does the Centre do?

Jeffrey Osland: It does a whole range of things. We opened <u>twenty-five years</u> ago but in the last ten years we've considerably expanded our activities and now we have lots of working displays. <u>These displays are built on the site which we occupy in the heart of the countryside and include ways to use the sun and wind for power</u>, as well as low energy buildings and different kinds of farming. We're open to the public all year round and last year we had over 80,000 visitors. Everyone is welcome. We get casual visitors, tourists, environmental specialists and lots of school children, especially <u>primary school children who are doing a project on some aspect of the environment</u>. We also run courses for secondary schools, universities and overseas students and these courses are residential, obviously, because people come and stay for short periods of time. <u>Most of the courses last three days</u> although in the summer we run week-long courses.

Interviewer: Goodness, I didn't realise it was such a big operation.

Jeffrey Osland: Oh yes. Altogether we have accommodation for about 70 people. When I say accommodation, I don't mean a luxury hotel! What we have are wooden cabins, which contain between two and five beds, and are very simply furnished, although we do have a few single rooms available. There are common rooms for relaxation, with facilities for making drinks. We also grow all our own food and meals are served in the Centre restaurant. As you might expect we only serve vegetarian food, no meat whatsoever. We don't allow people to bring meat in with them either. But we have an excellent chef who prepares really imaginative vegetarian food and I've yet to hear anyone complain. The atmosphere is very relaxed and informal, but we do forbid people to smoke in the buildings.

Interviewer: So, if I wanted to do a short course, what kind of thing could I do?

Jeffrey Osland: It would depend on your interests. You could do one of our general courses on Natural Gardening. You'd learn about nature – garden wildlife, herbs, climbing plants and plants which have particular scents or perfumes. Or you could do one of our more specialised courses on Waterless Toilets.

Interviewer: Waterless toilets?!

Jeffrey Osland: That's right. It's our most popular course. There's a big demand for it from countries where there are serious water shortages. We have designed a system which does not require water, it's a dry system. Our system helps people use their limited supplies for essential things like washing and drinking as water is very precious in many parts of the world. Other courses show people how to save forests, birds and animals.

Interviewer: How amazing. It sounds fascinating. Are these courses expensive?

Jeffrey Osland: Not really. In order to be fair we operate a varied price structure, which charges people what they can afford. For example, if you're in full-time employment, you pay more than if you're out of work and haven't got a job. And for people who are not able to pay anything at all we have a fund which was set up by the Centre a few years ago. This helps us to pay someone's costs, including their travel costs from home to the Centre. So we never turn anyone away, although we can only help a small number of people each year as we do not make a huge profit.

Interviewer: So if I want to go on a course, how do I apply?

Jeffrey Osland: You need an application form which you can get by ...

Test 1   PART 3

You will hear five different people talking about the importance of modern inventions. For Questions 19–23, choose from the list A–F the reason each speaker gives for the importance of the invention to them personally. Use the letters only once. There is one extra letter which you do not need to use.

1
I used to think television was the most brilliant invention because you could sit in an armchair and have a window on the world. But in the last couple of years I've changed my mind. For me now the best thing ever is the mobile phone. I mean they used to be so heavy and not that attractive to carry around. But now they're tiny and light – I never go anywhere without mine. And you can buy personalised covers and even change the covers to match what you're wearing. Some of my friends are so cool – they dye their hair to match their phones and their watch straps as well. I mean how amazing is that?!

2
There are so many things that I think I couldn't live without. My mum moans at me because I can't be bothered to cook. But I mean who needs to cook when there are so many takeaway places. Nor can I imagine life without radio and TV, but if there's one thing that's made a big difference to my life it's the cash machine. I can relax about getting money and not rush around trying to get to a bank before it closes. I was always running out of cash but now at any time of day or night I can turn up at a hole in the wall, put my card in and magic – there's the money! No hassle.

3
I know there are all sorts of wonderful inventions and it's easy to take everything for granted. Like electricity – life as we know it would be impossible without it, I mean we depend on it for almost everything. But for me personally it's the car which I think has massively changed people's lives. I know that holidays in space are more or less a reality now, and you can reach any part of the world by plane. But it's the ease of the car, the fact that it offers you such freedom. Like you wake up in the morning and think where would I like to go today? And you just do it!

4
I think some inventions are such fun. All these computer games, I really love them. And the fact that they're hand-held is great. They help me relax when I'm feeling stressed and take my mind off whatever's worrying me, although I suppose I could live without them if I had to. But there's no way I could live without my e-mail. When we all left school last year, I made sure I had everyone's e-mail address and that means we all keep in touch and get to meet up with each other. And if we can't meet, then at least we know each other's news and what we're all doing.

5
I hate being without my electric toothbrush, but I know that's silly because most people use an ordinary toothbrush and never think twice about it. But there is one invention which has really saved my life and that's my electronic diary. My girlfriend bought me one because she got so fed up with me forgetting arrangements. I've no excuse now for forgetting anything, even her birthday is programmed into it! They used to be dead expensive but now they've come down in price and I use mine all the time.

Test 1   PART 4

You will hear an radio interview with a research scientist. For Questions 24–30, decide which of the statements are true and which are false. Write T for True or F for False in the boxes provided.

Interviewer: My guest on today's programme 'What's New in Medicine' is Andrew Taylor. Andrew, welcome to the programme. Now I know there've been some pretty exciting developments recently in your area of work and one, in particular, which is close to your heart is the 'smart pill'.

Andrew Taylor: Well, I guess 'smart pill' is just a convenient term for what I think is going to be a pretty important development in medical technology. But what set us off looking at this in the laboratory is the fact that thousands of people each year are admitted to hospital because they have accidentally taken the wrong medicine or the wrong dose of medicine.

Interviewer: How come? Surely it must be quite difficult to do that?

Andrew Taylor: Not really. There're people who perhaps take quite a lot of medicine, tablets and so on, particularly elderly people, and so it's not difficult for them to pick up the wrong bottle or packet without realising. And then there're people with poor eyesight who can mistake one bottle for another, and for them the risk of taking the wrong medicine is even higher. People are very sensitive and they worry about getting things wrong and getting into trouble with their doctor.

Interviewer: I see – but it's not their fault.

Andrew Taylor: Of course not. So what we've come up with is a simple system for reading pill labels out loud. And this will be of great benefit to people whose sight is not very good. We've been experimenting with the system and generally speaking, most people are both amazed and delighted with it.

Interviewer: How does it work?

Andrew Taylor: Well, the system consists of special labels which contain tiny microchips. The microchip contains all the important information about the medicine for that particular patient. Their name, how many to take – if it's pills – and when to take them, such as before or after meals.

Interviewer: What if people are still unsure about something?

Andrew Taylor: Each microchip also has the name and address of their doctor as well as a phone number which people can ring if they have any questions.

Interviewer: So what is it that speaks out loud? The label?

Andrew Taylor: No, no. It's a thing called a reader. When a patient wants to take their medicine, they press a button on a small thing called a reader. You know the things that check-out assistants use in supermarkets which read the barcodes, the labels on whatever you're buying, well, the readers are like that. The reader sends out a radio signal to the microchip which returns the information recorded on the label. The reader then speaks this out loud.

Interviewer: Don't some people find that rather scary?

Angus Taylor: A few maybe. Admittedly the voice is electronic and some people are put off by new technology. But once they get used to the voice, which is quite soft – it doesn't shout at them – they become confident that they are taking the right quantity of medicine and at the right time and that's really reassuring. And everyone agrees that without the new technology they could end up in hospital.

Test 2 PART 1

You'll hear people talking in eight different situations. For Questions 1–8, choose the best answer, A, B or C.

1 .
You can't fail but be impressed by Marco Lyneham's latest achievement. At the International Stadium last night he managed to shave one tenth of a second off his fastest time yet. I mean not only does this man already hold three gold medals, but last month he was voted Sports Personality of the Year and presented with a handsome cheque as well as the splendid cup that he gets to keep for the year ahead. You'd've thought that things couldn't have got any better for him, but he's proved all of us wrong!

2
A: Can you let me have that recipe you promised?

B: Which one? The one for the orange and carrot soup we had last night?

A: No, I know how to make that, it's quite straightforward. It's the dish we had at Mike's party. It was delicious, d'you remember? It had potatoes, peppers and onions in it and we ate it cold with bread. I thought I'd make it and take it with us when we're out walking this weekend. We always take a packed lunch, and I thought this would be really nice with some salad and not too heavy to carry.

3
I know that many children are very keen to keep a pet. Some children are happy with a goldfish or a rabbit, others want a puppy and forget that it'll need exercising each day and they'll have to take it for regular long walks. Obviously some animals need looking after more than others. Cats are fairly independent creatures, and will disappear for long periods at a time, whereas dogs are more home-loving. Don't let your child spoil an animal by overfeeding it. I've seen some kids who think they're being really kind when they give a pet large helpings of food and then they wonder why the animal is so overweight.

4
I'm amazed at the number of people who turn up on the first day and know absolutely nothing about the places they're going to see. I mean when you think of all the travel programmes on the TV and the radio, the information on the internet, all the travel writers who fill columns in the newspapers and magazines throughout the year ... These people must have seen a brochure when they booked their holiday, surely? They sit there in the coach and expect me to tell them everything they need to know.

5
... so at the end I went up to him to ask him a question and he says, 'Where were you last lesson?' And I say, 'I was here. You gave me back my essay.' So he looked a bit embarrassed at that and I say, 'I need some extra help before the exams because I missed quite a lot when I was ill last month.' And he says he's too busy to fit in more lessons, I'll have to ask one of the other students. Well, I'm not going to, it's his job and I'm not going to take an exam which I know I'm not ready for so that's it, I'm not going again. I'll take the exam next year instead.

6
Hundreds of years ago actors wandered from town to town, village to village putting on plays in very informal surroundings. Sometimes they didn't even bother with costumes but there was always music, simple music probably played on a pipe like our modern-day recorder. For people in those days, these wandering players were a great treat and any performance was exciting. The plays took place outside, usually in the market place or somewhere central and this book is especially good on the different locations which could be anything from a wooden platform in the village square to a clearing under a tree.

7
A: … it was one of the most interesting exhibitions I've ever seen.

B: I couldn't agree more. I'd no idea people actually wore special clothes.

A: Well, those early vehicles didn't have a roof, so you had to protect yourself. And those poor people whose job it was to walk in front of the car in all weathers meant they had to be properly dressed, too. Even the first buses were open-top and, come to think of it, so were the first trains.

B: I suppose you must have been able to enjoy the scenery, though, and going so slowly probably meant you had a good view of everything!

8
I love this new season's fashion for little handbags. Mind you, they're pretty useless because you can't put more than a comb inside, so whoever designed them obviously didn't intend them to hold anything. The colours are nice but what's really attractive are the little glass beads which are sewn into the fabric. There are no real patterns on the bags, just thousands of these little things that sparkle and glitter as you walk. I imagine they're all hand stitched, which is why even the tiniest bags are quite expensive.

Test 2 PART 2

You will hear part of a radio programme in which a man talks about his childhood in Australia. For Questions 9–18, complete the sentences.

Interviewer: Each week we invite different people into the studio to talk about their childhood. This week William Cameron talks about growing up in Australia.

William Cameron: Australia is a huge country and I grew up on the north-west coast. The southern parts of Australia get snow but there is never any snow in the north. However, we do have a wet season and I remember when I was a child lying in bed at night, listening to the rain clattering on the tin roof of our house. Most houses were wooden but the roofs were generally metal. The noise was absolutely deafening and when I got up in the morning, it was usually impossible to get to school because the river had flooded. If the storm was really fierce, then we would stick tape across our windows in the hope that by making them stronger the glass wouldn't get blown out. My parents also had to keep supplies of candles and torches as the electricity supply would regularly get cut off at the height of a storm.

Another thing that happens in the wet season is that the tracks – there are no proper roads as such – get flooded and become impassable so we had to fly. In the dry season we travelled by jeep or pick-up trucks, but anything and everything that people needed at other times was delivered by air – food, the post, light bulbs, household things – there's no local shop. Even if your friends came to visit, they would come by mail plane, too. Looking back I suppose life was quite lonely, but one of the things I really loved was the feeling of space and the freedom of being the only person for miles around. The wildlife and the landscape were wonderful.

One of the best memories of my childhood was riding my bike around the sugar cane fields. After the cane was harvested the farmers would burn the land and I remember the rats running out from amongst the cane as the fire spread. The local name for them is bandicoots and my friends and I used to chase them away so they wouldn't get hurt.

When I was older we moved to central Australia near Alice Springs, where the summer was much hotter and drier. Winter nights were very cold, however, and we would have to put on the heaters at night and keep them on throughout the night. In areas like Alice Springs which are so far away from towns, young children don't go to school. At a set time each day they link up to the radio and have their lessons on air. The teachers send them work to do at home with their parents, but older children go away to boarding school, which may be as much as 1000 kilometres away, although that's not much by Australian standards. Six thousand kilometres is what we reckon to be a long distance!

As the summers are so hot people start work very early. By midday the temperatures are really high, so everyone remains inside for safety. It's so hot that it's not even possible to keep cool by swimming, although last thing at night we would swim in our pool in order to cool down. But even though the sun went down by seven o'clock, the water was still hot so it was like having a warm bath rather than a cooling swim!

Test 2   PART 3

You will hear five different people talking about what they like about their favourite restaurant. For Questions 19–23, choose from the list A–F what each speaker says. Use the letters only once. There is one extra letter which you do not need to use.

1
Where I live there are so many restaurants that I'm spoilt for choice. There are small, friendly bistros and large, noisy cafe bars. Where I choose to go depends on my mood and how I'm feeling. I quite like self-service restaurants if I want to be by myself and can't be bothered to speak to anyone. And some of the expensive places are incredibly posh. I do like dressing up occasionally, but the one that has everything, as far as I'm concerned, is nothing special to look at and is situated in a little side street. It's run by a woman called Silvia. Everything is freshly cooked and you're always made to feel welcome.

2
There are some days when all I want is to be spoilt, to be looked after by waiters attending to my every need! Good food is such a comfort. I particularly like this place where the service is excellent, the waiters know me and what I like to eat. It's a large

place but it has some wonderfully quiet corners where you can sit and watch everything that's going on around you. It's the best kind of entertainment, it's almost like being at the theatre and I get to have the best seat because I'm a regular.

3
Food and drink are very important but there has to be more if I'm going to have a really good time. I know people who will happily sit in a basement or a cellar because they like the cooking. But for me there's got to be a view, something to watch, like a sunset or waves breaking on a beach. That's why this place looking out across the water with just the cliffs and the pine trees for company is the perfect combination for me. Fortunately the food is excellent, too!

4
The supermarkets are full of exotic food and there's no shortage of cookery programmes on TV and cookery books in the bookshops. I think most of us eat and drink pretty well these days. It's not easy finding somewhere so special that it's worth the effort getting there, as well as the money it's likely to cost you. This place I know – in the middle of nowhere – is fantastic. Everything about it is original from the colour of the walls to the colour of the food. D'you know, last week the potatoes were blue!

5
I've never been able to see the point in having takeaway food. I mean, who wants to walk around eating? Part of the pleasure in eating is surely sitting somewhere comfortable, preferably with friends, soaking up the atmosphere and forgetting the rest of the world. I know of nowhere else other than this one place tucked away in the country and the moment you enter it's like being in another world. Everything is turned inwards and the focus is this enormous table simply covered with the most wonderful display of hot and cold dishes.

Test 2   PART 4

You will hear an interview with a woman who has left her own country to live abroad. For Questions 24–30, choose the best answer A, B or C.

Interviewer: Have you ever considered living abroad? Most of us these days get to travel to foreign countries either to work for a short time or, more commonly, for a holiday. The chances are you've thought how nice it would be to spend a longer period of time in that country. Well, Karin Newman has done just that. She left the UK a couple of years ago and is now back for a short time to see her friends and family. Karin, what made you decide to move abroad in the first place?

Karin Newman: Well, it was like you just said. I was on holiday in Italy with some friends and when the time came to go home, none of us wanted to leave. The weather was perfect, the scenery was wonderful and I simply didn't want to go home. And it suddenly occurred to me that there was no reason why I shouldn't stay. OK, I didn't speak the language but I had met lots of foreigners who were working there and I thought well, if they can do it, so can I.

Interviewer: You make it sound very easy.

Karin Newman: The decision itself was easy. But then it took quite a long time to make all the arrangements. Fortunately, I had some money, as I was living with my parents. I'd planned on buying a car with some of my savings so I used that money to rent a flat. But of course I still had to come back to the UK for a couple of weeks to deal with packing up my stuff and so on. The flat was a simple one-bedroom place but fully furnished and that meant I had a base to go back to. The flat my friends and I had been staying in was huge and it would've been great to stay there, but it was too expensive. So I handed in my notice at work and that was it.

Interviewer: Was there anything that you missed once you'd settled down?

Karin Newman: Well, my family certainly. Although if I'm honest it was all so different and exciting and I was so busy I didn't have time to think about things. Then after about six weeks or so <u>I began to be aware of being on my own a lot of the time</u>. People had been really kind and helpful when they realised I was new, but you can't expect that to last. And I hadn't found getting a job as easy as I'd expected. I wasn't particularly concerned because I had enough money but life was not as enjoyable as it had been.

Interviewer: So what did you do?

Karin Newman: Well, I was on the point of wondering whether I'd made a ghastly mistake when <u>my landlord, Pietro, called one evening to collect the rent</u>. He must have noticed I was looking rather down and asked me if I was all right. I said I still hadn't found a job, even though I'd written lots of letters to different language schools. <u>He clapped his hands and said 'perfect' – his wife was looking for some help in the restaurant she ran, he'd see to all the paperwork and I could start the next day.</u>

Interviewer: So, problem solved!

Karin Newman: Yes, in one sense. But my Italian was awful. I thought: I'll never understand what people are saying. I'll be hopeless and customers will get very impatient because they'll have to say everything so many times. <u>I was terrified</u>.

Interviewer: So did you turn it down?

Karin Newman: Pietro just laughed when I tried to explain how I felt. But his wife was very kind and to begin with I just worked in the kitchen, preparing vegetables, washing up, making salads and so on. She spoke very quietly and gently and I understood most of what she said, and in that way I suppose I became more confident, so <u>when the day came to take a customer's order I was fine</u>. I even smiled!

Interviewer: You've been there for two years now. Any plans to come home?

Karin Newman: Not for a while. My Italian's pretty fluent now and I've started doing some translation work for an Italian company. I've made plenty of really good friends and I'm enjoying life very much. It was certainly worth taking the risk but <u>I think I was very lucky to find myself in a situation where everything worked out. Some people have quite a difficult time, but my experience was just the opposite</u>.

Interviewer: Karin, thank you very much for talking to us.

Test 3 PART 1

You'll hear people talking in eight different situations. For Questions 1–8, choose the best answer, A, B or C.

1

Ah, good morning. I'm phoning on behalf of Marketing International. We're acting as agents for a car manufacturer. We believe that you, as a car owner, might be interested in a new model which the company is bringing out later this year. Yes, <u>your details were sent to my boss from the garage</u> where you bought your present car. Everyone who takes part in this survey has the chance to win a new car. All we ask you to do is to answer a few questions. It will take about 15 minutes ... That's great. Right, first question ...

2

It was so stupid. I've been playing netball for years and apart from a few falls when I've bruised my arms or legs quite badly, <u>I have never, ever run into anything or anyone before</u>. It was such a good match but we were one goal down and we only had about five minutes left. <u>So I caught the ball, turned to shoot it into the net and didn't realise how close I was to the post. The next minute – wham, I'd knocked myself out!</u>

3

A: Good morning. You are through to Maria. How can I help you?

B: I need to talk to someone about my mobile phone.

A: Can you tell me the problem, please?

B: Well, I bought my phone about four weeks ago and I think there must be something wrong with the battery. Even if I charge it up every night I only seem to get about 10 minutes' talking time. I took it back to the shop but they didn't want to know.

A: Oh. That sounds strange. The shop should really deal with it. <u>We'll let you have a special envelope so you can send it back to us and we'll check the battery for you</u>.

B: Right, thanks.

4

A: So, how are you fixed? Can you make next week?

B: It's not easy but I could manage an evening.

A: Evenings are difficult for me so I'd rather keep to a morning or afternoon.

B: Hmm. How long d'you think we'll need? About two or three hours, I guess.

A: At least. <u>I suggest we put this off</u>, unless you can manage the weekend.

B: You must be joking, weekends are out. OK, <u>this will obviously have to wait</u>, although it's essential that we deal with it face to face.

5

Welcome to the Royal Hospital Visitor Information Service. If you plan to visit a friend or relative in hospital, and are travelling by car, please allow plenty of time. <u>There is limited car parking space at the hospital, so you may find it more convenient to use public transport</u>. On arrival at the hospital, please check the information board at the front of the main entrance. This will give you directions to the wards. If you have a long journey and should wish to purchase light refreshments, there is a small snack bar to the left of the entrance. If you wish to find out about the condition of a relative or friend, please press 1 now ...

6

The thing is that however much you practise, you know you can always practise more. I got used to that at music college and you learn to discipline yourself to practise at least six to eight hours a day. There are days, of course, when it's more difficult than others, but <u>it's sitting there for hours by myself that is worse</u>. And then the same is true when you're performing and you have to stay overnight in a hotel. It's very rare that concert organisers will pay for anyone else to be with you.

7

I thought it was going to be interesting and I suppose it was in many ways. I've always found this particular lecturer to be really good and space travel is his thing, after all. It's how he made his name. <u>But what he said was so complex that I was lost before we were even halfway through. Quite a few people around me were whispering that they couldn't follow either</u> and they sounded quite irritated. I guess I'll have to buy his book and read and re-read it until I understand what he was saying.

8

I don't know what's wrong with her. Whatever I do she always finds something to grumble about. If it's not me, then it's my brother or her sister who's done something to upset her. I try to be patient because we'll all be old one day, and I know that since her operation she gets tired very easily. The other evening I left work late so I didn't get round to seeing her. The phone was ringing when I got home and, of course, <u>it was her complaining that most daughters</u> would make the time to call in and not work such long hours.

Test 3 PART 2

You will hear part of a radio programme in which a woman called Amelia Unwin talks about one of the most successful football clubs in the world. For Questions 9–8, complete the sentences.

Hi, and welcome to the programme in which we try to answer some of your questions about sport. A number of you have written in to ask what makes Manchester United Britain's most successful soccer club. Well, apart from the obvious answer – they've got lots of brilliant players – there're a lot of other things that go on to promote the Club which make it possible for 'Man U' to buy players for millions of pounds. And I mean millions. In the past they've paid 19 million pounds for just one player. So how come it is such a wealthy club?

Well, one way for the Club to earn money is to sell merchandise. If you look in their catalogue, you'll see you can buy anything from a pair of shorts to a woolly scarf. Some people think the prices they charge for this merchandise are quite high and I expect many parents would agree. A complete Manchester United strip costs almost 80 pounds – not cheap. But if you're selling this merchandise all over the world through a number of official shops or outlets, you begin to get an idea of the huge profits the Club can make.

Another big way to make money is to provide food and drink for fans at the football matches. And not just the fans who, for the most part want chips, burgers and hot dogs. The Club also offers entertainment on a grand scale for people who want to use the Club premises for their own purposes. For example, a large business might reward its employees with a company dinner and if it's held at a famous football club that's far more exciting than an ordinary restaurant, even if it is twice as expensive.

Then, of course, there's what's called the gate receipts – that's what the Club collects from the people who pay for a ticket to get in to watch the team play at home at Old Trafford – the name of Man U's football ground. The ground can hold up to 67,000 spectators and is usually sold out for all first team games. Many fans have season tickets, which means they've paid in advance for all the games in a particular period, but although an average ticket price is between 20 pounds and 30 pounds Man U's tickets are not as expensive as those for many other clubs.

Another hugely profitable area is the money the Club makes from allowing its matches to be filmed for television. There is an enormous demand for sports programmes from satellite channels as well as the BBC and independent TV companies and the income from this is increasing year by year. And if you think of all the football competitions and international championships, in addition to the regular matches, you can imagine how much money this brings the Club from all the programme rights.

Anything else? Well, yes there is – and that's sponsorship. If you look at the names of the products, and they're all different, which are printed on the players' shirts or on the advertising boards which are placed beside the pitch, that will give you an idea of what I mean. Any firm or business will benefit from its name being associated with such a successful Club, and as well as two main sponsors the Club has at least ten others.

By now you've probably got a pretty good idea as to why the Club is so wealthy. But where does all this money go? You don't need me to tell you that some top players are seriously rich and so the Club spends millions of pounds on its players' wages. Then there are the buildings and the ground to maintain, the cost of transport whenever the players travel either in the UK or abroad, all the staff who look after the running of the Club, the list is endless.

Test 3   PART 3

You will hear five different people talking about what they enjoy about going on a cruise ship holiday. For Questions 19–23, choose from the list A–F what each speaker says. Use the letters only once. There is one extra letter which you do not need to use.

1
I'm the ideal person to go on a cruise. It means I don't feel guilty about the fact that I should be walking instead of taking the bus or sitting behind the steering wheel of my oh so comfortable car. There's a limit to what you can do on deck! OK, I know there are fitness freaks who are out there each morning jumping up and down and trying to impress the rest of us. But I think if you 'choose to cruise', you do so knowing that it provides the perfect opportunity to lie back in the sun and not worry about climbing the nearest hill or running a marathon.

2
Cruises have something special. Something you can't get on a train and certainly not on a plane. It's that point at the end of the day when the sun is sinking and the sky is a wonderful mix of gold and red and purple. I stand on the deck and imagine what it must have been like for those early explorers sailing into the unknown. They must have been incredibly brave. Or I think about those battles that were fought on the sea or the ships that have sunk without trace, full of treasure. So romantic.

3
Cruises are great fun. You go on board knowing that everything you want is going to be there. You don't have to leave the ship if you don't want to. You don't even have to think about what to do. There's something organised if you want it from the moment you wake up to the moment you go to bed. Deck games, competitions, discos, cabaret, never a dull moment. And I join in everything, so that I sleep wonderfully well because I'm always so exhausted!

4
What I like most are the different ports we stop at and all the things that are on offer. The shops on board are nothing special. But all those foreign souks and markets full of all kinds of exotic goods. One port we stopped at I deliberately left my credit cards on the ship. I was determined just to look and not spend. So who was I kidding?! One look at the piles of the most gorgeous silk scarves and I was running around seeing who would lend me some money. I could've bought the lot!

5
To my mind the ship is like a floating hotel, but even better because you wake up each morning somewhere different and you haven't had to drag your luggage with you. I can't understand people who say they'd find a cruise boring and you're surrounded by water all the time. It's magical. You go to your cabin last thing at night having taken one final look at the palm trees on the beach and next morning you peer out of your porthole window and see towering mountains and a deserted coastline. The food is the best, because the ship takes on fresh supplies each time it docks. I couldn't wish for a more relaxing holiday.

Test 3   PART 4

You will hear a radio talk given by an TV actress called Zoe Fisher. For Questions 24–30, decide which of the statements are TRUE and which are FALSE and write T for True and F for False in the boxes provided.

When I was a little girl at school, I always used to say, 'I'm going to be a teacher when I grow up.' I really believed my dream would come true, even though I left school at 16. I had to leave because I was one of six children and my parents couldn't afford to keep me there. That was one of the saddest days of my life because I loved going to school.

Anyway, after leaving school I went to work in the chief accountant's office of a bank. I had intended studying in the evenings at college but I got involved with an amateur theatrical group and a few years later I applied for, and got a job in children's television.

When I started work on the children's programme, people asked me if I had trained as a teacher. I'm still asked the same question today. I suppose in a way I am a natural teacher, and my chance to communicate with millions of children across the world in the past 25 years has given me the opportunity to develop that ability. I love to bring knowledge into children's lives and truly believe that if we teach children well, they will lead the way in the future.

I was in a taxi on my way home one day from the TV studios and the cab driver turned round and said, 'I think of you every day.' 'Oh no, here we go,' I thought. But it turned out that he had a two-year-old son and his wife worked during the day, so when he looked after his son he would always turn on the TV so he and his son could watch my programme. That was the biggest compliment anyone could ever pay me.

I grew up in Trinidad in the West Indies and when I arrived in Britain in 1960 I had quite a difficult time to begin with. I had to fight to be accepted and I think that experience gave me a certain amount of drive and ambition.

In a way I think I've achieved my ambition to become a teacher through my work on television. I get letters from children whose lives I have touched in some small way and I feel my dream has come true. I'm hoping to write a book about my life and what I would want most is that children from all countries and cultural backgrounds will be able to identify with the emotions I have experienced.

I think I've been a very lucky person and I believe that our path may not always take the course we expect, but sometimes we reach the same destination by a different route.

Test 4   PART 1

You'll hear people talking in eight different situations. For Questions 1–8, choose the best answer, A, B or C.

1
Oh, good morning. I wonder if you can help me. I've just been looking at your book display on the history of trains and I see you've got the video of 'The Railway Children'. That was such a wonderful film. The trains might have been slower in the past but I'm sure they were more reliable. At least you could rely on the timetables. Which is actually what I'm after. I'm afraid I don't know how to use the internet, although I know that's what I'm meant to use. Do you keep one of those little leaflets or booklets which has all that sort of information, please?

2
A: Have you got the list of who's coming to the party?
B: Yes, I have. And I've told them to keep the date a secret. John hates any kind of fuss; do you remember when he found out that we'd bought him a birthday cake last year, he was furious. But this is different. Getting married is special and we've known him and Anna for years. I'm sure she won't mind, even if he does.
A: No, everyone's looking forward to it. I'll pick you up from the office and we'll drive there together, shall we?
B: That'll be fine. Thanks.

3
A: So I rang the surgery early expecting that they'd fit me in later that day. 'Is it an emergency?' this woman said, 'because if it is, you should go to your local hospital.' Her manner was quite rude. I said I needed to see my own doctor and she said he had no free appointments for the next seven days. I said I was going away on holiday and I needed a prescription. 'Well,' she said in the same tone of voice, 'you can write in to request a prescription and I'll get a doctor to sign it.' She was so rude, I think I might write and complain about her!

4
There're days when I can scarcely get out of bed. I'm so tired I could just sleep and sleep. It's not that I've been out all night or even gone to bed late. I wish. My disco dancing days are long gone. It's just the sheer volume of work. I spend all day in court and then when I get back to the office there are letters to write, documents to read, meetings with clients and so on. You can't

argue a case if you haven't got all the facts and thoroughly prepared yourself. It's never-ending and you tell me you're tired!

5
A: This is an excellent report, Henry. Based on what your teachers say you could apply to study almost any subject at university.
B: I'm not sure what I want to do yet. Perhaps medicine or business studies or even music.
A: You need to find out more about the courses. Don't decide until you've had a chat with one of the lecturers in the different departments. If you're going to study business, they might suggest you spend a year working in industry first. Go and have a look around and see for yourself. Ask people questions and find out all you can – that might help you to make your mind up.

6
This is a great opportunity, you know. The town's needed somewhere like this for ages. You're always getting tourists wandering around asking where they can eat. I mean most places close so early in the evening. Mind you, I couldn't have opened up if Jenny hadn't been prepared to come into the business with me, it's mostly her money that's gone into buying the restaurant. So if things go well, I plan on opening another place in the future – like a cafe bar, you know, more informal, serving coffees and milkshakes. Lots of comfy sofas with newspapers and magazines for people to browse through.

7
You won't believe me when I tell you but I had a reputation in my youth for being quite wild. We lived in a wonderful old house in the country, it was huge and my parents were very generous. I remember my father bought me a sports car for my twenty-first birthday – my mother was completely against it. But I drove all over Europe; I had so much energy in those days, we sometimes drove through the night. It's not that I want to drive nowadays, there's far too much traffic, but my goodness I wish I could still get around and see the world.

8
After last night's storms I am afraid things are not going to get much better until the end of the week. The storms brought with them torrential rain which is still falling in the south west. As a result, river levels are rising and police are warning motorists to stay at home. Unless your journey is absolutely essential, you should not travel as public transport services are already disrupted by the severe weather conditions even though last night's fog has cleared away. People living in low-lying areas are advised to move their possessions to upstairs rooms as some rivers are expected to break their banks in the next few hours.

Test 4   PART 2

You will hear part of a radio programme which talks about modern music. For Questions 9–18, complete the sentences.

Presenter: Next on tonight's programme is Lucy Byrne who's here to tell us about exciting new developments going on in one of our music colleges. Lucy …

Lucy Byrne: I spent last week sitting in on the rehearsals for a concert which will be given by final year students at the Royal Southern College of music in a couple of week's time. Now, I wouldn't normally spend one whole week doing this. But after the first day's rehearsals I was fascinated by what was going on and wanted to hear more. What was so special about what these students were doing? Well, if I tell you that the most important instrument in one piece was a huge, iron bucket, – played very, very loudly – you'll get some idea of why I was hooked. Not a violin or a clarinet in sight, I might add.

I've heard of composers using strange things like typewriters or hoovers, but this was a new one on me. In fact, for the composer Max Sinclair, it's a world first. What's more, he's getting the chance to have his piece, which is called 'Bang with Style,' played by one of the UK's finest orchestras and conducted by one of its leading conductors. The piece lasts 22 minutes and the bucket makes a forceful appearance at the beginning when it's struck 15 times. In the middle of the piece it's struck 46 times, and at the end it's given the hardest possible blows so that the sound it makes is as loud as possible.

When I spoke to the conductor, Peter Lloyd, he said that he enjoyed discovering what is going on in the music colleges and finds conducting experimental music very challenging. He said all the new pieces, six in total, being played at the concert represented a variety of styles, composed as they are by different individuals. However, he's also including two or three well-known popular pieces to keep the audience happy.

In one case, the piece of music had been written in the shape of a hockey pitch, which Lloyd admitted he had found a little hard to interpret at the beginning. He needed the composer to explain things to him and once they'd understood the way the notes were arranged, the orchestra had found it hugely enjoyable.

I asked Max Sinclair at one point how on earth he came to think of writing the piece in the first place. Apparently, he was sitting in his friend's room at college when he heard what he describes as 'a fantastic noise' outside the window. He looked out and discovered a builder mixing concrete and that was the start of his composition.

So, what does a professional musician think of the idea? The orchestra's percussionist, Tim Travis, who is more accustomed to playing the drums, seemed fairly good-humoured about it all. He admitted that he had played some peculiar things in his time. He's rattled chains, played a sharp carving knife and also played on funny whistles. In this piece he has to use a fairly heavy hammer and keep hitting one particular place.

I wondered how an audience would react to this kind of music and was reminded that in the nineteenth century people had walked out of concerts where music composed by Bruckner was played. People were horrified at such modern music.

Max Sinclair's music has been referred to as 'hard-line modern' and I wouldn't disagree. It certainly couldn't be anything other than twenty-first century music!

Test 4   PART 3

You will hear five different people talking about what they enjoyed best about their schooldays. For Questions 19–23, choose from the list A–F what each speaker says. Use the letters only once. There is one extra letter which you do not need to use.

1
I have very happy memories of my schooldays. I know some people can't wait to leave, but not me. I was never bored although I didn't like some of the teachers, especially the sports staff. I suppose that was because I hated sport and couldn't be bothered to make the effort. But I think it's the one chance you get in life to study things that interest you. I loved history and geography, science – everything really – and we had a brilliant art teacher. I wasn't particularly good at anything but I learnt a lot one way or another and I shall always be grateful for that.

2
I wasn't terribly keen on school and I was glad to leave. I couldn't wait to start earning my own living. The teachers were okay but I didn't like homework and stuff and I wanted to go out in the evenings with my friends. I guess that was the best thing about school really – my friends. We've all kept in touch and always will, and although a couple of people have moved away from the area we still manage to meet a few times every year. We have a good laugh when we think back to our schooldays, although I don't think it can have been much fun for our poor teachers!

3
It was only when I had my first proper job that I realised how much I missed being at school. Not because of the all the subjects we had to do and all the exams we had to take. No way. I think I was so used to having generous holidays that I couldn't believe it when I only had three weeks a year. I thought I would never get used to going without the chance to regularly escape boring routine. A group of us who were really keen on sport and outdoor life used to go off camping, whatever the weather, and when we left it never occurred to me that I wouldn't be able to do that sort of thing any more.

4
We had a teacher who taught languages and she was great at organising trips abroad in the holidays. Usually it involved staying in a family with a person your own age and then they'd come back the next year and stay with you. That way it kept the costs down and you only had to pay your travelling expenses. I never appreciated how much time and energy that teacher must have put in to setting up those holidays – you don't when you're a kid, you just take it all for granted. But without her I'd never have used the languages we were studying – Spanish and Italian – in the real world, and although I'm not fluent in either language, I've never forgotten what I learnt.

5
When I was a kid we lived in the city centre, and although there was a park close by we didn't have a garden. So when I went to secondary school which was on the outskirts of the city, I absolutely loved the fact that the school had its own grounds. It also had its own sports fields and a swimming pool and in the summer months some teachers took us outside for lessons. I remember sitting under the trees thinking how lucky I was to be somewhere so beautiful. I'm sure that kind of environment helped me enjoy school, even the most boring lessons.

Test 4   PART 4

You will hear part of a radio interview with a woman called Hayley Jones who spent a year in Antarctica. For Questions 24–30, choose the best answer A, B or C.

Interviewer: Hayley Jones has just returned from spending a year working in Antarctica. She's our guest on today's programme. Hayley, welcome to the programme. I suppose the first thing we all want to know is what you were doing for a whole year.

Hayley Jones: Well, I've always been interested in environmental problems and the university where I teach paid for my trip. My job was to produce a report at the end of my year. Although this may sound a little strange, the main thing I had to do was to look at rubbish. I spent most of my time with a binman who was responsible for making sure that everything brought into Antarctica is taken out again. I was based at Rothera, where most of the scientists are working but I travelled around quite a lot looking at what is going on. In a way Antarctica is like a laboratory for the world as all the research being done there will benefit us all wherever we live.

Interviewer: Did you miss anything whilst you were there? A year is quite a long time.

Hayley Jones: To begin with no, because it was so different and I found it really exciting. Then after a while I began to miss greenery, there are only a few plants like moss clinging to the rocks, and I found the lack of colour affected me and that made me feel quite low. I also missed my family but I had expected that would happen and although I didn't worry about not seeing television I certainly wished I could tune in to radio programmes.

Interviewer: Did the long hours of daylight affect you?

Hayley Jones: Well, I hadn't actually thought very much about that before I went. I'd wondered how I would cope with low temperatures but I discovered that because there's 24 hours of daylight I ended up sleeping a lot less and I didn't feel nearly as tired as I do when I'm at home. I must have worked twice as hard as a result. It was weird. Sometimes I forgot all about going to bed!

Interviewer: Good heavens! I can't begin to imagine what that must be like. What did you do to relax, then?

Hayley Jones: In Rothera I was quite lucky because there are a lot of things to do. There's a ski slope just up the hill from the base, so I could ski whenever I wanted. There's also a rock band and I would go and listen to them rehearse in the evenings and there're plenty of places to walk to and it's perfectly safe to walk by yourself, which was a new experience for me, after living in a large city. If I didn't want to be on my own, then I would go to the cafe bar and have a drink with whoever was there or watch a video film.

Interviewer: You mentioned low temperatures. How cold was it?

Hayley Jones: At times, extremely cold. Some days when the weather was calm it was only about minus 2, but if the wind picked up it could drop to minus 20 in a matter of minutes. I took care to dress properly to avoid frostbite, which is easy to get, and that meant wearing lots of thin layers of clothing – nothing too heavy – to trap the air and keep out the wind. A bit different from what I would wear for skiing.

Interviewer: Is it possible for people to go to Antarctica as tourists?

Hayley Jones: Well, getting to Antarctica is not easy for anyone, let alone tourists. But there are a few tours organised for those people who can afford to go because it's incredibly expensive, as you would expect. And I don't think the situation will change in the foreseeable future as there's not a huge demand from the tourist industry to develop Antarctica.

Interviewer: Would you consider going back to work there again?

Hayley Jones: Not straight away. Towards the end I felt very cut off and if I'm honest I was beginning to feel fairly restless. I'm glad I went because it was a tremendous experience and I wouldn't have missed it for the world. I certainly don't regret any part of it but there's so much to see and do that I'd like to work somewhere completely different if I go away again – perhaps a desert next time, where it's extremely hot!

Interviewer: Hayley Jones, thank you very much for coming ...

Test 5 PART 1

You'll hear people talking in eight different situations. For Questions 1–8, choose the best answer, A, B or C.

1
When they first offered me the job I couldn't believe my luck. I mean, there'd been loads of other people who'd applied so I was amazed when they said the job was mine. The hours aren't too bad, most of my friends seem to be working about the same number and everybody's very friendly and helpful. I didn't expect to earn much as I haven't got that much experience. But the best thing is that the pay is very generous, added to which there're all sorts of extras like free travel to work, cheap meals in the staff canteen and so on.

2
Some people'll forget their heads one day. I'm always getting people who jump into the cab and then look blank when I ask them where they want to go. They can't remember, so I say 'sorry you'll have to get out otherwise it's going to cost you a fortune'. So they get out and later I'll find their suitcase or whatever on the back seat. One guy last week gave me the wrong address and so when we eventually got to where he wanted to go, the fare was a lot. I had a right old argument with him over the price and in the end I said either he paid or I'd call the police.

3
A: I know my daughter can't wait for the day when she can afford to buy all the magazines she wants.
B: There are so many of them as well – surely they can't be all that different from each other.
A: Well, she tells me they are. They're certainly all full of glossy photos so I imagine that's why they're so expensive.
B: And I've noticed that most weeks they all have different free offers stuck onto the front cover – something like a CD or shampoo or cinema tickets.
A: Exactly. You can understand why they're so popular and they're full of advertisements. You wonder how parents find the money for everything.
B: They probably don't!

4
There was a lot of good stuff, things I'd never seen before. There was one room full of paintings, done in oils by local artists, not that I'd ever heard of any them, but there's obviously a lot of talent around. Then in another room there were pictures of local places, taken – oh I don't know – about sixty or seventy years ago and they were fascinating. I recognised quite a few of the old buildings and on one wall there was a collection of old advertisements, which must have been originals, they were so old and faded.

5
OK, now let's take this large sheet of paper. Lay it flat on the table, it's not going to be folded and you want to try and fit the complete drawing on this one sheet. Right. Now you need your pencils and a ruler and a rubber. We'll draw a wing first and then you can cut it out. That way you can lay the shape onto your piece of wood and draw around it. You'll have to do the same with the tail and the main body, and when it's finished you can paint all those little windows onto the wood.

6
A: I haven't seen him for ages.
B: Haven't you heard? He's been in hospital, although he's home again now.
A: I'd no idea. The last I heard of him he was on holiday with his wife. In fact they always seem to be going away somewhere. Winter sports, climbing, sailing ...
B: Well, apparently he had an accident when they were away. He slipped and broke his hip while they were walking, and although it's not serious it's going to take him quite a time to recover.
A: Poor man. It can't be a year since he had that fall when he was skiing and they thought he'd broken a bone in his foot.

7
If you're into finding out about the latest developments in industrial design, then this is the book for you. The topic itself might sound quite dull but the author manages to present the subject in a thoroughly imaginative way. What's more, the illustrations themselves are quite beautiful, there are ways of photographing buildings, bridges, arches and so on so that they almost become works of art in themselves. So don't be put off by the price – yes, it's expensive, but well worth it. It will open your eyes, so that the ordinary will never look ordinary again.

8
If they'd have told us what was happening, it wouldn't have been so bad. But we sat there for about an hour with no clear indication as to what was going on. Then finally we boarded the plane only to be told that there was an engine fault and there would be further delay. Well, finally it turned out that we wouldn't be taking off at all that night but the first we heard about it was when we were told to board the buses – the buses! which were waiting outside the terminal to take us to our hotel. OK, so it was a luxury hotel – but that was the least they could do.

Test 5 PART 2

You will hear part of a local radio programme in which a man is talking about a new college which has recently opened. For Questions 9–8, complete the notes.

Those of you living in this area will have been aware of all the building which has been in progress on the outskirts of the city during the last three years. Well, the good news is that Hardacre College was officially opened last week.

The college campus is built around a main square. This is at the heart of the college as all the paths and walkways lead out from this point. Standing in the centre you can see the signposts to all the departments, the library, the dining hall and the sports hall.

Car parking is limited and, in fact, students are not encouraged to come by car as the college is served by a new bus service. Buses run from the station and the centre of the city every six minutes throughout the day, and covered walkways lead from the college bus stop directly into the main buildings.

As you might expect with a new college, no expense has been spared and the facilities are amazing. The buildings are light and airy and there's a general feeling of space and calm. In part this feeling has been created by the trees and flowerbeds which break up the buildings. There is also a plan to build small fountains at various points.

The college is well supported with nursery and medical facilities. Young children under school age can be left in the college play centre, which provides free care for the children of staff as well as students.

There are also excellent facilities for disabled students and there is access for wheelchairs throughout the college at ground floor level, with special lifts to all floors at higher levels.

With the college being situated outside the city, it has been necessary to include major facilities like banks, shops and a post office. At present, however, only the banks and post office are open.

Money has also been made available for student clubs and societies, although it will take time for these to develop. There is a small theatre for drama and music and a large student common room with its own coffee bar.

So what about the work of the college? Once again, you can look forward to the latest design in laboratories and lecture rooms, all equipped with computers and interactive video teaching boards. This means that you can be in one room watching and listening, and your lecturer can be teaching somewhere else.

When the college is fully functioning and all the courses are running it is expected that the total student number will be about 8,000. This will make it the largest college in the region, offering 4,000 more places than its closest rival.

There have already been two open days and a third open day is planned for next Saturday. So whether you want to start studying or not why don't you go out to Hardacre and see everything it has to offer. Who knows, you might find a ...

Test 5 PART 3

You will hear five different people talking about their memory. For Questions 19–23, choose from the list A–F what each speaker says. Use the letters only once. There is one extra letter which you do not need to use.

1

I think I have a good memory largely because I was brought up to rely on doing things for myself. If I forgot something, like a book for school, I very quickly learnt that if I didn't remember things for myself, no one else would. The trouble is that I've found people are easily irritated if you have a good memory and that's really strange. They say things like: 'Oh, you never forget anything, do you?' in quite a sharp way. So sometimes I pretend to forget things in order to avoid being criticised. It's silly because I think having a good memory is really useful.

2

I've tried training myself to remember things in all sorts of ways. I make a list, then forget where I've put it. I once wrote a list on my hand and then without thinking washed it off. I've tried connecting things together, so that if I need to buy some stamps and some fruit, for example, I'll try to keep a picture in my head of stamps stuck onto apples. But nothing really works. I'm sure a good memory is something you're born with and there's not much you can do about it if your brain is wired up differently.

3

My memory is really strange. I remember a teacher at school telling me that I always remember the wrong things, and looking back she was right. If there was a piece of work which had to be learnt then I'd remember one or two unimportant details and forget the really significant stuff. I didn't do it on purpose, I couldn't help it. It's obviously the way my mind works and it's very embarrassing at times. I've had to find ways round it and write things down that I am expected to remember especially at work, otherwise I'd never be able to do my job.

4

My parents are artists and I'm sure that's influenced my ability to remember things. I'm hopeless at remembering numbers or how to spell a particularly difficult word, but if I see a picture of something, like a family group or even a map or a photograph of a building, I can remember every detail. And I only have to see it once – it's as if my brain photographs the image and stores it. But I don't understand why it doesn't work if I want to remember a friend's phone number or a list of verbs in a foreign language!

5

Some people say they have a photographic memory, which must be fantastic. I'd give anything to have a good memory, although I'm not so bad that I forget what day of the week it is or what I should be doing. I get cross with myself because I leave things around, like my keys or sunglasses, and then can't find them. But that's probably because my mind is elsewhere and I'm not concentrating on what I'm doing when I actually put my keys down. I think if I made a real effort I could probably be less forgetful.

Test 5 PART 4

You will hear part of a radio interview with a woman called Susan who runs a city farm. For Questions 24–30, choose the best answer A, B or C.

Interviewer: Susan, welcome to the programme. Now I imagine that many of our listeners might be wondering 'a city farm?' – that can't be right.

Susan: No, I suppose it does sound a bit strange. In fact, I often get that kind of reaction when I'm asked what I do.

Interviewer: So tell us, what on earth is a city farm?

Susan: Well, it is just that. A farm, quite a small one obviously, in the centre of a city. There are quite a few of these farms dotted throughout the country; most of them have appeared in the past five years or so.

Interviewer: But why? When we have so many farms in the countryside – which is where they should be!

Susan: Well, the idea came about when a teacher from a primary school wrote a letter to a newspaper in which she said she was horrified to find out that her class of seven-year-olds didn't know where milk came from. They drank it every day, they saw it in cartons on the shelves of supermarkets and when she asked which animal milk came from, one child said, 'Chickens'.

Interviewer: You're joking!

Susan: Absolutely not. Anyway, as a result, a local businessman bought a plot of land and eventually with the help of the farming community he opened a small farm to encourage children living in the city to find out what went on in the countryside which many of them never got to visit. And the farm was hugely popular with local schools and teachers but most of all with young children. It had been thought that people living nearby would object or that parents would feel that it was not necessary for their children to visit a farm, but nothing of that sort occurred.

Interviewer: What sort of animals did he have?

Susan: No bulls! But there were a few cows, some sheep, a couple of goats, and then chickens and ducks.

Interviewer: Amazing. So how did you get involved with the scheme?

Susan: Well, I saw a programme on the TV and I was fascinated by the children's behaviour. I used to be a teacher years ago but I gave up when my children were small and my husband worked away from home. Anyway, I watched some of these children who were apparently quite difficult to control in the classroom, but when you saw them with the animals they were so gentle with them, it was such a change.

Interviewer: Weren't they frightened?

Susan: Not at all. So I decided I could do the same thing in the city where I live. My house has quite a lot of land attached to it and I got permission from the local council to set up a city farm. I made sure that the local people knew what I was planning to do and there was a great deal of curiosity. Someone rang and offered me a couple of horses and we also have some ponies, as well as the more usual farm animals. People were very supportive.

Interviewer: How do you afford to feed all these animals?

Susan: Well, the council gives me a small grant, which surprised me as I thought people might object to money being spent like this, but now that the farm is established, most schools make a contribution towards the running costs when they visit. Local shopkeepers pass on fruit and vegetables or anything else suitable that they can't sell. As you know some animals will eat anything! Oh, and I sell the eggs direct to the public because they know they're really fresh. But what is really special is that many children come here in their own time, after school or during the holidays. They bring food for the animals and they help with the cleaning and general care of the farm. And some of them have been around when the lambs have been born and they become very attached to these young animals, which is lovely to watch.

Interviewer: Perhaps you'll produce a generation of farmers!

Susan: No, I don't think that's very likely somehow.

Interviewer: Sue, thank you very much for coming into the studio today and good luck with ...

Test 6 PART 1

You'll hear people talking in eight different situations. For Questions 1–8, choose the best answer, A, B or C.

1

My previous car was running really well – after all, I'd only had it for about six months and I bought it brand new. But this letter from the car manufacturers was such a good deal, it was difficult to resist. The difference in price between what I would get for my old car, and what I would have to pay for a new model was so small – I'd have been silly not to accept. And I'd always wanted a silver car, although colour doesn't really matter that much.

2

I only left the office for a short time. I popped into the canteen to get a coffee and was back at my desk within five minutes. It wasn't until lunchtime when I went to pick up my bag that I realised it wasn't where I always leave it. Someone had obviously stood on my chair and instead of putting the bag back under my desk had left it on a very high shelf where we keep the plants – needless to say my purse wasn't in it and I had quite a lot of money in it, unfortunately.

3

A: Where were you? I waited ages outside the cinema.
B: So did I! I couldn't find you anywhere.
A: That's ridiculous. You said seven o'clock and I was there, especially early so we could have a drink before the film started. In the end I just went home.
B: But we agreed on the late night showing at eleven, so that's the one I went to – alone I might add!
A: Oh, no, and it was the last night that film was on and I was so looking forward to it.

4

It's interesting to look at the latest research into the importance of a baby's first year. Some early findings suggest that by the end of the first year a child's character has been formed for life. In fact some of the researchers claim that these tests show whether a baby will grow up to be a shy or a bold person. However, part of the problem surrounding this research is the fact that babies can't speak for themselves and so the researchers rely on experiments which involve the baby's parents and brothers or sisters – if there are any. I'm surprised they don't bring in the grandparents as well!

5

A new health and fitness centre opens this week in the heart of the city, close to the local technical college. It's been built on the site of an old department store and has been developed with money raised by local businesses. It's hoped that the facilities which include a swimming pool and gym will enable office workers to make the most of their lunchtime break. It will open early and close late five days a week; there are no plans to stay open at weekends, which will disappoint the students who live close by. The centre manager feels that at weekends families and friends are the priority, not exercise.

6

A: So why are you going?

B: No one particular reason, really. I've been fed up with the pressure for some time – but that's true of many jobs these days – and although the money's important it's not everything. In fact, I shall miss my generous salary and the working conditions.

A: So why not stay then?

B: Well, if I don't make a move now I might regret it in the future. It's so comfortable and it'd be the easiest thing in the world to stay. But there has to be more to life, something more challenging. And who knows: I might find a job where I earn even more!

7

Well, I've no complaints really, just one or two little niggles. The weather, which had been quite cold, turned out to be just right that evening – warm and cloudless. The organisers had laid out the tables and chairs under the trees in the shade, to keep the food cool, I imagine. Incidentally, the food was much better than last year. Anyway, I don't suppose anyone could've done much about the mosquitoes. And once it got dark and the candles were lit, along came the moths to join in the fun as well!

8

I think this new hotel is brilliant. It's right on the beach and provides everything you need. Obviously it's pretty basic – no luxuries, no fancy furnishings. There are single and double rooms, all with their own bathrooms, TV and internet access. I know some people don't like the idea of hidden cameras, but if you're coming back late at night, it's really good to know there's a system out there to make sure you're safe. It gives the night porter a view of what's going on and that for me is probably the best thing of all.

Test 6   PART 2

You will hear part of a radio programme in which a man called David North talks about an animal called a bay cat. For Questions 9–18, complete the sentences.

I must confess that I had never heard of the animal called the bay cat. Apparently, it's one of the rarest animals in the world and on a recent trip to Borneo I got to know a lot more about it.

Borneo is the third largest island in the world – something else I didn't know – and is in the Far East near Malaysia. I went there to make a geographical film on the mountains and the jungle which make up such a large part of the island.

One night while we were out in the jungle planning where we would start work the next day, we heard a rustle in the undergrowth, in the long grass. My immediate thought was snakes and I was getting ready to run. But the guide who was with us told us we had just missed seeing a bay cat. This small animal only ever appears at night when it's out hunting and even the local villagers say that it can be ten years between sightings. But the forests of Borneo are shrinking as more and more trees are cut down, so where will the bay cat have left to hide and where did it come from in the first place?

It was first recorded in the last century in 1874 and after that there was no mention of it until 1950. At that point in time, a traveller noticed the fur was worn by the local Dayak tribes people on their ceremonial caps. But once again, despite attempts by animal photographers and zoologists to try and see the animal, nothing more was heard of it until 1992. In that year some local hunters saw a bay cat for long enough to describe the animal in more detail. This particular bay cat had a small head and a long tail that was white at the tip. The coat was brown with faint markings all over.

A number of other reports followed this sighting, but the reports were scattered and not very reliable. Then in 2000 there was news that a bay cat had been caught by local tribespeople. As a result of this news a wildlife photographer flew out to Borneo in the hope of seeing and photographing the animal. He travelled with the director of SOS Care, an international cat conservation organisation. According to the photographer they both had mixed feelings. He had dreamt of being able to take photos of the bay cat, but the fact that one had been caught told him that the environmental pressures on the animal were increasing.

What had driven this particular animal out into the open, however, turned out to be a fire; the bay cat had been forced to break cover and had then been caught. After it had been photographed, it was set free. Nothing has been seen of it since. Fortunately, the location of the animal was kept secret and nothing was published in the world's newspapers until it had been safely released into the jungle.

I didn't manage to see a bay cat and perhaps I never will. No one can be certain about the future of the animal, but scientific researchers are hopeful that if the bay cat has survived this long, it may succeed in finding ways to survive even longer in the hill forests of Borneo.

Test 6   PART 3

You will hear five different people talking about what puts them in a good mood. For Questions 19–23, choose from the list A–F what each speaker says. Use the letters only once. There is one extra letter which you do not need to use.

1

I think I'm a fairly well-balanced person, although there are days when I feel a bit down. Even listening to my favourite music doesn't help, and I like being alone until I feel more positive. One thing that does help me feel better is what people call 'comfort food'. I know it varies from person to person but for me something like chocolate or a sugary bun – that instantly cheers me up. It's crazy, I know, but I think there are good scientific reasons for the way it affects one's mood – something to do with body chemistry I'm told.

2

I used to love getting letters. If the post came before I left for school, I'd be in a good mood all day. That's all changed now. I rush back from work to see if I've got any e-mails as they have exactly the same effect on me. I still spend quite a lot of time on the phone to my friends but it's easy to run up huge bills and that's hardly likely to put me in a good mood. One of my friends has got a video phone but I'm not sure I fancy one of those. The good thing about using a computer is that you can contact people in your own time and it doesn't matter how you look.

3

My friends say I'm quite a moody person. I'm convinced it's to do with the weather and that if the sun's shining, I automatically feel better. But that's completely outside my control. If I need to pick myself up, I reach for my walkman, put on my headphones, shut out the world and listen to my favourite groups. I've tried listening to music on the internet but it's not the same because I don't have that feeling of being enclosed in my own private world. I can guarantee that I'll be in a good mood for the rest of the day.

4

There's nothing worse than sitting around wondering why you feel moody, and if I don't get out there and do something, I'm sure I'd just carry on feeling depressed. I generally go for a long run, whatever the weather and I come back exhausted – but my mood's changed completely. Perhaps it's to do with tension or the need to get rid of energy. But it's weird because I don't actually like organised sport. I hated it at school and I made every excuse to avoid having to run anywhere, at any time!

5

I spend hours on the internet, e-mailing my friends and joining in chat rooms. And then there's suddenly a day when I don't even bother to switch on my computer. I might feel really fed up and although going shopping cheers me up, the good mood doesn't last long because I get home and decide I don't like what I've bought – so I feel depressed again. Then I rely on my friends and I'll phone around to see who's free. We might just stay in and chat or we might go out for a coffee but either way I go home feeling heaps better at the end.

Test 6   PART 4

You will hear a radio interview with a young man called Ollie Smart, who is an artist. For Questions 24–30, decide which of the statements are TRUE and which are FALSE and write T for True and F for False in the boxes provided.

Interviewer: Ollie Smart, I know you've always been interested in painting even when you were a young boy. Now, I'm particularly interested in this new project of yours which is aimed at encouraging the under-16s to paint.

Ollie: Yeah – I can't imagine life without painting. But you're right, my main passion at the moment is getting through to kids. A few months ago I was doing a TV show and at the end of the programme I asked kids to write in and tell me how many of them spent time at home painting.

Interviewer: Did you get many replies?

Ollie: I was amazed at the response. I thought if I get a 100 replies I'll be pleased, but do you know, I got more than 4000 and from kids all over the world. They wrote and told me what they paint, whether they use oils, watercolour, crayons or even make their own special paint mixtures! And in a way it proved my theory because I was convinced that there must be loads of young people out there painting, even though most TV art programmes are targeted at adult audiences.

Interviewer: And have you discovered things about this age group that do surprise you?

Ollie: Yeah! I guess I thought these kids would be painting for their friends but what's really nice is that they're painting for their families. In most cases kids put up their pictures on the kitchen walls, stick them on the fridge door or a cup cupboard somewhere, but if everyone really likes it, they'll get a frame and hang it somewhere it can be admired by all. I think that's great!

Interviewer: I can remember when I was a kid that my mother used to get fed up with me if I spread things all over the kitchen table and then didn't clear away. Do you think this generation is any different?

Ollie: Probably not! But some kids mentioned a great idea which is that their parents set aside special times for them to take over the kitchen. One lad said he'd been painting since he was eight and that he'd learnt good practice automatically and now clears away and washes up his brushes without being told.

Interviewer: Is it difficult trying to experiment with mixing your own paints?

Ollie: Hm – expensive, if not difficult! I used to ask my parents to buy all sorts of different kinds of oil paints so I could try out new ideas. They were pretty good about it but I know they weren't happy if I wasted the paint or it was such a disgusting colour that it had to be thrown away. They preferred it if I played safe.

Interviewer: So what happens now with all the information you've collected?

Ollie: The next thing is to select about twenty kids and involve them in my own TV art programme but using their ideas and pictures. I'm reading through things to see who sounds adventurous and who has really tried to create something individual. It's also important to get a good range of ages into the programme, from about 8 to 16 and obviously a mix of boys and girls.

Interviewer: I thought the advice was to never work with animals or children!

Ollie: Yeah, I think it is. You'll never see me on an art programme with animals, that's for sure! But what I'd like is to create a relaxed atmosphere where viewers can learn as well as enjoy what's going on. I can imagine we're all going to get in each other's way, but then that's what an artist's studio is usually like. My Dad would offer to help and just get in the way, messing up my paints and trying out different colours before I'd finished. It was maddening.

Interviewer: Ollie Smart, thank you for talking to us today and good luck with your ...

Test 7   PART 1

You'll hear people talking in eight different situations. For Questions 1–8, choose the best answer, A, B or C.

1

Anyone's who's serious about their music should check out Topnote. It stocks music from techno to experimental including hip-hop, house, garage, funk and reggae. The staff are really knowledgeable and able to point you in the direction of music you might want to hear but don't yet know about and the customers are as wide-ranging as the music. What makes this shop different from all the others are the shows when artists come in in person and play their new compositions on their laptops. There are about 8000 sound samples on the shop's website so you can listen before you buy.

2

I wasn't sure what to expect when I decided to do my week's work experience in our local hospital. But it was really interesting. Although I wasn't allowed to handle the patients, I could watch the doctors and nurses at work and I learnt loads of new things. Some of the elderly patients who'd been there for some time were very chatty. I think it must be lonely to be in hospital, because although people are kind they're too busy to sit and talk with you for hours. They all said that they'd miss me and that made me feel quite sad.

3

A: I'd never been to a political meeting before, but I was pleasantly surprised.
B: Weren't you bored?
A: Not at all. I thought he was very good. Some of the people putting the questions were determined to give him a hard time and were actually quite rude. But he kept his cool and didn't lose his temper. In fact, he was, clever, really, because the ruder they were, the more sweetly he smiled.
B: That's an old political trick. And in any case if you go into politics you can't expect to be treated any differently.
A: That's not the point. I was just impressed by the way he answered the questions which he could've refused to do.

4

The best thing about camping is being outdoors. I know that seems obvious, but there's nothing better than that sense of being in touch with nature. I don't even care if it rains, in fact I love lying in my sleeping bag listening to the rain pattering on the tent. Although I suppose it's better when the weather is dry. And with all the modern equipment there's no reason why you can't be just as comfortable as you can in a hotel. Probably more so because you can stay in your tent all day if you want and nobody will bother you.

5

Well, to begin with I thought I'll never be able to keep up. I felt so exhausted and the session was only half an hour long. It seemed a good idea at the time because I'm so busy and although I say I'll make time to go to the gym, I never do. But if I'm paying someone to come and keep me fit that would force me to exercise and I wouldn't be able to make excuses. Trouble is that it's such hard work and I'm now looking for excuses to cancel the sessions! Perhaps I'm just basically lazy – wish I could be fit without the pain!

6

A: I really enjoyed that course.
B: So did I. When you see a film at the cinema you never stop to think about how the film got made in the first place.
A: No, and the huge financial investment people have to make before anything can happen.
B: It must be good fun to work in the film industry.
A: I don't know, I got the impression that people can spend hours hanging around doing nothing but waiting for things to happen. That must be pretty boring. Especially if you're shooting outdoor scenes waiting for the weather to improve. Or things don't go right and they have to keep re-doing the same scene.
B: Yeah, I hadn't thought about that.